The Creative Introvert

How to Build a Business You Love On Your Terms

by Cat Rose Neligan

About the Author

Cat Rose has been exploring what it means to be a creative introvert and thrive in this noisy world since going freelance in 2013. Her podcast, The Creative Introvert helps thousands of creative introverts every month to create confidently, show their work and acknowledge their wins.

Born in South-east London, she moved to the colourful seaside city of Brighton, in 2016. Happy to be alone in a new city, but it wasn't long before Cat found herself forming a creative community and stepping further outside her introverted comfort zone.

Since then she has delivered talks and workshops on self-promotion, community and creativity for corporate clients, universities and creative organisations. A regular contributor to the Huffington Post, her work has also featured in Thought Catalogue, Elephant Magazine and countless others. She has been interviewed on The Janet Murray Show, The Introvert Entrepreneur, The Creative Penn amongst other podcasts.

Cat has travelled to dozens of countries, craving the mixture of peace and excitement that solo travel entails. She really does love cats, but doesn't own one (yet) and enjoys drawing mandalas to relax and recharge.

Website: www.thecreativeintrovert.com
Twitter: www.twitter.com/creativeintro
Instagram: www.instagram.com/creativeintro

Table of Contents

About the Author 2

An Introverted Introduction 1

Part 1: Prepare **11**

    Chapter1: Know Thyself 12

    Chapter 2: Get Your Mindsettings Right 16

    Chapter3: Who the Heck Are You? 24

    Chapter 4: What Do You Need? 42

    Chapter 5: What Are Your Superpowers? 64

    Chapter 6: What Is Your True North? 78

Part 2: Plan **91**

    Chapter 1: The Gap 92

    Chapter 2: What Do You Do? 96

    Chapter 3: Who Do You Serve? 115

    Chapter 4: What Do You Want? 124

    Chapter 5: What's Your 90-Day Goal? 136

    Chapter 6: What's Your Business Plan? 152

    Chapter 7: How Much Will You Charge? 163

    Chpater8: Who Do You Need To Be? 178

Part 3: Promote **186**

    Chapter 1: Authentic Promotion 187

    Chapter2: Why Do You Struggle With Self-Promotion? 192

    Chapter 3: How Does Content Marketing Work? 201

    Chapter 4: How Do You Build Your Online Home? 213

Chapter 5: What the Heck Do You Say? 233

Chapter 6: How Do You Plan Your Promo? 242

Chapter7: How Do You Grow Your Audience? 252

Chapter 8: How Do You Collaborate (and Why Would You?) 263

Chapter 9: How Do You Network? 278

Chapter 10: How Do You Speak in Public? 287

Part 4: Progress 292

Chapter 1: How to Keep on Keeping on 293

Chapter 2: How Do You Review Your Progress? 297

Chapter 3: How Do You Deal with Discouragement? 303

Chapter 4: How Do You Handle the Haters? 308

Chapter 5: How Do You Work With Difficult Clients and Customers? 319

Chapter 6: How Do You Change Direction? 324

Chapter 7: How Do You Keep To Your Word? 329

Chapter 8: Who Do You Go To For Help? 333

Chapter 9: Who Do You Surround Yourself With? 340

An Introverted Introduction

The woman leaned over, smiling kindly as she offered me a fruit pastille. I graciously accepted candy from a stranger, as though in doing so the sugar would somehow absorb into my bloodstream and make life sweet again, rather than simply causing an insulin spike.

If this isn't evidence of the kindness of strangers, I don't know what is. To really set the scene: this was a rainy day in October of 2010. I was still proverbially wet behind the ears, having recently graduated from the University of Reading with a BA in Graphic Communication and Typography.

I was three months into my internship at a small digital agency in London's West End, and I had stormed out of the office in tears approximately 45 minutes prior. I was still sobbing, red-faced, as I sat on the train, urging it to leave the station and take me away from the hell of Victoria train station as swiftly as possible.

Come to think of it, that kind, sweet-bearing lady didn't have much choice. You can't really enjoy your fruit pastilles if you're sat opposite someone showing signs of hysteria, her face turning as red as her hair. Might as well offer one to the sorry mess.

So... what was the reason for the waterworks and the storming out, two hours before the day's end? There were a multitude of reasons, from unfair salary to a narcissistic CEO, but what persisted – and what sparked this book into being – was the dawning of a discovery I wouldn't fully grasp for another three years.

I left that sadistic internship the next day – yay – but the underlying problem causing my chronic distress and dissatisfaction followed me into my next job. There, I found a much more fair, friendly and above-board company to work for. Yet whilst my circumstances improved on paper, the storm brewing inside me did not.

Let's piece the evidence together and see if we can diagnose the Cat of circa 2010–2013 with the real underlying problem:

- The highlight of her workday is the first hour. Quiet time to herself before the remainder of the office (comprising 30–40 individuals at any given time) clocks in.
- After this, she starts to exhibit signs of quiet distress. Her brow furrows, and grooves get deeper throughout the day, until 5:30pm comes and she resembles a raisin you might consider putting on your cereal.
- She is in a state of constant lethargy, despite the fact she spends approximately 80% of her day sitting.
- The kindly co-workers around her, who mean well with their table football and darts, just can't understand why she is spontaneously crying. Is it something they said?

When I looked at these symptoms in the thick of my malaise, I assumed that I was fatally flawed. A broken human who couldn't hold down a respectable job that plenty of other young graduates would have given their left eyebrow for.

I actually never figured it out whilst I remained (miraculously) employed there. It took a leap of faith and a plane ticket to Japan for me to finally pack it in and save my boss and colleagues the discomfort of keeping Mount Cat from erupting.

I didn't have much of a plan beyond clearing my head in Japan, then returning to London to give this thing called freelancing a go. I had about six months of savings to get me through it, but I can honestly say I had no idea what I was doing. I just had to test my hypothesis: that the 9–5 office grind was not a match for me.

It turns out, I was on to something. Overnight, I discovered energy I hadn't had in over three years. I woke up without the need for an alarm (and several snoozes), eager to open my laptop, inspired to start creating and refining and emailing and tinkering each and every day.

So what changed? What was it about my newfound lifestyle and work day turned me from Sourpuss to the Cheshire Cat? Did I just hate people? That didn't seem fair: I liked my colleagues very much. Plus, the more 'difficult' clients hadn't disappeared: I was still dealing with some of the same people and arguably some even more prickly characters now.

Was I just spoiled with years of schooling and university that sheltered me from the grind of commuting each day to an office full of diverse characters and pressure to demonstrate initiative? But I've always been highly conscientious, hard-working and tolerant of rigid routine. Again, this didn't add up.

Eventually, discussing my confusion with a friend, he casually diagnosed me.

"You're an introvert, then."

"An introvert?!" I balked. I could admit that I was a shy child, and had my own share of social anxieties, but on the whole I'd made huge progress in my social skills and increased my confidence over the years. I couldn't be an introvert!

Then he explained what the original definition of introvert is, coined by the Swiss psychoanalyst Carl Jung, and later expanded upon by Katharine Cook Briggs and her daughter Isabel Briggs Myers.

The confusion I had over my work history – and much of my school years – started to vanish. Upon learning this definition of introversion, a whole world of self-knowledge and understanding of others opened up to me.

An introvert, defined in this book is:

- Someone who gets drained by socialising in groups and recharges by being alone.
- Someone who processes information slowly and deeply.
- Someone who is NOT necessarily shy or quiet!

Newly armed with this information, my fascination grew. I started to understand why networking was so exhausting. I realised why in-house freelance contracts were not ideal, why I couldn't stomach networking, why I grew tired long before my more extroverted friends at the pub. I started to shape my business around remote work and clients who could accommodate that. I started turning to more strategic ways of getting my work in front of people. I started letting my friends know why I had to pull an 'Irish Exit' so often.

The biggest relief was knowing: I wasn't broken. I wasn't a freak. I was in the 30-50% of the population who also fell on the introverted side of the spectrum. A real ah-ha moment came as I started to see a correlation specifically between the creatives I knew and my newfound self-diagnosis. I was finding that the vast majority of these creatives; illustrators, animators, writers, even musicians (who I had assumed were all extroverts, if they performed on stage) were also introverts.

We lamented over tepid pints of dutch courage, how much we wanted to relax into a hermit lifestyle and commit to our art. Self-promotion, social media, talking about what we do, pitching clients and agents... that was the drag, the painful side of our creative path we would do anything to avoid.

I felt this pain acutely. I also felt called to do something about our conundrum. I committed myself to first working out an introvert-friendly way to make a career that suited my personality type and preferences, then to helping my fellow creative introverts. I committed myself to finding a way we could have our cake and eat it (alone) too. In this case, our cake is creating work we love, and eating it is... well, making a living from it without selling our soul to our extrovert overlords.

This became my obsession, the one that kicked off the Creative Introvert Podcast, the League of Creative Introverts and the book you're reading.

Are you a creative introvert?

There are a plethora of tests online that will give you your introvert diagnosis, but really it's very simple. Do you identify with more than three of the following?

- You restore your energy when you spend time alone.
- You generally dislike being at the centre of attention.
- It takes you some time to get involved in social activities with a new group of people.

- You usually find it difficult to relax when talking in front of more than one person.
- You prefer to express yourself through writing or other non-verbal forms.

Well my friend, you're an introvert in my books! Or, more accurately, book.

Misconceptions about introverts

Common misconceptions about introverts are that we're *all* shy and socially anxious. Whilst these traits do overlap, and it is very common to be both an introvert and shy, I do want to clarify that these are separate traits. Even if you consider yourself shy, you probably recognise that your shyness is situational: **it depends on the context.**

Introversion however, is less fickle. I can't control whether or not I feel my energy drain after a few hours in a large group situation. I can't control how my brain processes information and how long it often takes me to find the right word when I'm speaking (especially compared to when I'm writing).

In addition, this isn't a book about becoming more of an extrovert: that isn't my goal and I don't believe it needs to be yours either. Nor is it a simple description of what it is to be a creative introvert, and an excuse to rant about our struggles.

Instead, you'll be given tailored, experience-based and evidence-based guidance on building a thriving creative career, taking into account your introversion.

Now to define creativity... Oh my.

This is a little trickier to pin down than introversion. Unlike personality tests, I'm less fanatical about 'creativity' tests that get you to think of multiple uses for a pencil, and decide your creativity based on that.

I'm a believer in creativity being in the eye of the beholder. You can feel creative in a niche area like flower arranging, whilst regarding yourself as unmusical, a terrible painter with two left feet. Creativity comes in myriad forms and outlets, and more than anything it's a description of how we connect the dots, how we generate novelty, and how we play.

I'm not going to ask you to take a test to bolster your belief in how creative you are: I'm going to take a guess and say that you ARE creative. How you utilise that creativity and bring it to fruition is entirely up to you, and I would love more than anything for this book to reveal how you can best do that for your specific personality type, preferences, skills and desires.

If anything you've read so far about introversion and creativity resonates then there is a good chance this book is for you. The clincher is this: have you experienced challenges in your career ambitions? It might be communicating with your boss or coworkers. It might be feeling exhausted in an open plan office space. It might be clarifying your target market and building a coherent body of work.

All of these challenges – and many more – you might face as a creative with a degree of career ambition will be explored in this book. The difference from other career advice books is that this will take into account **your introverted nature**. It will take into account your preferences for alone time, rich conversation with one person at a time and other subtleties that make being an introvert different. You'll learn how to use your introverted strengths in your creative career and mitigate the blind-spots that you might experience.

If that sounds like something that might help you, then this book is most definitely for you.

How to make the most out of this book

This book is divided into six sections: the key areas I've identified in working with hundreds of creative introverts in coaching and teaching settings.

They are:

1) Prepare: Learn What You Need to be at Your Best

This section shows you how self-knowledge is foundational to creative career success. We will explore self-limiting beliefs, what you value, what your hidden strengths are and how to make the most of them. Without this foundation, taking action and applying all the nitty-gritty strategy will likely fall flat; you'll run into all sorts of sticking points and tie yourself in knots, if you don't have these firm foundations.
You'll find out what you need in order to thrive: to be at your creative best, both internally and externally. There will be multiple quizzes so you can identify more about your own personality type and we'll explore the various routes to learning more about yourself, and how to apply this knowledge.

2) Plan: Get the Clarity to Move Forward With Confidence

Next, you'll learn how to break down the daunting tasks of planning a career shift, starting a new project or building a creative business from scratch. You'll be guided through a process specifically tailored to creative introverts: including a new take on business planning that is not going to induce sleep.

You'll gain clarity on what kind of life you're carving out for yourself, and how to remove the overwhelm from that grand concept, breaking down any size of dream into practical, actionable steps. This section will include practical worksheets which can be filled in online or downloaded to print.

3) Produce: How To Actually Get Things Done

If you've ever struggled with the procrastination gremlin, you'll be relieved to know that the battle ends here. You'll learn strategies and tools you can use in any situation to finally get it DONE. Regardless of your old habits and limiting beliefs, this section will help you find a way to make strides in anything you set your mind to: on your terms.

4) Promote: Time To Get Your Art Out!

This is the section that many creative introverts will be most challenged by: but I promise you that this is where the biggest rewards lie. You'll learn how to market your work without feeling sleazy or pushy. You'll learn how to identify, attract and sell to your dream clients or customers and get the exposure you so deserve. Plus, you'll do it all in a way that suits your introverted nature.

5) Progress: Taking Stock and Correcting Course

Throughout this book you'll find an emphasis on experimentation. This section is where this scientific approach comes into its own. You'll learn how to run your own experiments that will show you exactly what you're doing that is working, and what you need to tweak. The point is to have fun: this is more like the Mento and Diet Coke type of experiment than the Hadron Collider type of experiment.

6) People: Introverts Need Them Too

Just because we're introverts doesn't mean we can do this all alone. People are on every corner of your creative journey, and learning how to manage these relationships effectively is going to be the make or break difference in your success. This section delves into collaboration, communication and energy management.

Note: This is not a straight-forward how-to guide book. I encourage you to find your own formula. All I can give you is ingredients (Tips + Tools) and recipes (Action Steps) that myself and others have tried, and have found helpful. This is a bit of a 'choose your own adventure', in that I want to give you as many options as possible to find what works best for you with *your* personality type and preferences.

This was the good news I so badly wanted to be true when I first started to understand myself better: that just because something that works for someone else didn't work for me, does not mean I'm a lost cause. It just means **there is another way to get there**. This book aims to show you the other way.

If you're ready to get started and finally build a successful creative career that fits you like a tailor made glove, then let's get going!

Part 1:
Prepare

Chapter 1:
Know Thyself

The ancient Greeks were on to something when they had the words *gnōthi seautón* (or, 'know thyself') inscribed on to the Temple of Apollo. Philosophers, psychologists and neuroscientists alike haven't stopped studying this inquiry: the inquiry of... us.

Who am I? What do I believe? Why do I do what I do? These are questions most of us ponder on some level throughout our lives; I started making an active effort to 'know myself' in my mid-twenties. I suppose I'd had enough of my bizarre, tearful outbursts on public transport, and once the dust settled, I started to look inwards for answers.

Introverts are especially good at this introspective pondering. Sometimes, it can be more of a curse than a blessing: if you've ever tried getting to sleep whilst analysing your own feelings, thoughts and behaviours of the day past or what's in store for you the day ahead, then you'll know what I mean.

I've slowly but surely been creating a detailed map of my personality, preferences, values, strengths and blind spots. From this map, I can get much closer to where I want to go.

Heck, even knowing where I want to go would be bloody hard without this map.

"I would not for anything dispense with this compass on my psychological voyages of discovery."
~ Carl Jung

This is a long process, and we're never done. After all, we're always evolving so our maps will too.

Note: I am not interested in changing who you are to become someone else. I'm interested in you discovering who you *really* are, and bringing that to the forefront.

In the pages to follow, you'll learn about:

1) Get Your Mindsettings Right

Regardless of whether we are born as blank slates or not, we quickly get programmed into certain 'Mindsettings' throughout our lives. Some of these are helpful for getting what we want from life and finding fulfilment. Others are... less helpful. The first step towards sorting out the ones that help from the ones that hinder, and doing something about the latter, is becoming aware of what your Mindsettings are.

2) Who the Heck Are You?

There are records of personality typing since the days of Ancient Greece. Even though there is valid criticism about the various methods of personality typing, I believe that if you approach this as just one more lit candle in a dark room, you'll gain invaluable clarity and insight about yourself and others.

3) What Do You Need?

We all have our quirks. Being aware of them doesn't mean you need to change them either: no one who wears a size four shoe should start wearing a size seven because that's what their best friend wears. Learning your unique needs, your preferences, whether it's your ideal working style, your best time of day for creative work and other quirks, will help you get the most mileage on your journey – and enjoy it a lot more.

4) What Are Your Superpowers?

Seeing our own Superpowers (or skills) isn't always easy: sometimes you need someone else (or maybe a book) to point them out. This chapter will help you discover your Superpowers: what comes naturally to you and, regardless of how useful you deem them; how to make the most out of them.

5) What is Your True North?

This is the part where you'll get clarity on what you really want. Moreover: *why* you want it. When you have that, you will have your guiding star. The 'how' will start to show up. You'll be able to orient yourself in this tricky world and move onwards, full steam ahead.

There are Action Steps at the end of each chapter so be sure to have a pen and paper next to you! You can also download your accompanying Creative Introvert workbook and all the resources mentioned throughout the book at: www.thecreativeintrovert.com/book

You will also find Troubleshooting chapters peppered throughout the book, to help you overcome any challenges that may arise in working through the exercises. And if you have any questions for me at any point, don't hesitate to email: hello@thecreativeintrovert.com

Chapter 2:
Get Your Mindsettings Right

'Mindset' is likely a term you've come across before, but I can't say I'm a fan of it. It suggests that our minds are set: that they're rigid or fixed. Instead, I like to use the word 'Mindsettings.' These are simply our *current* settings, much like our phones have; that we're free to change them at any time. Of course, some settings take a bit more time and energy to change than others, but I'm a firm believer in your ability to make that change.

What Mindsettings do you want to change?

The first step is taking stock of what your current Mindsettings are. Our Mindsettings are comprised of messages, beliefs, biases and judgements that we've been collecting since we were children. We picked them up off family, friends, teachers and TV. We picked them up in books, podcasts and experiences we've had, both pleasurable and uncomfortable.

Some will be helping us and some will be hindering us, even though at one point in time they formed because our mind was doing its best to make sense of the world and operate as best we could in it.

Common unhelpful Mindsettings can be categorised in the following ways:

1) Fear of failure

We start our lives by doing a lot of failing. A baby's first steps come out of a jumble of stumbles and falls (or fails) but that doesn't put baby off. No one reprimands the baby for falling: we know it's part of the process.

But somewhere along our journey, we learn that failing is to be avoided. For most of us, experiencing the fear of failure might bring up memories about school: we knew that success meant getting lots of answers right on a test, and failure meant getting lots of answers wrong. We tried not to fail. Failure meant disapproval, and sometimes punishment. Yet we still fell short, because we were (and are) still learning.

Whilst fear of failure can be helpful in motivating us towards doing our best and learning and growing: an extreme fear of failure, when it crosses the line to phobia (known as 'atychiphobia') is crippling. This is when we allow our fears to stop us from doing something altogether, so that neither success nor failure can be risked.

You might have experienced this level of fear if:

- You are reluctant to try something new, even if part of you wants to.
- You sabotage projects you start – for example, through procrastination or failing to follow through with goals.
- You commonly speak to yourself using critical statements such as "I'll never be good enough to get

that job," or "I'm not good enough to publish my work."
- You are only willing to try only the things that you know you'll finish 'perfectly' and successfully.

Overcoming our fear of failure means taking action in the face of risking failure. It's acknowledging that we can't guarantee our desired outcome, but that it's better to have tried and failed than to never have tried at all.

The next fear that comes our way, once we take up our challenge is...

2) Fear of judgement

At the core of social anxiety is fear of judgement. This can range from the slight knee-knocking of nerves before going to a networking event to the trauma of a panic attack. Millions of people all over the world suffer from this devastating and traumatic problem every day, either from a specific social phobia or from a more generalised social phobia, so if this is you: know that you are certainly not alone.

Experiences that are particularly triggering to our fear of judgement:

- Being introduced to new people
- Being teased or criticised
- Being the centre of attention
- Being watched while doing something

Once we overcome our fear of judgement, and start to consistently move forward in the face of critics, both internal and external, we might just have something we're proud of:

something we value. That's when our third fear raises its head, as we risk losing what we've risked so much to build.

3) Fear of loss

From big life-altering decisions like leaving a job or a partner to smaller, daily quandaries, fear of loss is often there, lurking in the background and preparing the path for us to feel uncertain about our choices and actions. If I do this, will I lose that opportunity? If I say that, will I lose their respect? If I say no, will I lose my security?

It may come as no surprise that the psychological impact of losing is thought to be twice as powerful as the pleasure of gaining. Because of this bias, we're at risk of making poor decisions based on the weighty impact of our fear of loss.

You might have experienced fear of loss and acted on it by:

- Buying things you don't need (or Groupons you'll never use) because a sale is ending soon.
- Kept a gym membership you weren't using just in case you won't be able to get that same rate again.
- Turned down opportunities that could be rewarding to avoid the risk of losing something else.
- Refused to invest in yourself because it feels painful to part with your money.

Fear of loss can be overcome once we acknowledge that with every loss comes opportunity for new starts, growth and change. Which is all good and well, until we realise that actually, change can be rather scary...

4) Fear of change

"I'm not afraid of change!" I spouted triumphantly, before my sister pointed out several times when I've explicitly demonstrated my fear of change. My confusion was simple: I wasn't scared of changes I could control. It was the change that occurs regardless of my will that I feared.

It's understandable, like all these fears. We make sense of the world by spotting patterns and making predictions. It's a pretty neat feature of the brain. But when something changes and we are missing the information we've become so accustomed to relying on... we panic.

What we fear is not being able to cope with the change: something new doesn't present itself as an opportunity to explore and learn, instead it looks threatening to our safety.

Fear of change often follows from overcoming our fear of loss, making a decision that leads to an upheaval in our lives, and panicking. At this point, we often get struck with our next fear: fear of success.

5) Fear of success

The sense that if we get to a point of contentedness, when we're flying high and all our dreams are coming true, that the 'other shoe is going to drop', is likely familiar to most of us. It's the child who drops her ice cream cone, just before taking the first lick. It is the lesson we're told by a well-meaning parent 'don't get your hopes up too high.' So we learn to stay down, where it's safe.

Things we tell ourselves when we're fearing success:

- I won't be able to cope with the pressure
- If I'm successful, people will think I'm selling out

- I'll become a jerk if I get too successful.

In overcoming these concerns, and achieving what we deem a success, we move onto our next challenge. And no doubt, with it comes the fear of failure... and we complete the cycle to return to fear #1!

I'm not going to tell you all you need to do is to face your fears and they'll go away; I know that these fears have built up over time, and I won't pretend they will vanish completely overnight. Going forward though, you'll be armed with more understanding, acceptance and strategies that you can use to gradually ease those fears, and eventually: change your Mindsettings.

If however, you're really suffering with any of these fears, I strongly recommend seeking out a therapist who understands what you're going through - and yes, I guarantee they're out there. Cognitive Behavioural Therapy (CBT) is particularly well-researched and proven to help with these anxiety disorders.

ACTION STEPS:

1) Fill in the following blanks. Don't spend any time deliberating your answer; try to write as swiftly as possible, you can always analyse later:

I'm afraid of not having enough...
I'm afraid I can't...
I'm afraid of someone finding out I...
I'm afraid I don't have...
I'm afraid I will never...
I'm afraid of getting...

I'm afraid of someone seeing...
I'm afraid I will...
I'm afraid my family will...
I'm afraid my friends will...
I'm afraid I only have...

Remember: none of these need to be true or even be rational. These fears have been baked into us through our life experiences, and our mind was trying to protect us by learning from them.

Now these fears have done their job, you can start to put them aside, and take on new Mindsettings.

2) Next, for each fear you can identify as distinct and troublesome, try re-writing the fear as an affirmation of what you're willing to face.

For example:

"I'm afraid of public speaking" becomes, "I am willing to face my fear of public speaking."

3) Next, for each affirmation, try writing down a small (microscopic if necessary!) step you can take towards facing that fear.

For example:

"In order to face my fear of public speaking, I will attend a Toastmasters meeting." If that feels too big, it might be, "I will record a 30 second video of myself speaking on my phone, and delete it immediately if I want."

We'll explore micro-steps like these more in Part 2, so don't worry if you get stuck here, just give it a whirl and see what comes out. This exercise is one of the most empowering things you can do for changing your Mindsettings.

Chapter 3:
Who the Heck Are You?

Being self-aware is very different from being self-*conscious*. Being self-conscious is to feel insecure, like a deer under the gaze of a lioness. But being truly self-aware can help give you confidence and inner strength, especially when it comes to being creative and following through on your creative dreams.

We are always learning about ourselves: from an early age we get to know what food makes us gag, how hot or cold we like to be, what kind of games we like to play and so on. But to make a conscious effort to reflect on our personalities is something that not everyone gets to do.

When I first began my path of attempting to become a 'professional' freelance illustrator, I figured part of the journey was to shmooze with other illustrators and go to networking events. Which I did... briefly. It wasn't easy. I had to *drag* myself along to these events and after a drink or two, I'd usually make a stealthy exit. I would feel so drained, all I wanted to do was to get home and sit in my PJs.

They call this the 'Irish goodbye' or 'Irish exit'. But in my case, it wasn't my inherited Irish propensity for booze that was prompting my dash for the door: it was me being an INTROVERT that made me behave this way.

I've never considered myself as shy, and I hated being called 'quiet' as a child. In my head, I was super loud. I wouldn't shut up! Being labeled as shy or quiet didn't deter me though, and after getting better at going to these networking events and talking to more fellow creatives, I started to notice we had a lot in common.

Most of us loved to work alone, had highly active imaginations, expressed our ideas better on paper than in speech, had a tendency to overanalyse... Indeed, most of us were introverts. We choose our profession, not just because we love to draw or paint – but because we love to work alone.

While I was tempted to make the assumption that introversion and creativity went hand in hand, I've since rested on the theory that I was just drawn to the introverts at these events. I'm sure there were extroverted creatives there - we just stood at opposite ends of the bar. Which makes sense: us introverts could relate to each others struggles, we wouldn't talk each others heads off, and we knew when to end a conversation.

Whilst introversion may or may not affect how creative we are, our personality type does seem to determine what form our creative work takes, what environment we creatively thrive in, and the way we perceive and record our world.

Creativity takes courage and self knowledge, and the best way to develop these qualities is through learning about your personality and preferences.

Knowing your personality and preferences will:

- Determine the environment in which you come up with your best ideas

- Help you realise and make the most of the unique way you see the world
- Give you insight into how you make decisions
- Help you understand your own creative process.

Everything we create is a result of our personality and how we relate to our inner and outer worlds. Combined, these traits and preferences affect so much of our daily lives: but until we're aware of what they mean, simply knowing our 'label' is meaningless.

Knowing about your tendencies, preferences, behaviours and quirks allows you to communicate better and to grow as creatives and humans in general: it does not have to confine you. It's like having an inner compass orienting yourself. You know where you stand, where's up and where's down. It means you can filter the information you get and tailor it to your needs when you're learning something new. From there, you can truly know and show your most authentic, creative self.

Plenty of people know what creative process has worked for them in the past, and with the best intentions go about teaching their roadmap to others. The trouble is that their roadmap is theirs and only theirs. It isn't designed for your specific personality type and whilst you may share some of their traits and characteristics: you're likely vastly different in other areas. It's as if they are giving us directions to get home but their instructions lead us to their house, not to ours. Directions that don't match with our creative personality type are so frustrating that many of us lose confidence and give up altogether on our creative journey.

I've done this plenty: following instructions designed by – and for – extroverts who couldn't possibly understand that an introvert might need a different roadmap. Of course I don't expect every teacher to translate what they know to suit each and every single individual: this might work if you have one-to-one time with someone, but if you're learning from a book or an online course, no one can expect anything but generic advice.

Even this book can't take into account your precise personality type – as much as I'd love it to – but I do want to encourage you to take matters into your own hands. This is exactly what self-knowledge will allow you to do.

When you know yourself, you can take on lessons in a new light. You can pick and choose what you do and how you do it. For example, you can use your Tendency in completing a creative project. If you know you're an Obliger: you can get accountability from a friend; checking in with each other until you've completed your project. We'll cover these terms in this chapter.

One thing this book will do is give you tailored advice for creative introverts: even though there is much variation between us, there are certain qualities we share that inform how I've gone about building a thriving creative career, and can now share with you.

Limitations of personality typing

You might have taken a personality test before, whether it was at school, at work or on Buzzfeed.com for fun. You might have learned something surprising from it. You might have agreed with it – or disagreed. You might hate the fact that it labels us. That it puts us in a category and boxes us in. Which is understandable. Yes, we like to think of ourselves as unique snowflakes. No, we don't want to be seen as predictable to others.

But the utility in grouping us in best-possible types outweighs the subtle limitations of these tests. It helps us to make sense of ourselves and the world around us when we have names for things. Is it limiting to call all chairs 'furniture'?

These tests aren't designed to prove to us how unique we are: they're designed to prove **what we have in common** with folk like us. They're designed to help us spot patterns and blindspots we may otherwise miss: putting names to complex behaviours and beliefs that in turn help us spot them in ourselves and others. From there, we can best determine how we're going to use our self-knowledge to be at our best.

It's also worth remembering that the labels we're given in the results of these tests are not *all* we are. **You are not JUST an introvert.** Instead, these are just words to describe how we mostly – but not always – behave or think or feel.

It's helpful to think of any labels we are given, whether it's via these test results or in other uses of language, as verbs rather than nouns. For example, you aren't angry, you're *experiencing* anger. You aren't an introvert, you're *behaving* in an introverted way.

Thinking about labels this way allows us to be flexible in our decisions: helping us to respond to the moment rather than react instantly or go into autopilot. It helps us remember what our patterns are, but also that we have an option to choose whether to follow through or break the pattern in that moment.

This is partly why many books on introversion I've read have been largely unhelpful: they only encourage us to continue to use introversion as an excuse or an obstacle, rather than working within our natural state as well as extending it to become more adaptable, when needed.

It's also worth remembering that no type – regardless of what test you take – is better or worse than another. For example, I'm right handed. That doesn't make me better than my friend who's left handed. It might have done in medieval times... but that's besides the point.

Can you change your personality?

There's a scene in a T.S. Elliot play where a woman at a cocktail party turns to a man and says, "I hope there's something wrong with me."
"Why?" Asks the man.
She replies, "Because at least I can change myself."
Implying that it is the world that is out of her control, not her self. This is the same for all of us: knowing we can control our own responses is incredibly freeing. It also means we must take responsibility for ourselves in order to be rewarded with that freedom.

When you can honestly say that you've done everything to change your response to a situation, that's when it's time to move into acceptance. But until you know that for sure, don't settle with a situation you aren't happy with. As you learn more about yourself in the coming chapters, remember you always have a choice. If you aren't happy with something, be curious about what you can change, whilst acknowledging that no one else can tell you what you should or shouldn't be. This book is about understanding yourself and embracing that creature, working with it and for it, to create whatever you choose.

There is an abundance of personality type tests out there online, some more scientific than others... but it's more important that you find ones that help you see yourself more clearly. Here are some of my favourites:

Your Creative Type

This is my adapted version of the Myers-Briggs Type Indicator (MBTI) that looks at all the 16 types through the lens of creativity. It's based very much on the work of David B. Goldstein and the late Otto Kroeger, co-authors of *Creative You*.

You'll find out how your type affects your creative process, how you work and get things done, based on the personalities, styles and habits of varying types of creatives. You'll learn what your strengths are, as well as your blindspots, in terms of your creative process. It's particularly helpful in working out who you might want to collaborate with or get help with.

If you aren't familiar with the dimensions of personality that the MBTI tests, here's a brief overview. The test reflects your preferences in the following areas:

1. Introvert or Extravert

This describes how you expend and how you get your energy. Compared to the Big Five model, the MBTI is very closely derived from the work of Carl Jung, who used the terms to explain the different ways in which people direct their energy. The MBTI recognises a clear distinction between shyness and introversion, and that we all fall somewhere on a spectrum; each of us spends some time 'extraverting' and some time 'introverting'.

People who are considered Extraverts (E) in this model are not as sensitive to outer stimuli and actively seek to connect with their outer environment for energy. Introverts (I), on the other hand, are more sensitive (though this is not to be confused with Highly Sensitive People, which we'll get to) and can quickly exhaust their mental energy reserves, preferring to get their energy from the ideas, pictures, memories, and reactions that are *inside* them. They also like to take more time than extroverts to reflect on things before acting.

Questions to ask yourself include:

- Do you prefer to spend time in the outer world of people and things (extraversion), or in your inner world of ideas and images (introversion)?
- Do you feel more comfortable in groups and enjoy working in them (extraversion), or feel more comfortable being alone and enjoy things you can do on your own (introversion)?
- Do you sometimes jump too quickly into an activity and don't allow enough time to think it over (extraversion), or spend too much time reflecting and don't move into action quickly enough (introversion)?

2. Sensing or Intuition

This next pair of preferences describes how you get information from your environment. Much like the terminology introvert or extrovert can be misunderstood, sensing is not to be confused with sensual and intuition does not necessarily mean you can read people's minds...

There are far more people who prefer sensing than intuition (a 2:1 ratio.) When you boil it down, the difference between Sensors (S) and Intuitives (N) is this: Sensors prefer reliability of information, and Intuitives prefer speed and depth of insight. Intuitives learn to trust pattern recognition to help them understand information quickly and get a 'big picture view' from just a few data points.

Sensors have this same ability but they don't trust it as much, so they don't hone it. Instead, they trust reliable information – things that can be seen and measured.

Questions to ask yourself include:

- Do you pay more attention to information that comes in through your five senses (Sensing), or do you pay more attention to the patterns and possibilities that you see in the information you receive (Intuition)?
- Do you trust experience first and trust words and symbols less (Sensing), or trust impressions, symbols, and metaphors more than what you think you experienced (Intuition)?
- Do you start with facts and then form a big picture (Sensing), or like to see the big picture, then to find out the facts (Intuition)?

3. Thinking or Feeling

These traits describe how you make decisions. More misunderstandings can bubble up here: Feeling is not to be confused with emotion and Thinking is not to be confused with intelligence. Everyone has emotions about the decisions they make and intelligence varies within Thinking types too.

People with the Thinking (T) trait seek logic and rational arguments, relying on their head rather than their heart. Interestingly, people with the Thinking trait are often just as emotional as those with the Feeling trait – but they tend to subdue and override their feelings with their rational logic.

People with the Feeling (F) trait make decisions with their hearts and guts and care little about hiding their feelings.

These individuals tend to be outwardly compassionate, sensitive and highly emotional.

Questions to ask yourself include:

- Do you like to put more weight on objective principles and impersonal facts (Thinking) or do you put more weight on personal concerns and the people involved (Feeling)?
- Do you look for logical explanations or solutions to most everything (Thinking) or look first for what is important to others and express concern for others (Feeling)?
- Do you make decisions with my head and want to be fair (Thinking) or make decisions with your heart and want to be compassionate (Feeling)?

4. Judging or Perceiving

The final pair of preferences describe how you prefer to appear to others; your orientation in the outside world. This is the only trait that clearly distinguishes between the outside world and our inner world: this trait only describes how we appear to the outside world.

One person may feel very orderly/structured (Judging) on the inside, yet their outer life looks spontaneous and adaptable (Perceiving). Another person may feel very curious and open-ended (Perceiving) in their inner world, yet their outer life looks more structured or decided (Judging).

Questions to ask yourself include:

- Do you prefer a more structured and decided lifestyle (Judging) or a more flexible and adaptable lifestyle (Perceiving)?
- Do you like to have things decided in advance (Judging) or like to stay open to respond to whatever happens (Perceiving)?
- Do you plan work ahead of time to avoid rushing just before a deadline (Judging) or are you stimulated by an approaching deadline (Perceiving)?

When you have your chosen preference from each pair, the result is a four-letter code, and that's what your Myers Briggs 'type' is. For example, an ISFP is an Introvert, Sensing, Feeling, Perceiving type. In my Creative Type test, I've assigned each of the 16 types different names to help express what each type stands for in terms of their creative potential.

Take the quiz:
https://www.thecreativeintrovert.com/your-creative-type/

The Big Five

Currently, the most commonly agreed upon model for explaining our personality is the Big Five Model. Whilst not everyone agrees with the names of the traits that the model is comprised of, you might find it helpful to use the acronym OCEAN (openness, conscientiousness, extraversion, agreeableness, and neuroticism) when trying to remember the big five traits.

Let's look at the five traits one by one:

1. Openness

Those high in this trait also tend to have a broad range of interests, a great imagination and deep insight. They also come across as more adventurous and creative. People low in this trait are often much more traditional and may struggle with abstract thinking and taking on new ideas.

2. Conscientiousness

Typically someone with high trait conscientiousness have high levels of thoughtfulness, good impulse control and very driven towards goals. Highly conscientious people tend to be more organised and mindful of details.

3. Extraversion

I'm going to spend a bit longer on this trait than the others, because, well, this book is for introverts and I want to explain the different ways introversion is classified by different classification systems. With the Big Five, Extraversion is characterised by excitability, sociability, talkativeness, assertiveness, and high amounts of emotional expressiveness. People who are high in extraversion are outgoing and tend to gain their energy in social situations. People who are low in extraversion (or introverted) tend to be more reserved and have to expend energy in social settings.

It's worth noting here that the way the Big Five model describes the introversion/extraversion scale is quite different from Myers-Briggs, which follows more closely the descriptions Carl Jung laid out from his research and personal experiences. With the Big Five, this trait relates to how people respond to dopamine and reward: those high in extraversion respond very positively to activities that give us an increased dopamine response (a reward.)

Introversion here is defined as a preference for quiet, being reserved, and more cautious about your environment. But it has nothing to do with introspection and creativity, which are more likely related to a secondary reward system concerned with potential information-based reward. This is not the same as the value we get from status; the older reward system. The newer system, one that makes us uniquely human, is gaining information, pursuing our curiosity and there's no reason that this newer, curiosity-seeking drive is less high in introverts.

In addition, shyness, which many confuse with introversion, actually comes from neuroticism, not trait extraversion as described by the Big Five model. Extraverts can also be high on trait neuroticism (and therefore more socially anxious, despite being driven towards social reward.)

These are just a handful of the items have been found to accurately capture these major aspects of the introversion-extraversion domain of personality. Rate each item from 1 (doesn't apply to me at all) to 5 (really applies to me):

I am hard to get to know. ___
I keep others at a distance. ___
I reveal little about myself. ___
I rarely get caught up in the excitement. ___
I am not a very enthusiastic person. ___
I lack the talent for influencing people. ___
I hold back my opinions. ___

If you scored more than 17, you're likely an Introvert according to the Big Five model.

Personally, I don't see a lot of correlation between the Myers-Briggs definition of introversion, which I personally find more empowering and accurate in describing the introverts I know. You might find you come out as relatively high in Extraversion on the Big Five model, even if you come out as an introvert using the MBTI.

4. Agreeableness

This personality dimension includes attributes such as trust, altruism, kindness, affection, and other prosocial behaviours. People who are high in agreeableness tend to be more cooperative while those low in this trait tend to be more competitive and even manipulative.

5. Neuroticism

Neuroticism is a trait characterised by sadness, moodiness, and emotional instability. Individuals who are high in this trait tend to experience mood swings, anxiety, irritability and sadness. Those low in this trait tend to be more stable and emotionally resilient.

The results of this test give you percentages of each trait, which are relative to the overall population.

Take the test: https://openpsychometrics.org/tests/IPIP-BFFM/

The Four Tendencies

Gretchen Rubin, author of *The Happiness Project* and many other titles, has created a way of distinguishing people according to how they meet inner and outer expectations. For example, an Upholder easily meets inner expectations and outer expectations: so if an Upholder decides in her own mind to go to the gym five days a week, she'll do it. Similarly if a friend suggests she starts going to the gym five days a week, she'll equally comply: no questions asked.

A Questioner however, will need to know why they are doing something: responding best to inner expectations. An Obliger is the opposite: responding best when someone is dependent on them: outer expectations. Finally, a Rebel is someone who challenges both inner and outer expectations.

My experience is that we can flit between Tendencies depending on the nature of the expectation, but generally we have one that we fit most naturally into. This is an incredibly useful test to understanding why you do what you do – or don't do.

Take the test:
https://www.surveygizmo.com/s3/4232520/gretchenrubinfourtendenciesquiz

The Enneagram

This is more mystical as well as more complex than the tests we've covered so far, but well worth exploring. There are nine personality types described by the Enneagram, and each have distinct strengths and blindspots.

It can become complicated, depending on whose interpretation you study (I have a podcast series that might be helpful in walking you through this) but if you're enjoying yourself: by all means explore till the cows come home!

There is also an emphasis on self-improvement: that in knowing where you are on a spectrum of healthy to unhealthy for your Enneagram type, you can better yourself in the direction it suggests. Not for everyone, but worth checking out.

Take the test:
https://www.eclecticenergies.com/enneagram/test

The Creative Introvert Podcast series on the Enneagram:
https://www.thecreativeintrovert.com/en01-what-is-the-enneagram/

Your Birth Chart

Astrology is a bit of an oddball here, as it is the one lens to see yourself that doesn't require any self-purported data. You don't get to enter your preferences here or rate your likelihood to act in a certain way. The Birth Chart (a 2D, geocentric map of the sky at the moment you were born) is predetermined and fixed. Your only job is to report as accurately as you can the time, date and location of your birth to an experienced Astrologer, and that's where the science ends (in my opinion.)

A challenge we face when taking the other personality type tests I've mentioned is that we tend to answer in the way we want to be; rather than how we actually are. For example, if asked whether or not you care whether you're late to meet a friend, there's a good chance you'll answer 'yes' even though your behaviour (mostly running at least five minutes late) would suggest otherwise.

This is partly down to how these questions are worded, but also down to how honest we can be about our own behaviour and thought patterns. For this reason, I find Astrology an incredibly valuable tool for providing us with much more objective statements for us to reflect on, in a way that these other tests simply can't provide, due to their subjective nature. It can also be used to shine a light on other dimensions of our lives, including the people around us, our career path, creativity as well as challenges that we may encounter.

This is a topic too big for me to cover in this book, but if you're interested in learning more about what the sky can tell you, you can email me directly to discuss Birth Chart readings and ask any questions you have: hello@thecreativeintrovert.com

Get your own birth chart drawn up for free:
https://www.astro.com/cgi/genchart.cgi

How to use your results

Regardless of what route you decide to explore first, let's say you have been given results that describe traits you would rather not have, or deny having, ask yourself: Is something I'm prepared to work on? For example, I'm an INTJ in the Myers-Briggs Typology. This means I'm an Introvert, Intuitive, Thinking and Judging type. What does this mean?

Well, I learned that my creative process follows a 'plan A' but always has a 'plan B.' I learned that I spend a lot of time looking ahead to possible outcomes, and leaping ahead when I think one path might work. But I also love to reflect, analyse and make adjustments based on data I am constantly collecting. I fail to savour victories because I am already looking ahead to the next project. My attention to detail suffers; I'm a big picture thinker.

With this knowledge, I can choose to ignore it, use aspects of it as excuses as to why I can't do something or do something well, OR I can use this knowledge to double down on my strengths and try to mitigate my weaknesses. This might mean I challenge myself sometimes; pushing my comfort zone. For example, acting more spontaneously and letting go of the need to have a detailed plan. I can also have more compassion for others who don't share my qualities: having patience for the friend who arrives late (a 'P' to my 'J') or collaborating with an extrovert who can tolerate social demands of our project better than me.

There are unlimited ways we can embrace our personality type and use our knowledge to enhance our creative journey and all aspects of our lives.

ACTION STEPS:

1) Explore at least one of the self-knowledge tools mentioned in this chapter.

2) Reflect on your results. What surprised you? What did you agree with? What did you disagree with? What do you feel is in your control? What is not in your control? Is there anything you'd like to work on or change?

Chapter 4:
What Do You Need?

When I was working at my office job in London, it wasn't long before I adapted my routine to fit my highly sensitive, introverted nature – even before I knew what those terms meant.

This was largely triggered by my outrage with London transport. My commute from Croydon (which I implore you to visit if you have a penchant for concrete and human suffering) into the heart of the West End, took me to a new level of hell. I'm not sure if it has improved since, but trying to get on to a tube at London Victoria at 8:30am was as close to warfare as I ever want to get.

So, I started to tweak things. I tried different routes to get to work, including a one and a half hour bus ride, followed by a 20 minute walk, which was surprisingly soothing, even if it meant getting up at an ungodly hour. I also discovered that the earlier I got into the office, the better I felt. Starting in a quiet, gentle manner before the rest of the crew arrived meant I could bask in my relative privacy and get my best work done in those early hours.

Through this process of trial and error, I was learning valuable lessons about myself: what I needed to be at my best, what I could tolerate (early mornings) and what I couldn't tolerate (crowds.) Being able to reach our optimum settings doesn't come without sacrifice: getting up an hour or two earlier than you're used to is likely to cause you some pain – at least to begin with.

Then there are the people around you: you might not be able to change your work schedule at all. In these cases, but you can find still tweaks to improve your environment, efficiency and overall contentedness, like using noise-cancelling headphones to create a sense of calm. You might not be able to change your commute, but maybe you can take a soothing walk on your lunch break.

The biggest hurdle is **realising what you have control over.** It's likely much more than you think. This chapter will explore some of the tweaks you can make, according to your personal preferences and creative wiring.

Your ideal daily schedule

"Observing what you do best at particular times of day and then allocating your workload accordingly can really boost your confidence. You will feel that things flow better, that you achieve more and that you are not pushing against a dead weight of resistance because you are trying to do the wrong thing at the wrong time."
~ Pete Mosley

One of the problems I have with the traditional office place, is the assumption that we can work at our full capacity consistently between the hours of 9am and 5pm (or much later.) The truth is, our energy levels fluctuate throughout the day, and varies between person to person.

I personally think the tradition certain cultures have of taking a daily siesta or long lunch is a great idea: rather than the more common tradition in the USA or the UK where most office workers quickly munch lunch at their desk. It's actually *less* efficient to try to power through our working day in an effort to get as much done as possible. It's not only unrealistic, but it's counterproductive. We don't do our best, most creative work when we're exhausted.

I had an inkling of this when I was trying to be hyper-productive in my office job, but failing and ultimately feeling very burned out. It wasn't until I read books like *The 4-Hour Work Week* by Tim Ferriss and read about Daniel Pink's discoveries in chronotypes that I realised it's not so much *what* we do but *when* we do it. Simply timing our activities in our day can be what gives us most energetic leverage.

Time of day doesn't just affect how many lines of code we can write or how well we can solve a puzzle, Pink has revealed how Judges are far more likely to grant prisoners parole in the mornings and after breaks and how students score better in maths tests when they study in the morning. Timing matters.

Pink has also applied what he saw in these studies to his own life. For instance, he learned that for the majority of adults, our mood and thinking styles follow a common pattern. Our ability to focus and analyse peaks in the late morning, takes a plunge in the afternoon, and recovers in the late afternoon and evening, which is when we're more likely to be in a good mood, and therefore primed to think creatively.

With this information, Pink planned his day as the following:

Morning: no calls or emails, creative work only
Afternoon: administrative tasks, meetings and interviews
Late afternoon/evening: brainstorming, planning

As an early bird, this also suits my chronotype, and I plan my days similarly. I also schedule in bouts of light movement to keep myself perky and in a stable mood; I'll often take a brisk walk or do a bit of yoga in the late morning and/or late afternoon. When I return, I'm usually able to bust out another short but effective work sprint. However, I know not all creatives are early birds, and many do their best work in the dead of night. Rather than trying to bend yourself into someone else's ideal schedule, I want to encourage you to be honest with yourself, and honour your own unique inner clock.

I know from experience that bad things happen when I try to power through my exhaustion. I make dreadful mistakes in emails and more technical tasks and in my web design work. This is far from ideal. When I have a full tank of energy however, I feel enthusiastic, willing and able to do my best work. I also use these mini-breaks as time to generate new ideas. How often have you found your best ideas come to you when driving or walking or in the shower? Scheduling in leisurely time for this is key for creativity.

To find out your chronotype and what schedule might work best for you, take the quiz here: https://thepowerofwhenquiz.com/

Your ideal morning routine

I've been an early bird for as long as I can remember; I was never a big fan of sleep as a kid, and nowadays I fully embrace my early bird nature. I think part of it is just having a chunk of the day that's just mine: it's the most quiet, peaceful time and when I miss out on it, I feel wonky for the rest of the day; like I've somehow been cheated on an hour or two of 'me' time.

The point of this is actually to say: early starts are overrated if you're not an early bird! Know thyself. If you know (as in, you've tried it out for a period of at least a week) that you feel like crap in the morning and don't come alive until 11am, then you can totally work with that. I have several friends who do their best creative work at 2am.

Regardless of your chronotype, starting your day right, whenever you start it is really the key to having a productive day. The obsession with morning routines and rituals is probably not new to you, and if you haven't read Mason Currey's book *Daily Rituals: How Artists Work* I highly recommend it. It contains truly fascinating little insights into the sheer breadth of routines and rituals that some of the worlds greatest creatives, thinkers, doers have had.

So what is the best morning routine? Annoyingly, my answer is: it depends! It depends on your personality, your preferences, your circumstances. But I won't leave you there.

I'll share with you a few tips on creating a morning routine that actually sets you up to be more productive: that doesn't stress you out – that would defeat the purpose – and that leaves you energised for the rest of the day.

Tip 1: What sounds good to you?

If you've tried meditating and it just left you feeling frustrated and or you fell asleep, then skip it. It might not be for you. The point of this is to work out YOUR needs, and to honour them. There are plenty of ways to start the day. Some ideas include but are not limited to:

- A gentle yoga routine
- A walk around the block
- Drinking a warm glass of water with lemon juice
- Listening to music
- Reading (a book, not social media!)
- Playing with your dog
- Petting your cat
- Journalling
- Drawing
- Writing a gratitude list
- Setting your intention for the day
- Setting your number one goal for the day

So there are lots of things you can do that aren't necessarily productive in terms of work out-put, but they are energising, and it's that energy that is going to carry you through your day and help you get the things you need to get done.

Tip 2: Allocate whatever time you have

I'll confess my morning routine spans almost two hours between me waking up and me sitting down to work. That's pretty long, considering I don't commute anywhere. But yours could be a tiny slice of that: whatever time you feel comfortable with scheduling in. On that note: DO schedule it.

Protect it with your life: this is YOUR time, and if you want to start getting stuff done, it takes that level of protection to actually do the things.

Tip 3: The smallest of wins add up

It may seem that the habits comprising morning routines, the individual tasks, don't really amount to anything. There isn't one big, measurable goal you're working towards. But that's not the point. The point is simply the act of taking time out for yourself that makes you feel energised, calm and prepared. It's in carrying out the daily routine – whatever it is – that helps set you up for a day full of bigger wins.

If you see it like the first domino in a row, you know that just knocking that first one down, will set off a chain reaction that is much greater than the sum of its parts.

Tip 4: What tools can you use to make it easier?

No, a good workman does not rely on his tools, but they really do help! Some of the tools – the apps, the technology – that make my morning routine so much easier to knock out are:

1. Insight Timer - useful for being more consistent with meditation. It has a meditation timer, various sounds and bells, plus guided meditations from teachers all over the world. https://insighttimer.com/
2. Youtube channels for yoga - I love Yoga with Adrienne. https://yogawithadriene.com/
3. 365 Gratitude - an app to prompt me when I'm feeling a little blank as I sit down to journal. https://365gratitudejournal.com/

Tip 5: Experiment

I've don't think I've had exactly the same morning routine for more than six months. It's constantly evolving. Each time, I see it as an upgrade. Change usually comes from wanting to add something in, but realising that three hours is already excessive, I switch one activity for a new one. I test it out for a few weeks, and see if it makes me feel better or worse. If I feel better, I keep it!

So if you do read these articles about the 'best' morning routine or someone recommends you try something: go for it. But don't bet the farm on it. It doesn't have to be forever: it's not a lifelong commitment. It might become one, but it doesn't *have* to. Just note how it makes you feel: and give it a fair try for a few weeks.

Your ideal level of stimulation

High sensitivity

Ever had anyone say to you: you're too sensitive? I have. A LOT!

But, much like introversion, high sensitivity is becoming to be seen more as a trait that is highly nuanced and can be a huge advantage, particularly in this age where people are becoming more aware of the need for empathy, sensitivity towards others and to the world we live in.

Note: Not all highly sensitive people (HSPs) are introverts – around 70% of HSPs are introverts. This means there is 30% that are highly sensitive extroverts – which can lead some to *think* they are introverts.

Some characteristics of HSPs:

- **You're easily overwhelmed.** HSPs tend to notice the stimuli in their environment more, so they can easily become overwhelmed by too much intensity, chaos and noise. If you are an HSP, you might often feel the need to take a time out in a darkened room or some other quiet sanctuary where you can find relief from overstimulation. For example, I wear sunglasses most days from March to November. In ENGLAND. Which is a testament to my sensitivity to light, not just my wanting to hide from the gaze of strangers.

- **You are aware of subtleties that others miss.** HSPs tend to process more information in a given situation. They also have a tendency to reflect more deeply on what they see and sense around them.

- **You have a rich and complex inner world.** Most HSPs have a deep appreciation for contemplation and introspection. They tend to enjoy creative activities, philosophical thinking and might have a spiritual side.

Some of this may sound a lot like introversion, but it's important to distinguish these characteristics. For one, you might relate to some, but not all. Also, like introversion, the trait of high sensitivity exists as a spectrum of subtle levels of sensitivity.

If you think you're highly sensitive, then you might find making subtle changes to your environment greatly improves your day. Many HSPs are extra sensitive to caffeine, so limiting themselves to one caffeinated cup a day or swapping to decaf or herbal teas can help them feel more energetically stable and less anxious.

If bright lights are a problem in your workplace, you could bring this up with your boss. Do all the lights need to be on? Would they consider bringing in some adjustable uplighters? Can you make any adjustments to lighting at home?

Simply noticing how we respond to aspects of our environment can come as a relief as it reminds us we aren't total victims of our bodily responses or mental anxieties: all our body is doing is alerting us to what's happening outside, and we're able to either accept that or make some changes.

Take the test to find out if you're a Highly Sensitive Person: https://hsperson.com/test/highly-sensitive-test/

High sensation seeking

Sensation seeking is the drive for varied, novel, complex and intense experiences and well, sensations. Basically, High Sensation Seekers (HSSs) require more sensory stimulation to reach their optimal level of arousal.

How to know if you're an HSS:

- **You seek novelty.** You crave new or novel experiences, simply for the sake of the experience itself. This may or may not entail some risk.
- **You're highly open**. Much like trait Openness discussed in the Big Five Model, you are curious and open to new experiences.
- **You consider yourself creative.** Creativity, particularly divergent thinking, has been shown to be correlated with high sensation seeking.

- You like adventure. Skydiving, paragliding, rock climbing etc
- You seek new experiences. Exotic travel destinations, mind-bending drugs, funky new restaurants etc.
- **You get a kick from disinhibition**. You're prone to acting like a bit of a loon at parties, drinking to feel drunk, skinny dipping etc.
- You can be drawn to risky experiences. Thrill seekers may be more prone to indulging in drugs, booze, parties, multiple sexual partners etc.
- **You are bored easily.** You have a low tolerance to repetitive, non-stimulating people and places and things. If your optimum level of arousal isn't met, you get in a crappy mood. For many HSSs, boredom is so despised that they will go to great lengths to avoid it.

When I read about this I had that same feeling I had when I first read the description of an introvert, and of an HSP: 'OMG yes - that is ME! Mostly...' Whilst I'm not much of a risk taking, inhibited HSS, it's this more adventurous, easily bored side of me that had me convinced I was an extrovert for many years. It's the part of me that made me 'fun Cat' throughout university years.

You may not have ALL of these traits. In fact, it's quite likely you don't, especially if you're also a HSP and an introvert. Dr Ken Carter of Emory University has research that takes further the work of Japanese psychologists who have been researching sensitivity for many years.

Dr Carter takes into account four different subsections of sensation seeking, which he describes are:

- Thrill seeking

- Experience seeking
- Disinhibition seeking
- Boredom aversion

The idea is that we can score high on some of these attributes but not necessarily all. It's this strange rational that seems to account for my own twisted need for adventure as well as the need for downtime. For example, you might be all for sensation seeking but not a big risk taker. You can do parties, rock and roll and intoxicants – but you know your limits and recharge much better by reading a good racy novel in bed.

This push-pull tug of war can be quite a struggle in day-to-day life for high sensation seeking introverts especially if they share the traits of high sensitivity too. It might sound ridiculous: how can someone who is seemingly so sensitive to their environment, who thinks deeply and processes slowly and carefully can also be someone who seeks out novelty, adventure and gets bored quickly? It's more common than you might think: at least 30% of HSPs are also HSSs.

Dr Tracy Cooper has some interesting self-reported survey data that suggests why there are many traits that overlap, particularly if you consider yourself to be creative:

- **Curiosity/exploring.** HSPs, due to their ability to notice subtleties before others may also be encouraged in their curiosity, finding reward in exploration – even if it can get overwhelming.
- **Creativity.** In two studies from 2014, Cooper established and reinforced empirical links that indicated over 90% of participants in a qualitative study were creative.

- **Boredom.** The need for stimulation is also strongly present in HSPs, despite their tendency to get overstimulated.

If you think you have some or all high sensation seeking traits, don't worry: I'm not going to tell you to book your next sky-diving holiday in order to fulfil your creative dreams. However, I am going to suggest you create as many opportunities for novelty, exploration and sensory stimulation in your life as possible. This could be as simple as cooking a new, exotic dish every week. Or trying a new coffee shop to work from on the weekend.

One of my discoveries was my need for adrenaline doesn't require extreme sports: all I need is a bit of risk in the form of social awkwardness. For me, this means trying new classes at the gym (Zumba is perfect for this - and surprisingly enjoyable) and it even led me to improvised comedy. Instead of feeling my fear and deciding that discomfort was too great to stand, and not worth the experience (which I've done plenty of too) I embraced the fear as a sign that the reward (the afterglow of having done something scary) would be worth all the discomfort.

Knowing this about myself has been a huge help in feeling the fear and not only acting in spite of it, but acting because of it: because it tells me "Oh yeah - you're going to like this one! Well... when it's over anyway." If you find yourself prone to inexplicable boredom or despondency, it could mean that you just need a bit more of this stimulation in your life.

Take the test to find out if you're an HSS: https://hsperson.com/test/high-sensation-seeking-test/

Your ideal learning style

I remember clearly being in school and being taught about learning styles. The teacher went through the model taught to her, which boiled down to auditory, visual or kinaesthetic.

It made sense to me that I must be a Visual learner, given that I was the designated class cartoonist, at least when there was a Rugrats character to draw.

Later, I learned that this was just one of many models to describe our preferred learning style. It's also possible – in fact very likely – you have a mixture of styles. Some may be best used in certain circumstances. For example, learning how to put an Ikea wardrobe together requires different processing than learning a language. Plus, you can develop or change your preferences over time: in fact I did this through listening to podcasts. Now, I process audio much better than I did at school.

It's useful to explore learning styles, and not just the ones you think you have a preference over. It's useful not just to help you learn stuff more effectively, but to communicate better with others. When you know what style someone else prefers, you can accommodate them. It's something I try to take into account in my online courses, as well as when I'm coaching someone or consulting with a client. If I realise that they're a visual/spatial learner, I scribble down images to represent my ideas, or use visual analogies to give form to any of my more nebulous concepts. Or is they're kinaesthetic I try to slow my speech a bit. This is another weird fact: apparently kinaesthetic types speak slower on average.

There are seven styles that have been developed since the 1970s, which give a slightly more detailed range of preferences than we may have been taught at school. These are

- Visual - prefer pictures
- Auditory - prefer using sound
- Verbal - prefer speech and writing
- Kinaesthetic - prefer doing with your body, touch
- Mathematic - prefer logic, numbers, systems
- Social - prefer working in groups
- Solitary - prefer working alone

Most of these learning styles are self explanatory but I'd like to mention the last two. I'm going to assume you sit into the latter category: working solitary, but... I know this will not be the case with everyone, even if you are an introvert.

I know I do my most creative, productive work first thing in the morning: crack of dawn, no one around. But I find it very hard after lunchtime to get that same level of focus and enthusiasm back. Granted, I'm more productive than I used to be when I work from home than in my office days, but: I still have my limits. Naturally, most of us start to peter out in the afternoon - and this I've discovered is the best time to do people time.

This 'people time' might sound draining even at the thought of it for some of you more hardcore innies, but stick with me. The idea is to get a blast of social connection just for a couple of hours or whatever your personal energy budget is, to shake things up. This could look like scheduling any calls to the afternoon instead of the morning, taking meetings in the afternoon, working from a bustling coffee shop or – my personal favourite – having a work buddy to meet up with and work independently side by side. Obviously this is for folk who work for themselves, students, freelancers or solopreneurs; as it's this group who – especially if you're an introvert – tend to isolate themselves and after a while, this creates real limitations in our progress.

Don't judge your optimum learning style so fast. I learnt that as visual as I am, audio suits me really well, especially when combined with doodling or written notes. In addition, I learnt I do very well working alongside someone in a quiet cafe as it keeps me accountable during my afternoon slump.

Take the test to see how you learn best: https://www.learning-styles-online.com/overview/

ACTION STEP:

Once you've taken the tests outlined above, you should have a good idea about your ideal daily routine, your requirements for stimulation as well as the way you best take in information.

From what you've learned, jot down some ways in which you can use your results to optimise you daily life. This can be actions like:

- Go to bed an hour earlier
- Wake up an hour earlier
- Don't check emails till noon
- Go for a 20 minute walk in the morning
- Buy some noise-cancelling headphones
- Schedule a fun activity for the weekend
- Take visual notes in meetings
- Listen to an audiobook

You might consider creating a morning routine for yourself too, jotting down what time you would like to do what at. For example:

6:30 - Wake, drink some water

6:40 - Meditate using an app
7:00 - Shower, get ready
7:20 - Read, drink tea
8:00 - Breakfast and head to work

Troubleshoot: Lack of Willpower

Willpower is best understood as a very old battery in a smartphone. It lasts a shockingly short amount of time, and no amount of encouragement will restore it. The only way to recharge it is by plugging it into an energy source. The human equivalent of which is sleep... but we'll get to that in a bit.

You might have heard that willpower is a finite resource, that gets refilled after a good night of sleep. This also means that our willpower peaks in the morning – regardless of whether you're an early bird or not. Throughout the day, we expend energy on all kinds of things, some are incredibly willpower intensive, some not so much.

Things that drain willpower, much like Bluetooth for your smartphone battery, are:

- Lack of sleep
- Refraining from desire (like being around a jar of cookies all day and trying not to eat them)
- Stress
- Certain people (the 'go on, just one more pint?' people)
- Certain language (using phrases (like 'I have to' instead of 'I choose to.')
- Decision making

Without willpower in the tank, tackling any demanding task from finishing a commission for a client to writing website copy to practising guitar, becomes excruciatingly energy draining. As a creative introvert, energy is a vital resource, so we need all the help we can get from our will.

Keeping in mind that this willpower stuff is finite and fleeting, how can you make the most of it while it lasts?

1) Create a routine

Even after I left the design agency and went freelance, I kept to my early start. This was partly because I feared turning into a layabout who slept for 12 hours and never changes out of her pyjamas. Which I did try for a few weeks, just to make sure.

Don't misunderstand me: I love my layabout days, and actively take at least one a month. But... I'm naturally prone to laziness (actually, we all are) and for this very reason, I knew I would have to enforce some kind of regime on myself: I was my boss now, and I run a tight ship. The result of this was, after the initial wake up call shock, a much easier time when it came to my creative work.

Now, I use a day-per-page diary to plan out my day, more or less to the hour. This might be a bit too restrictive for you right now, so may be try a week-at-a-glance planner. You can also experiment with online tools like Asana or Trello.

<PIC OF PLANNERS>

2) Get your sleep

I can't stress this enough, and I know I'm not the first person to try to ram this down your throat and I likely won't be the last. But it really makes a difference! Science says so...

You see, a team of researchers looked at the interaction between sleep and willpower. They reported that sleep deprived individuals are more likely to give in to impulses, have less focus, and make other questionable or risky choices. The conclusion was that when we're low on sleep, we have a lowered ability to exercise willpower. In addition, it could diminish the energy we have for self-control.

As someone who has experienced their fair share of insomnia, I do have plenty of sympathy for anyone who struggles in this area. But I am convinced that a handful of bedtime rituals I've come to adopt could help 90% of folk out there, if you're willing to give them a go.

In short, my sleep formula is:

- No caffeine after 3pm (caffeine stays in your system for up to six hours)
- A magnesium citrate supplement (any magnesium will do, just NOT oxide unless you want disaster pants)
- A regular bedtime and wake time (my granny hours are set to 9 pm–5 am but I'm not recommending the same for you, just pick one block of 8–9 hours and try to be in bed for that time as regularly as possible.)
- A bedside journal (for jotting down those 3am thoughts that just won't quit.)

3) Do hard things first

If we know our willpower depletes throughout the day, it makes sense to get the most challenging things out of the way first. This could be something you don't find challenging of course, and doesn't have to be stripped from enjoyment. But putting the most important task first will be a massive benefit to your overall day.

I believe creative pursuits are best tackled as soon as possible in the morning (though for some, creativity strikes later in the day; you'll know what works best for you if you found your daily rhythm in the previous chapter).

That said, if I find that I'm procrastinating on a certain task, I'll bump that up to my first thing in the morning spot. I don't like diving into my emails first thing because it tends to derail whatever day I have planned. But I do like to write emails first thing, while I'm still sharp and have enough willpower to do something challenging, like hitting 'send' on a daring pitch to a bigwig.

This applies whether you're working for yourself or for someone else. Even if your boss or clients dictate the content of your day, there are plenty of opportunities to structure when you do what, even if it means waking up a bit earlier.

4) Reduce decision fatigue

There's a good reason Steve Jobs wore the same thing to work everyday. I personally have spent an embarrassingly long time pondering over my outfit for the day; hours upon hours I'll never see again.

The same goes for planning what to eat, what to work on and how to spend free time. Each micro-decision you make is lapping up willpower resources that you desperately need if you want to reach your creative goals. Have a think about some of the decisions you have already made today. How could they be reduced in the future?

Some ways I've reduced decision fatigue are: having a handful of choices for clothing (usually leggings and a funky shirt, optional knitted cardigan. Not much different to my seven-year-old self.) I also have themed days: I assign a certain theme to each day of the week. For example, Monday is always podcast day. I always write my weekly Museletter on Friday morning. Having a meal plan for the week or fortnight might also help reduce some micro-decision making for you (and save bags of time.)

5) Set up your environment

On the subject of food... Resisting the temptation to snack on the cookies your colleague brought into the office, or the leftover cake from your flatmates birthday just meters away in the fridge... all of that eats up willpower. Yep, the energy it takes to resist something or just generally do something that goes against our animal instincts is really costly on willpower.

So, how to put less stress on your willpower? Remove temptation altogether. Kindly ask a colleague to stop offering you cookies, or put them out of sight. Give your leftovers to your dog, and stop keeping sugary snacks in the house.

Another big distraction for most of us is social media. Trying to resist the temptation to have a Twitter break or a scroll through Instagram is very honourable, but is only costing you unnecessary willpower losses. To curb the craving, remove the temptation: use an app like Self Control that prevents you from accessing the sites you tell it to block. Delete certain apps from your phone. It may seem arbitrary, but these little changes make a big difference to keeping our willpower up.

6) Stop the snowball at the top

If you say yes to a drink with that 'fun' friend, how likely are you to say yes to another? And then another? With each 'Yes', we get exponentially more likely to keep going down a path that ultimately leads to a nasty hangover.

It's the same with a creative project. If you find yourself missing a day of working on your creative pursuit, don't let it get to day two. It's more tempting to continue to slack when we 'break the chain', and each day it gets harder to gather our willpower up again to start.

Just remember you're never starting at ground zero once you've got just one day of work under your belt. Yes, you'll slip up. But starting afresh the following day is the very best thing you can do. No berating yourself, please.

ACTION STEP:

Take one of the tips from above and take action. This could be starting your new bedtime routine, downloading an app to block certain websites or planning your weekly uniform. Take action now - you likely won't have the willpower left later!

Resources mentioned:

Asana - https://app.asana.com/
Trello - https://trello.com/en

Chapter 5:
What Are Your Superpowers?

If you were a Superhero, what would your Superpower be? I always struggle to pick between being able to fly and being invisible. Typical introverted answers: picking the two superpowers that would let me escape extroverted situations...

More than being a fun game to play when you're six, this is a great question to ask yourself throughout life. Your Superpowers don't have to be extraordinary or win you any awards, let alone save the world... they are simply the abilities you have that come easier to you than most, and when put to use, energise you.

Individually, they may not strike you as special at all. In fact, until you go through this chapter, you might not be aware of them at all. But when you do identify them and start to harness them more, you will start to see evidence of your true capabilities.

Stop focussing on your Kryptonite!

Introverts tend to be especially critical of themselves, because of our tendency to focus inward so much. Unsurprisingly, treating yourself too critically can easily reduce your self-esteem. Low self-esteem makes life a lot more challenging. In short: you want to bolster your self-esteem, not tear it down.

It does serve us to be critical when it comes to honing our skills; being able to accurately assess where you're at is one of the core ingredients to getting to where you want to go. But there will be nothing to assess and improve upon, without first acknowledging what your Superpowers are.

Not sure what your Superpowers are yet? No problem! Here are some ideas to get the cogs turning, based on what is known about the nature of introverts.

1) The Superpower of Thoughtfulness

This is particularly helpful when it comes to communication with others. It means an introvert doesn't blurt out any old thing, and can be more deliberate and diplomatic in their speech. It also means we're less likely to make hasty judgements and risky decisions that we might regret later.

2) The Superpower of Focus

Introverts can pay close attention to those they are speaking to. This is great if you're speaking to one person, but even at a larger scale this can be picked up. For example, a speaker on stage will often be able to notice if there's someone paying true attention to them: and this will mean a lot to them. You get to be that day-maker!

3) The Superpower of Introspection

The bedrock of this book is indeed self-knowledge, which may be because I'm an introvert who values introspection so much. But I don't know of any type of person who wouldn't acknowledge the value in being self-aware, and introverts are naturally primed for self enquiry. The philosopher Plato asked, "Why should we not calmly and patiently review our own thoughts, and thoroughly examine and see what these appearances in us really are?" Maybe he was an introvert too.

4) The Superpower of Independence

Compared to extroverts, who very much rely on the responses and feedback of others, introverts are not so concerned with the outside world. This is particularly true for the more left-brain, analytical introverts – usually ISTJs, INTJs, ISTPs and INTPs. Marti Olsen Laney goes into greater depth on left-brain introversion in *The Introvert Advantage: How to Thrive in an Extrovert World*.

In addition, this gives introverts an ability to be less self-oriented: to create from a place that is not driven by vanity, or muddied by the opinions of others.

5) The Superpower of Empathy

Empathy is a great skill, whether it comes naturally to you or you learn to develop it. It means people are quicker to trust you and feel less threatened by you. However, I should point out that not only introverts are empathic, because we all experience empathy to a greater or lesser degree (unless you're a psychopath of course!)

It's worth noting though, that there are two different types of empathy: cognitive and affective. Cognitive empathy is also known as 'shallow empathy.' It means you can look at people and sense their mood, you can notice and respond to body language cues, but you don't really *feel* it or internalise what you pick up. Extroverts tend to use this type of empathy more.

Affective empathy, also known as 'deep empathy,' means you are slower to 'read' a person or a crowd, but once you're aware of it you start feeling the same way; you begin to feel as the other person does and try to deeply understand what they're feeling. For better or worse, introverts appear to have a preference for affective empathy and will feel things more deeply.

What are YOUR Superpowers?

Now, let's talk about your *unique* Superpowers - the ones that set you apart from the next creative introvert. You might have some or even all of the introvert Superpowers mentioned already, but you also have your own unique Superpowers, ones that will make you the perfect fit for your life purpose.

Not sure what your unique Superpowers are? That's understandable. One of the mistakes people make when identifying their Superpowers is that they immediately think of their abilities in areas that society tends to deem the most important. You might think of your academic history... and how difficult you found maths. You might think of sporting achievements... and remember you were always picked last for teams. You might think of your workplace history... and remember how you always got passed by for promotions.

In focussing on the big, obvious (and actually less significant) roles society has suggested you play, you end up missing the Superpowers you do have in other areas.

It can help to think about something that doesn't feel emotionally loaded. For example, playtime when you were a kid. What about you shone then, that's still true today? Are you endlessly imaginative? Are you dedicated to detail? Are you considerate and generous when it comes to sharing your resources?

It's these little moments that bring us joy, boost our energy and feel so easy to us, that point to our actual Superpowers.

ACTION STEPS:

1) Have a Superpower brainstorm by jotting ideas down from the following questions:

- What are you really good at?
- What comes naturally to you?
- What activities make you feel energised?
- What quality do you bring to an activity?
- What do you get asked for help with by others?

2) Put your Superpowers to use in daily life

It's one thing to have a nice list of Superpowers you can keep in your wallet when you need a pick-me-up (which I do recommend) but it's another to actually put these skills and talents to use as much as possible in your daily life. Now you have your list (you can also add the typical introvert Superpowers too if they resonated with you) start to note down real life ways you can use these Superpowers.

For example, if one of my Superpowers is being attentive, I know I can bring this to occasions when I meet new people. These aren't usually the most introvert-friendly events, but if

I know I have my Superpower in my back pocket, I have more reassurance that I can use this to my advantage.

Think about how these Superpowers can help you through day-to-day life as well as the more challenging occasions we might face. Try the following sentence structure to work through each Superpower:

"I can use the Superpower of _____ when I _____."

For example: "I can use the Superpower of listening when I go to that networking event."

3) Put your Superpowers to use in a current project

Go one step further and think of an event or upcoming project where you can really put your Superpower/s to use. Make a point of using this as your intention in going into that event/project. This is often a much better way of setting goals than focussing purely on the end result.

Troubleshoot: I'm Not Good Enough

One of the most frustrating challenges I see as a coach is my clients' fear of not being 'good enough.' This might be an illustrator who feels their portfolio is inadequate, so they stall on creating new work entirely. Another troubled client might be a musician who keeps making music, but won't let anyone hear it because he's afraid it isn't 'perfect.' The secret to overcoming these roadblocks doesn't reside in perfection, however. I want to tell you about the magic of mastery.

Mastery, in this context **does not mean perfecting anything**. What I mean when I talk about mastery, is the *process* of mastering something. A process is no more than a series of actions taken in order to achieve a particular end... and with mastery, you get to decide what that end is.

The problem we face as sensitive creative souls, is feeling unsure about that end. In many cases the end keeps moving: we continue to move the goal post. Or we start believing the end is determined by an external force or figure. The result? A creative who stops a project or backs off a goal because they feel they can never ever reach that far. Someone who hides their work all their lives because they're afraid that it will fall short of the fantasy standards of others.

When we drop these beliefs and actually claim ownership on where our end point or our goal post stands, then we can approach mastery with grace and ease. That's what I'd love to encourage you to do, starting today.

I see the process of mastery like a training plan. I've never been an athlete (I openly confess to being the last-picked-for-the-sports-team kid...) but as I understand it, you have a set of daily exercises or weekly exercises. You also have periods of rest, as well as regular checkins to see your progress. Your mastery training plan is no different.

How to begin your mastery training plan

1) Decide what area/s you want to work on

So far I've been discussing mastery in general terms; but now it's time to get clear. What is it that you want to master? What do you think is holding you back?

Note: it doesn't have to be something directly related to your creative career. Many skills will indirectly but very noticeably have an impact on your creative career, even if you don't expect it.

Have a brainstorm about what areas you feel are holding you back. These could be technical:

- My portfolio
- My social media strategy
- My photography
- My editing

Or they could be 'soft' skills; the kind that are harder to measure but still very real. For example:

- Confidence
- Negotiation
- Public speaking
- Communication skills

Some could just be niche interests that you're curious about but haven't got an obvious use for. Interests that I've dedicated (arguably far too much) time to:

- Astrology
- Philosophy
- A language
- Quantum physics

You get the picture. Have fun with this! Consider dedicating one day a week to one area, one to another. If you're easily bored I recommend mixing it up, but if you really are limited on time, just take one and dedicate as much time as you can to it.

2) Decide how much time you can dedicate to mastery

Of course, there will be times in life when you can dedicate more or less time to mastery and personal projects. But I urge you to consider allowing time for mastery, regardless of how busy you think you may be.

The reason? Parkinson's Law. This is the adage that 'work expands so as to fill the time available for its completion'. It was thrown at me for the first time at art school, when I was moaning to a professor about how much work I had... and how little time. Needless to say, I put his 'law' to the test, and found that I was capable of much more than I'd previously imagined.

Don't limit yourself! The worst case scenario is: you miss your mastery session once in a while. No big deal. But when you start to incorporate mastery regularly, you'll start seeing the benefits. In most cases, the time you spend on mastery will pay off exponentially down the line: meaning you'll increasingly make yourself MORE time.

For example, the more I write, the better I get. The quicker I get. The easier the words flow. When I take a long break from my writing practise I notice the effects. And not just in the written word. I find it more difficult to organise my thoughts and my spoken words become stunted. All in all, I become one unhappy creative introvert.

My personal sweet spot for mastery is aiming for one hour a day, Monday to Friday. Outside of that time, I also try to attend one or two workshops or in-person training sessions each month. Do I always hit my mastery quota? Heck no. Do I beat myself up over it? No. But I do know it's worth missing out on catching up on whatever Netflix series is the distraction du jour.

3) Invest in yourself

Not just in time, but financially. I know, I know – the typical creative doesn't have tonnes of excess cash lying around to spend on an aromatherapy course just because. It may sound a bit arbitrary, but I've found this piece of advice to be a good rule of thumb:

"Here is a rule that will guarantee your success – and possibly make you rich: Invest three percent of your income back into yourself."

~ Brian Tracey

Considering that 3% of a £25,000 yearly income is around £58 per month, there is a great deal you can do with a small percentage of income, similar to what many spend on a gym membership or just one evening out eating and drinking.

I would recommend starting with books. A Scribd subscription is around £7/month - leaving another £50 to spare. Then you've got online courses, which vary greatly in price but you can find some fantastic low cost offers on Udemy.

Of course I'd be remiss if I didn't mention The League of Creative Introverts, my own membership community that connects you to like minded creatives from around the world, monthly Masterclasses and coaching from yours truly.

When you invest in yourself, and do the work, you level up. You gain skills that employers are blown away by and create opportunities to meet people who open the doors to your wildest dreams. I've never regretted a personal investment. What I have regretted is not making the most of the opportunities in front of me.

4) Make a date with yourself each week to review progress

If you're constantly making an effort to master something but not checking in with yourself, you might be doing more harm than good. I know that it isn't easy to see progress when you're chipping away at something over time, and not seeing progress means it's even harder to motivate ourselves. That's why regular checkins are so important: we see the chipping add up!

A simple weekly checkin, which might consist of reviewing your notes or the work you've done that week, is plenty. Over time, you'll be able to look back further and see your progress – and that's incredibly motivating.

The only question you ever need to concern yourself with on this journey is: have I done my best? No amount of criticism (self-generated or otherwise) can affect you when you know you've done your best.

Still stuck for ideas on your own mastery curriculum?

Ideas for mastery training plans:

1) Read for an hour in your chosen field

This could span from reading about creative superstars of your industry – it's amazing what insights you can pick up from reading the biographies or, even better, autobiographies of the people you most look up to.

Or this could be about a subject totally unrelated to your industry. The important part is to digest what you read. I like to take hand-written notes (as the action of writing helps us integrate the words better) and every now and then, re-read my notes. Even better if I can teach it. If you can find an opportunity to share your newfound knowledge with someone – take it!

It's possible that reading isn't your thing. In which case I really recommend audiobooks and podcasts, which you also have the luxury of listening to on-the-go.

Finally, there are video classes, which are my favourite way to learn. Find out how you learn best (see part 1, chapter 3) and get learning!

2) Life drawing classes

Particularly for visual artists, life drawing classes are without a doubt the most effective way to increase your skills in hand-eye coordination. Even if your 'style' is far from what you might produce in a life drawing class, you'll be able to see your overall perception and control vastly improve (if you can get past the painful early classes!)

Most cities will have workshops and many colleges open their doors to the public for taking part in life drawing.

3) Focus on a meta-skill

I found out about this technique from Scott Adams, Dilbert creator and author of *How to Fail at Almost Everything and Still Win Big*.

It's the idea that by learning a mixture of certain skills, you can maximise your mastery in most other skills. These are like the levers that separate you from the next creative regardless of what experience in your creative industry you have.

The best part? You don't need to be a pro in any of these areas; it's a case of jack of all trades actually being an advantage.

"Luck has a good chance of finding you if you become merely good in most of these areas...

Public speaking
Psychology
Business Writing
Accounting
Design (the basics)
Conversation
Overcoming Shyness
Second language
Golf
Proper grammar
Persuasion
Technology (hobby level)
Proper voice technique"

~ Scott Adams

Personally, I'd trade golf for cooking, but that's just my own bias.

ACTION STEP:

1) Decide what you're going to master and how much time you can allocate to it each week.

2) Commit! Declare yourself a student of your personal mastery plan.

3) Download or print out your Mastery Training Plan from the Resources and use this to keep track of your progress at at www.thecreativeintrovert.com/book

Resources mentioned:

Scribd - https://www.scribd.com/g/7anpba (get 2 months for free when you use that link)

Udemy - https://www.udemy.com/

The League of Creative Introverts - https://www.thecreativeintrovert.com/lci

Chapter 6:
What Is Your True North?

"Having a clear idea of where your 'true north' lies is one of the major underpinnings of confidence in yourself and your actions. It's the point from which you calibrate your compass for everything else in life."
~ Pete Mosley

Let's be honest: letting ourselves feel the intensity of fear isn't easy. It's much easier to let ourselves off the hook. To stay home, preferably under the covers with a pint of Ben and Jerry's.

We tell ourselves things like:

"Well, I guess there'll always be another networking event..."

"Yeah, I didn't really want to get a stall at that craft show anyway. Next year will be better."

The excuses we allow ourselves are usually totally rational. They are very logical in many ways, and the part of us that they come from simply wants us to bow out and return to where you feel safe... and stay stuck where you are.

We introverts have a tendency to get 'stuck in our head' and attempt to think our way out of a sticky situation using our mighty logic and reason. However, this will only take you so far. To overcome your fears and doubts, you need to fight like with like. I can rationalise why there isn't a monster in my cupboard, because I'm not actually feeling any fear about their being a monster in my cupboard. However, reasoning my way out of a situation I actually feel fear about – like public speaking – will only get me so far. I might feel it as tightness in my chest, a pit in my stomach, or sweaty palms. To change how I feel, I need to find another *feeling*, one that's even greater.

Even if you're more used to using your logic to get out of a sticky situation, and you may be dubious about this feeling stuff... stick with me. The process I use to do this starts in a familiar, comfortable land of logic, and will take you gently into the realm of feelings. It's perfectly possible for anyone who's new to listening to that gut instinct.

This process is called...

Your True North.

Your True North could also be referred to as your 'Why' (if you're Simon Sinek) or your 'Purpose' (if you're Tony Robbins) but because of the associations many of us have with these words, it is helpful to drop them for now. Your True North is your weapon for facing the inevitable fears, doubts and discouragement.

You've probably been asked the question: 'What would you like to be when you grow up?' You were likely much younger when you heard this, and might have been excited by the possibilities. For the record: I wanted to be a Coca-Cola truck driver because I loved the fizzy sugar water so much. Later, I settled on being 'someone who draws cats', because that was also a passion of mine - and this was met with more approval from the big people.

For you, the answer to that question might have shifted over the years, so much so that you aren't certain you even have the answer. After all, school and college and the workplace are not designed to help you truly find your calling: instead, you're left with the socially acceptable options and those most beneficial to the institutions needs.

A question you're much less likely to have been asked is: "*Why* do you want that?" I think I probably was asked that actually, when I gave my answer that I wanted to be a Coca-Cola truck driver, but since then, my reasons for wanting something, whether it's a career or anything else for that matter, are rarely met with 'why?'

So... what does this Why have to do with facing fear and other uncomfortable emotions? Well, when you're clear about your direction, even if something big and scary lies in your path, you know when to face it and why you're facing it. If it lies outside your path, a few towns over: you can avoid it. It's the ability to know when to plough ahead, and when to take a detour.

More often than not, people struggle to get something done because they don't fully know *why* they're doing it. If someone asked me to do a stand up comedy show tonight: I'm likely to decline. Other than testing my fear-facing capabilities, I can't imagine getting much else out of it. Compared to the discomfort I would feel, it simply isn't worth it because it doesn't align with my direction: it likely won't get me closer to my True North. However, if they asked me to speak in front of the same audience about being a creative introvert and give them some actionable advice, I'll say yes. I would still be nervous, but I'd know that it is on route to my True North.

When you know your True North, you can justify the discomfort, and remember the bigger picture at times you feel you want to give up. Your True North isn't something you can create out of thin air: you already know it on some level. You just need to uncover it and get clear on how it relates to your dreams and desires.

The problem with goals

I love goals: don't get me wrong. You'll be setting your own goals in the next part of the book, in fact. They help me focus, find clarity, get me pumped up and it feels good when I check one off my list. But without a True North, a goal can feel like a pointless target.

The belief that once we've got the goal, we're 'done', that all is well and we live happily ever after... is simply never true. We're never done - and that's a good thing! We creators are in the game to always be creating: not just to create once and be done with it.

Your True North will always look different, depending on where you are in life and only goals that are congruent with it will feel satisfying to you. It isn't something you can ever 'have', in the same way you can't actually get to the end of the rainbow (trust me, I've tried...) It simply guides you; and helps you get back on track when you've veered off course.

To pursue your True North you need to know:

- Your Values (how you want to feel, why it matters)
- Your Mission (what you'll do and how you'll achieve it)

- Your Touchstone (your measurement of success)

Let's have a look at all of these:

Your Values

To start, it helps to define what a Value is, at least in this book. I'm calling a Value something that we prize or regard with high importance. More than physical material things – such as my bed or my laptop – the Values I'm referring to here are closer to feelings or modes of being. What do I wish to feel? How do I wish to behave? How do I wish others to treat me? The answers to these questions can often point us in the direction of our Values.

When we hit on a Value that's true for us, we feel good about it. We feel congruent; like every part of us is nodding 'yes' in agreement. Oh and regardless of whether you do this Values-seeking exercise, you already have Values because you make decisions every day, with in adherence to or in contradiction to them. We're just not always aware of what those underlying Values are.

"Your values are the energy behind your goals. It's hard to sustain any activity that isn't congruent with the personal values at your core. If you keep suffering from a sense of paralysis or keep grinding to a halt then the chances are that what you are doing is out of phase with your innate personal values."
~ Pete Mosley

So, why is knowing our Values so important? Researchers believe part of the benefits from journalling about our Values is that it helps you to connect meaning with the more challenging events in your life. For instance, taking care of your family can be tiring and difficult, but if you connect this with your Values, you're able to overcome the challenges.

"It turns out that writing about your values is one of the most effective psychological interventions ever studied. In the short term, writing about personal values makes people feel more powerful, in control, proud, and strong. It also makes them feel more loving, connected, and empathetic toward others. It increases pain tolerance, enhances self-control, and reduces unhelpful rumination after a stressful experience.
    In the long term, writing about values has been shown to boost GPAs, reduce doctor visits, improve mental health, and help with everything from weight loss to quitting smoking and reducing drinking. It helps people persevere in the face of discrimination and reduces self-handicapping. In many cases, these benefits are a result of a one-time mindset intervention. People who write about their values once, for ten minutes, show benefits months or even years later."
~ Kelly McGonigal

Ordering your values

You might have a long list of Values, and that's perfectly fine. The tricky part is making sure our Values aren't in conflict with each other. All the little to-do's we set for ourselves become much more difficult when our Values are conflicting with each other. Tony Robbins, a big proponent (literally) of using your Values to live by, experimented with ordering:

"What if I took someone whose number-one value was security, and whose number-fifteen value was adventure, and I switched the order, not only intellectually but so that adventure became the new highest priority in their nervous system?"

Of course, this made a big difference. He re-ordered his own values (for example, bumping up Health into first place, and knocking his old #1 Passion down six places.) He discovered how much this influenced his decisions on a day to day basis:

"I asked a question that kind of scared me, a question I had never asked before: 'What could having passion at the top of my list cost me?' In that moment, the answer became obvious. I had just recently returned from conducting a seminar in Denver, where for the first time in years, I had felt unbelievably ill. Health was always on my values list; it was very important. But it wasn't very high up on the list. I began to realise that by having passion as the highest value on my list, it would cause me to burn out and therefore potentially cost me the very destiny that I was pursuing."

So, whilst passion was still important in Robbins' life, he realised that it was no longer his priority. If your current number one Value is Security, what might that be costing you? What would happen if Creativity or Adventure took its place?

It doesn't mean you need to change your Values altogether: by their nature, they're hardwired into us. But over time, we can make an effort to reorder them and reap the benefits. Just by becoming aware of what your Values are and what order of priority they rank in can help to uncover why you might be feeling stuck in certain areas.

1) Make a list of what your current Values are.
Ask yourself: What do my Values need to be in order to live a contented, meaningful life? What do I need to feel at my best? How do I wish to treat others? What do I appreciate?

2) Now reassess your list of Values.
This can be done with questions like: What Values are at cross purposes? What Values might actually be someone else's Values, not my own?

3) Rank your Values in order of importance.
Double check your order by asking for each Value: What benefit do I get by having this Value in this position on my hierarchy? Will this Value be sabotaging any higher Values?

Your Mission

Now it's time to put your Values into practise. This begins with making statements that you will start to internalise. For example, if one of your core Values is 'Family' you might say 'My family comes first. Even if it means my career and independence suffer, I know that as long as I can care for and spend time with my family I am doing my best.'

"If I realize my focus is off, and certainly when I'm experiencing any negative emotions, I ask myself, 'Where should my attention be right now?' Almost always, the answer is 'my mission,' which is like a beacon that always beckons."
~ Adam Robinson

Your Mission is the path to attaining your Values, or living them on a more consistent basis. You can think of ways your Values affect different areas of your life, which could be:

- Career
- Health
- Finance
- Leisure Time
- Spirituality
- Romantic relationship
- Family and Friends

Your Mission is different from your Values in that it sets you into motion: it is the route you're mapping out to fulfil your Values. It usually looks like "To help X, I must achieve Y." For example, the eyewear company Warby Parker's Mission is: 'To offer designer eyewear at a revolutionary price, while leading the way for socially conscious businesses." I don't know their Values, but you could guess at:

- Equality (making the eyewear affordable)
- Creativity (leading the way in their industry)
- Contribution (building a socially conscious business)

So, how do you uncover your Mission?

This enquiry can take more work than you think, because your Mission has multiple layers - and depending on what area of life you're focussing on, you might have multiple Missions. I want you to get as close to the core Mission as possible.

This is because the deeper you go, the more important and powerful it is: it's just like fear. On the surface level, our fears seem quite light and sometimes irrational. But when we keep digging, our ultimate fear (fear of death) is a strong, deeply embedded motivator. So if your surface level Mission is to pass a driving test, it might not stand up to the convincing voice of the inner critic who might reason there are more important things than driving tests, and that it's safer and more pleasurable to stay home today.

However, if we dug deeper into this Mission... It might be because driving will allow us freedom (a core Value) to get to where we want whenever we want. Whatever it is you're trying to do: clarifying your Mission, and underlying Values will be your most trusty weapon against your inner critic when you find yourself giving into its reasoning.

To uncover your Mission, lets take a leaf out of the Toyota car company's book, which was the source of the Five Whys exercise. When you go through the Five Whys exercise, you're likely to wind up with something that resembles one of your core Values. That's how you know your Mission is aligned. Sometimes it might take another Why or two, but it's more than likely you'll get to a simple word that represents a deep, important aspect of your life. For example:

Why #1?
First, what is your Mission in each life area? A good place to start is by jotting down some goals or 'love to have' in each area.

Examples: Speaking in public, Changing career, Applying for a new job, Contacting journalists, Selling your artwork, Networking at events, Learning a new skill...

Why #2?

For each item on the list, write down why this is important to you. What will this item lead to? What will that lead to?

Example: Speaking in public will allow me to get my message across to more people, help them and in turn make a difference.

Why #3?

Now, dig deeper! For each item, ask why this matters to you. This is where it starts getting tricky. But stick with it. This one will likely be the deal breaker when it comes to facing your biggest fears, aligning with your biggest Values and make the difference between following through or backing out.

Example: Helping people and making a difference in the world will allow me to leave a legacy and make a change in the wider world.

You can continue digging for Whys #4 and #5 – though you might get to the nubbin sooner. If I continued asking why with this example, I might get to the simple word 'Impact' which might be one of my Values.

Your Touchstone

While Values have an intangible quality to them, and your Mission serves you well as your plan to fulfil them, they mean very little if we can't measure our progress. That's why the final piece of the puzzle is your Touchstone.

Your Touchstone is your standard or measurement by which your success is judged. This term comes from an actual thing: a touchstone is a small tablet of dark stone like slate, which is used for determining how pure a metal alloy is. It has a finely grained surface on which soft metals (like gold) can leave a visible trace.

Similarly, your 'gold' – your Mission – can be measured, using your Touchstone. It can be as simple as checking in with yourself at the end of the day and asking if you stayed in alignment with your Values (how you want to feel) and if so, you know you're on track with your Mission. If you feel misaligned from your Values, you can start to think of ways to adjust your Mission to keep you on track.

Your Touchstone is an important step, because without it, we can easily end up pursuing a Mission that is not fulfilling our Values. By using a Touchstone, you can constantly adjust and realign to make sure your oriented to your True North.

There are many ways of checking in with yourself, and it is up to you how often you feel comfortable in doing so. I do recommend daily journalling if possible, ideally at the end of each day. You can also have a weekly review, on a Sunday evening.

You can write about whatever comes to mind, basically answering the questions:

- What evidence is there of my keeping aligned with my Values?
- Did I experience the feelings I value? Did I work to create them?
- Did I do my best to carry out my Mission?
- What could I do differently tomorrow or in the future?

ACTION STEP:

Write out your True North. Go through this chapter again if necessary, but the overall aim is to get a record of your current Values, Mission and Touchstone.

For example:

"My Values are...

My Mission is therefore to...

I will check in using my Touchstone by..."

Find the workbook for this in the Resources at www.thecreativeintrovert.com/book

Note: these can and likely will change but the clearer you get, the more fulfilled and motivated you will feel, even in the face of fear. You can make this as visual and creative as you like, getting out the coloured pens and stickers and glitter... Or making a note in Google Docs or Evernote and keeping it simple.

Part 2:
Plan

Chapter 1:
The Gap

No matter who you are or how far on in life you are, if you're dreaming big enough: there will be a gap. The gap between where you are, and where you want to be. This gap, by default, does not feel good.

Victor Frankl, neurologist and psychiatrist famous for his work *Man's Search For Meaning*, believed that at the spiritual level, someone with depression is someone who faces that very tension created by the gap. Frankl referred to this as the 'gaping abyss.' He suggested that if goals seem unreachable, you lose your sense of possibility and meaning – which can result in depression.

Most of this book is geared towards challenges: hopefully none of which will appear so vast that you find yourself staring into a 'gaping abyss'... but if you do: then this part is the one you need to bookmark. No matter how big that gap is, this is the process that can allow you to face your challenges, connect with meaning and move forward.

In the pages to follow, you'll learn about:

1) What Do You Do?

Most of us creative introverts have diverse interests and like to dabble in a heady mixture of artistic outlets. This is great when it comes to creating original work... but less good for building a solid body of coherent work, that makes sense to your clients and customers. In this chapter, you'll find your focus so you can get on with doing what YOU do best.

2) Who Do You Serve?

Whether or not you *think* you have any Superfans, I want to assure you – you will soon! We'll get to the bottom of exactly who it is you're creating for, where you can find them and how you can best serve them.

3) What Do You Want?

In this chapter you'll learn my patented (not really) Bridging process. This is the simple, safe and surefire way to 'bridge' the gap between where you are and where you want to be. It's designed to suit you regardless of whether you're a big dreamer or if you're someone who feels queasy at the thought of 'five year plans.' We'll get you across that bridge!

4) What's Your 90-Day Push Goal?

Goal-setting is an art in itself, and I don't want you to screw yourself over by setting an unachievable or unhelpful goal. This chapter will help you get focussed and get clarity on what exactly you want to achieve, and help direct the rest of your working through this book.

5) What's Your Business Plan?

Business plans aren't usually the first thing creative introverts I work with want to get stuck into when they have an awesome idea for a new business or project... but a good one can be the difference between a flying success and a belly-flop. I'll outline my unique way of building a business plan – one that doesn't leave you bored to tears.

6) How Much Will You Charge?

Yikes! Money! Oh jeez... This is not for the fainthearted creative, I know. But it really can't be avoided and I want to make sure you finish this chapter feeling like you can command the rates you deserve, and receive proper payment for all your valuable work. Let's bust the myth of the starving artist once and for all!

7) Who Do You Need To Be?

Finally, we'll put this all together and design your very own Alter Ego. This is the version of you, your very best self, the one that existed before you can remember, the one that existed before people and society made you think or behave a certain way. This version of you will always keep you on track – if you learn to listen to them.

There are Action Steps at the end of each chapter so be sure to have a pen and paper next to you! You can also download your accompanying Creative Introvert workbook and all the resources mentioned throughout the book at: www.thecreativeintrovert.com/book

You will also find Troubleshooting chapters peppered throughout the book, to help you overcome any challenges that may arise in working through the exercises. And if you have any questions for me at any point, don't hesitate to email: hello@thecreativeintrovert.com

Chapter 2:
What Do You Do?

Looking back through old journals, I can see evidence of a very lost, very confused and somewhat distracted young Cat. I'll give her one thing: she was INTO stuff. Handmade lettering, graphic t-shirts, illustrated children's books, stop-motion animation, VJing... And not just interested in them, she wanted to DO them all. At the same time.

I made a good attempt at it too. My efforts to juggle all of my diverse interests after going freelance fills pages of my old journals. Monday = pitching clients, finishing a never-ending website project, practicing lettering, researching animation programs, life drawing class... It sounds fun, in retrospect. But it was also incredibly stressful and as a result of spreading myself so thing across multiple disciplines... my ability to master any one of them slowed to a snail's pace.

It wasn't until Fig Newton reviewed my illustration portfolio that I was finally shaken into the hard, cold reality of: being a Jack of all trades, master of none. Womp womp.

"In trying to please all, he had pleased none."
~ Aesop

In my case, trying to satisfy all of my interests led me to satisfying none of them fully. And I'm probably not the first one to tell you something like 'you need to niche' or 'you need to specialise.' That's because it's good advice. At least in the early days.

When we try to do all the things, we lack the ability to develop true skills in any one thing. In addition, when it comes to trying to attract clients or customers, we risk baffling them with our diversity. A little diversity is wonderful, and I encourage creatives to keep a range of tools in their toolbox, especially if you're freelancing or have your own business. But if your portfolio to online store is a jumble of disjointed, half-hearted whims, it's hard for anyone to have that feeling of "YES! This is the exact thing I was looking for. This person is clearly for me." Instead they leave feeling a bit unsure of what the heck you are, and whether or not you can supply them with what they need exactly.

I went away after that portfolio review and had (another) early-twenties crisis. Beginning the process of specialising meant I had to go through the following stages:

Stage 1: Despair

Okay. It hurts to realise that you need to kill some of your darlings, as I imagine Stephen King would encourage us to do. But it's a necessary sacrifice if you want any one or two of your creative projects to survive.

Another feeling that might arise is anxiety about the potential lost opportunities that come from not being quite so diverse. For example, when I realised I couldn't keep pitching myself as a generic web designer and would have to specialise in some way, I couldn't help thinking about all the potential clients I could serve but would be missing out on.

The trick is remembering that when we do pick a particular client to serve, or a platform or tool to work with and so on, we end up attracting way more (and usually way more awesome) clients to us.

When I specialised in serving health coaches and those I alternative healing professions, my life became tremendously more easy and the work I produces made for much happier clients who were much more confident in my abilities and appreciative of my work. Remember this possibility in your moments of despair.

Stage 2: Contemplation

Once you've mourned the inevitable loss that's coming, it's time to get quiet. It isn't always obvious as to what stays and what goes. Who are you without X, Y and Z? What is at the core of your work, that you couldn't remove? What is the essence? What are you most proud of and most enthusiastic about? What are people willing to PAY YOU FOR?

All important questions to sit in contemplation about. You might also want to contemplate through drawing. Here's a process that has been used by many a confused creative of entrepreneur:

Grab a blank sheet of paper and a pencil, and draw three large circles that overlap in the centre. Then devote each circle to one of the corresponding subjects:

1) Your Superpowers

We covered these already in the previous section (see: Part 1, chapter 4) but you might think of more when you go through this exercise. In the first circle, jot down whatever skills, attributes or abilities you feel you can offer in the world.

2) Your Passions

What do you actually enjoy doing? Often, some of our Superpowers actually bore the bejeezus out of us, and some of the things we are passionate about... we aren't very good at. So some of your Passions will be duplicates of your Superpowers, and spoiler alert: that's a good thing! We'll get to the refinement part in a bit, for now just list everything you're passionate about in the second circle.

3) Your Opportunities

This is a very important circle that many creatives are prone to forgetting: what are other people willing to pay us to do? These opportunities can be things like industries you can serve that are booming right now, or clients you know are looking for the skills you have. This might take some added research, including reaching out to some people who currently work in these industries. I made a big effort to ask as many professional illustrators as I could about their line of work when I was first dipping my toe in the professional realm. It's in asking these questions you can work out whether the area you're thinking of niching in is even profitable in the first place. Again, keep listing ideas especially the ones you know overlap with your Superpowers and your Passions.

Stage 3: Refinement

Now you have your jumble of words in each of these circles, it's time to think about where the three merge. What ideas cross your Superpowers, Passions and Opportunities?

If you're missing one of the three, it might be worth thinking about what you need to prioritise. Now let's be honest: unless you're rolling in cash right now, the two most vital to prioritise will be your Superpowers and your Opportunities, at least for a little while. Ultimately, things we're not so passionate about CAN become genuine loves simply from serving the right clients or customers. I highly recommend *So Good They Can't Ignore You* by Cal Newport for more on this theory.

I find that the more I can focus on and develop one area, I can build up resources (repeat clients, automated workflows) that will free up my time so I can splurge on my Passions again, and sometimes even integrating them. In other cases, my Passions become Superpowers that become Opportunities. This is what happened with the Creative Introvert Podcast. I started it because I was passionate about the content I wanted to share, it eventually became something I had a level of skill in and I was asked to give workshops on how to podcast for a local business, which generated some income. For this reason, it's worth remembering you can always return to this exercise and reevaluate your categories.

Stage 4: Testing

Up until this point, we've been playing with theory. It's incredibly important to give your hypothesis a real go. For example, 'I'm going to specialise in beaded jewellery only and sell my work at local craft fairs for the next 8 months.' It doesn't count if you make a few changes to your website, and after seeing no new sales after 3 weeks, pack it in. This requires a healthy dose of patience (I know this because I lack it) and a degree of scientific distance. Once you run your experiment, you need to evaluate the results. Did that niche produce some fruit? Maybe it did but you despised the work, and need to find a way to integrate your passion. In any case, set yourself some parameters: what are you hoping to see at the end of this first trial run? One new client? Two? A 20% increase in sales? Or if you're like me, any improvement is a sign you're moving in the right direction, and you can call it good.

This process has been something I've returned to regularly since that fateful day. I'm still prone to being a total magpie when it comes to shiny object syndrome. I still juggle multiple projects and passions, but now I know my limit. I know how many proverbial balls I can have in the air without dropping one. I know how much time a new love takes to nurture and grow, before I can divert some of my attention to another new, shiny object. There will still be occasions when I miss the mark, or find out I wasn't focussed on the best target. This is why these stages of specialising are something I keep close at hand.

So don't fret if you've come to the end of this chapter and you feel overwhelmed at the prospect of nailing what it is that you do... This is an ongoing process, and the good news is: you can always change your mind.

ACTION STEPS:

Work through the Stages of Specialisation, and set yourself a deadline to access your results. If your resulting niche isn't working for you, simply return to Stage 2 (unless you insist on returning to bask in Despair again) and move forward.

Troubleshoot: How to Talk About What You Do

It's one thing to know what you do personally, but how do you actually express that to others? If you're someone whose mouth gets dry as soon as you hear the words "Now let's go around the room and introduce ourselves!" you're you're not alone. Creatives tend to struggle when it comes to summarising what they do, because as we all know: it's a

LOT. Sometimes it's kind of weird and hard to explain. Sometimes we just can't be bothered with trying to justify what we deem as the vital outlet of our creative spirit. Sometimes... We just want to be in bed with a good book.

Regardless of your objections, it doesn't seem possible to go through life avoiding the question: "So what do you do?" The best solution I've found is to find ways to make answering this question as painless as possible. Here are some things I've learned over the years of grappling with my creative identity:

1) Different strokes for different folks

It's fascinating to see how many different reactions the words 'creative introvert' get from people. Some people light up, and fervently declare they too are creative introverts, and want to learn more. Others, confused, ask me to repeat what I said. Then I explain what an introvert really is, and their eyes glaze over like cold custard.

The trick is reading what the situation calls for. I've never been in a position where I've had to pitch someone in an elevator, so I've safely decided that the 'elevator pitch' is not for me. And it may not be for you either.

Instead, consider a handful of situations, some you might have been in before, some you might anticipate being in in the future, and write an introduction for each.

I keep a long document on Evernote with all my different bios from one liners to longer life-stories. The more I add to it, the more comfortable I become in declaring what I do and who I do it for. I recommend having five documents which can be used for a range of different situations; the guide to writing these will be coming up in this chapter.

2) Practise makes progress

On that note, the more you do this, the easier it gets. It's that frustrating thing about all kinds of creative pursuits. Actually, all pursuits in general. The more we do something, the more comfortable we get. Of course you'll get more confident in your ability over time too, but simply the act of saying what you do and talking about your latest project, even to friends and family, will help your confidence massively.

Give yourself as many opportunities as possible to be in circumstances where people will ask "So what do you do?" I know that sounds a lot like networking, but it doesn't have to be. Chances are there are some great Meetup groups, classes or workshops near you that are low pressure, but with enough new people that the opportunity to talk about what you do will arise.

3) Research your creative heroes

What are the people you love and respect doing? If they can do it (regardless of how challenging it might have been for them) then you can too, right? Some examples to get the ball rolling:

- Austin Kleon sends a weekly newsletter out to 55,000+ subscribers which is packed full of great little tidbits from around the web, but he always remembers to pop in a little call to action to check out his own products at the end of each email. For that great free content, of course I'll click a link.

- Andy J. Miller of the Creative Pep Talk podcast uses his art as promotional graphics for his podcast, and his Instagram feed looks dope as a result. He's doing what he does for his clients: illustrating their message, and helping spread his own word about his show.

• Atticus the poet has used Instagram – traditionally a very visual platform – to showcase his written words to great effect. Though 80% of his posts are poetry, he doesn't shy away from occasionally mentioning his paid-for books and adds giveaways as incentives for followers to support his work further.

How to find your voice

Part of talking about your work is finding a voice you feel comfortable with. Hint: that voice is YOUR voice. The one that connects you with your tribe, the one that accurately and powerfully expresses what you're about and helps the world understand your art. But how do you find this elusive voice of yours?

Fortunately, that voice is already within you. While I don't know if I can point you to the exact location, I can tell you, you won't find it by wandering around in the dark asking "Are you my voice...?"

You find your voice by actually *using* it. It might not be fully formed and functioning on day one, but over time - it will develop. Writing is the way I recommend starting for most introverts. After all, most of us find expressing ourselves through the written word much easier than off-the-cuff speaking. I open my mouth and instantly get critical, needing more time to gather my convoluted thoughts than speech allows. I speak quickly too, which doesn't help, my mouth moving faster than my brain can access the words.

Even if you don't think of yourself as a particularly good writer, that's not a problem. We aren't being judged anymore for how well we string a sentence together; this isn't school. I find that some of my favourite writers online and in books have a very simple, conversational style, that probably didn't come from formal training but from the sheer practise of finding their voice.

Here are some ways to start finding your voice:

1) Start a blog

It's OK if no one reads it except your Aunt Pauline. This project is about discovering your true voice, what matters to you, and what you can uniquely bring to the table. If I'd have cared too much about grammar and spelling (skills I left behind the day I graduated university), I'd never have started a blog. Even worrying about originality of my writing would have stifled my flow (and on many occasions, I let it.)

I did my best to keep myself focussed on the process: the daily practise of writing a little bit, chipping away at an idea I had on the train, and finally the sweat-inducing moment where I would hit 'Publish' and hope for the best.

Starting a blog taught me more than I could have ever imagined, and not just about finding my voice. It helped me with commitment (I've published a post at least weekly since 2013) as well as vulnerability, with some posts pulling out secrets from me that I never thought I'd air even with my closest friends.

2) Journal

If you can't bring yourself to start a blog just yet, you're not off the hook. The privacy of a journal is a great way to get tuned into your true voice, because you're less likely to edit yourself (the inner critic tends to be quieter on the page of a journal) than on a public blog. But at some point I want you to go public, partly for the accountability and partly because this is about promoting your bloomin' work!

If you would like some guidance on how to start journaling, a fun little acronym I've found helpful is W.R.I.T.E:

W – What do you want to write about? What's going on? What are you thinking about? What do you want? Name it a 'what' that has been flitting through your mind and won't quit, even if it seems insignificant.

R – Review or reflect on it. Take three deep breaths. Focus your attention inward. What emotions are coming up? You can start with "I feel..." or "I want..." or "I think..." or "Today...." or "Right now..." or "In this moment..." This is the time to apply your subjectivity (again, even if it seems irrational) to your chosen subject.

I – Investigate your thoughts and feelings. Now you've started writing – keep writing! Let any judgements (or 'blurts' as Julia Cameron would call them) out onto the paper. Ponder what's going on underneath your surface thoughts, feelings and desires. I don't recommend stopping to read what you've written at this point - just keep swimming.

T – Time yourself. It helps me, particularly when I'm feeling reluctant to journalling, to give myself 5–15 minutes to write. It gives me a goal so I don't quit too soon, and a reason to write speedily, without too much hesitation. You can set a timer on your phone.

E – End it. I try to write one or two wrap-up lines to sum up how I'm feeling at the end of the session. How do you feel that went? You could also take a minute to read through what you've read, and reflect on that.

W hat topic?
R eview/reflect
I nvestigate
T ime yourself
E nd it neatly

I also include a journal prompt every week in my Museletter email, which you can receive when you sign up at www.thecreativeintrovert.com

3) Blogging on someone else's platform (Huffington Post, Medium, Linkedin)

This might sound intimidating, but it is actually a really low maintenance and low commitment way to start writing more. For one, you have the advantage of reaching a decent audience, by using someone else's platform. Depending on where you submit your articles, this can also be a stamp of authority you can use on your own site or further down the line.
    Part 3 will go deeper into my strategies for pitching other people's blogs or magazines, but for now you can start getting your writing chops up on Medium.com.

4) Social media

Writing long-form posts on Facebook or adding long blog-like captions to your Instagram images are a great ways to start sharing authentically. Even though Instagram has historically been known as a purely visual platform, I've seen good results recently in posts that have lengthy captions. It's worth experimenting with.

My only caveat here is how tempting it is to fall into the comparison trap. If you get distracted by the perfectly finished, framed and sold work of another, or bamboozled by someone's flawless selfie, only to remind yourself you are not where you want to be, consider taking a different approach with social media. Scheduling tools like <u>Later.com</u> or <u>Buffer.com</u> let you post your gorgeous work and words, all without scrolling through your feed on your platform of choice.

Five documents that say it all

Here are the five documents I mentioned earlier. These are great time and energy savers to have at hand, not just for other people to understand what you do, but for yourself. This process strengthens your own understanding of what you're here for, what your aims are and how far you've come.

When you have these five documents, I have no doubt you will feel more confident about your creative pursuits, and feel much more ready to show and tell the world.

Note: these will evolve over time, just like you. Keep writing and rewriting, and make a regular habit of returning to them, especially if you get the feeling you're outgrowing them.

1) The Quick Pitch

I may not be a fan of the elevator pitch but this quick pitch is worth having. Having a 'slash' career – doing multiple things at once for work – makes for a cumbersome and random answer, which I try not to subject anyone to. For fellow multipassionates, I recommend having a handful of quick pitches at the ready.

A myth many of us trap ourselves with is that once we have this elusive, perfect pitch, we'll be able to reuse those exact words over and over again. In reality, depending on who you're speaking to, the context of the situation and what you're hoping to gain from the conversation, you can have a custom pitch for each.

When I was mostly working on website designs, yet wanted to grow my pet portrait business, I often gave the pitch: "By day I design and build websites for small businesses, and by night I draw people's pets." The latter usually got eyebrows raised, and provoked a much more interesting conversation than the website stuff alone. This isn't because pet portraiture is inherently more interesting, it's because my passion for that came through in my pitch, and that's what people connected with.

As long as you can talk about your work with some degree of passion, even if it's a weekend-only thing, you have material for a great pitch. Try to keep it to a sentence or two; expect follow up questions to explain the rest.

For inspiration: Look at who you follow on Twitter or Instagram. What are people expressing in their bios? These are usually the right length for a quick pitch.

2) The 'Professional' Bio

Often written in the third person, this is the kind of piece you send to people who might want to interview you – I have one ready to go for all podcast hosts who are kind enough to have me on their shows.

It can also be added to a media pack; a document you send off to press or people who want to feature your work. The idea is to include your past as well as your present, giving an overall arc to how you've come to do what you do now, and pack it with achievements, awards, training and anything else you have bragging rights on.

I find this easier to write in third person for this very reason – often bragging about ourselves isn't exactly the most comfortable job for an introvert. Pretending to look at yourself from the eyes of a benevolent, outside character – may be a favourite grandparent – helps to get the accomplishments part in.

For inspiration: Mark Levy gives two versions of his bio, one is more formal, and one is more like the About Page I describe next. Check it out:
http://www.levyinnovation.com/about/

3) The About Page

This is a great place to go deeper and share your story. This is coming from someone who insisted for the longest time: she did not have a story.

It's difficult to see our own story; especially when we're in it: we're the protagonist - and all around us looks like a bit of a messy muddle of dull anecdotes and sad one liners.

That was until I discovered the archetypal structure, outlined in Joseph Campbell's *The Hero With a Thousand Faces*. The Heroes Journey is a multipart structure, seen in literature from around the world, myths and legends, as well as modern day cinema: from the Bible to Star Wars.

There are multiple ways of structuring a story, and you don't have to wedge your own life history into this format just because Mr Campbell says so. However, it's worth having a google for the Heroes Journey, and see if you can identify any common themes in your own life. Was there a time of struggle? Most of us can recall at least one dark patch, if not many.

What about the high times? The discoveries and changes that led to better times? Who were the people involved? The archetypal teacher, the bully, the best friend?

In your creative work, where can a story emerge? Were you making art in a certain style, struggling away until you made a breakthrough? Or did you get bored of your 9–5, deciding you weren't fulfilling your calling, and changed paths completely?

There's a story in your history, and it ain't over. You can write about where you hope to go, what you've got your sights set on: all of which is so much more captivating than telling your audience where you went to school and your favourite flavour of ice cream (unless there's a story in that...)

For inspiration: It's got to be Derek Sivers: https://sivers.org/about

4) The Résumé

Traditionally the dullest of the lot, but that doesn't mean it's not an opportunity to get creative. Depending on what line of work you're going for and the nature of the company, you can break out of the traditional approach to the two-page, black copy on white paper approach.

You might not need a résumé or C.V. For your current career: you might be happy with your current workplace, or you have your own business and you're the boss for example. But you never know what might come up, and having an up-to-date résumé isn't a bad idea. If you're a service-based business and attracting new clients, simply having a résumé of your project history is a worthwhile document to have available to download on your portfolio site.

For inspiration: There are loads of online résumés to eyegasm over, if you search on Behance or other portfolio-style sites. Personally, I love the simple yet clearly branded style that Kyle Robertson has accomplished: http://kyledesigner.com/wp-content/uploads/2018/09/CV-2018-09.pdf

5) The Manifesto

This is probably the least common document you'll find from a creative, but it's one I highly recommend, partly because it can be so fun, partly because it gives you clarity, and partly because it's fantastic marketing for your work.
You get a chance to share what you stand for, what you'd like to see in the world, how you'd like to shape it, and attract people who think like you do.
So what goes into a manifesto? Naturally, there are no rules here – it's whatever you want (that's kind of the point.) Here are some points to think about:

– **Intentions** (what you intend to do, for example what you'd like to do with your body of work, what you'd like to create)
– **Opinions** (what you believe, your stance on a particular topic such as your particular niche of the creative industries)
– **Vision** (the type of world that you wish to see, any lofty ambitions you have about the impact you hope to make.)

For inspiration: New Belgium Beer make it clear in telling their company story, and tying it in with their values and

vision:
https://www.newbelgium.com/brewery/company/history/

You can also refer back to your True North (Part 1, chapter 5) in which you laid out your personal Values and your Mission. It can feel like a statement that gets set in stone, which may make you hesitate to express your manifesto, but I urge you to let go of that! You can update this as regularly as your underwear if you like - as I said, there are no rules here! Have fun with this one.

ACTION STEPS:

1) Research your creative heroes. Spend 15–20 minutes thinking about who you admire. It could be someone from your specific industry, or someone from further afield. Ideally, you want someone whose marketing you can study. Where do they show up online or offline? How do you hear or see them? Do you receive a weekly email newsletter, or do you watch their Instagram stories? Make a mini case study on one or two of your creative heroes.

2) Daily voice finding practise. Note: this is a practise, not a search for perfection. If you need to make something perfect, make it a perfectly enjoyable experience. Get comfortable. Eliminate distractions. Make your favourite beverage to entice you to do the work. I used to bribe myself with a perfect cup of coffee in reward for doing my daily blog writing, and to this day if I have to cajole myself into doing anything... coffee still works.

3) Pick one of the above five documents and get a first draft out. Time yourself . You don't have to spend longer than an hour on this: just get something out. The more you write these, the easier (and better) they become.

Chapter 3:
Who Do You Serve?

There's a good chance you've already been asked or pondered the question: "Who is my ideal customer or client?" before. It might have even cost you the odd sleepless night too. When I first started pursuing my dreams to illustrate professionally, I ran headlong into this question, and it quickly became an unsolvable problem or gargantuan size.

For one, I had no existing clients or customers - so how could I possibly know who would want my stuff? When I was given the advice to just 'make one up' I couldn't help but feel I was playing make believe. I decided what many conclude: **everyone** is my ideal customer! If they have money in the bank, they're my type. Before long, I realised the mistake I was making by believing this to be the case. To illustrate this folly of mine, I'd like to tell you a story about Pete, a furniture maker, which I've adapted from a story in David Parrish's excellent book *T-Shirts and Suits*.

Pete is also a creative introvert, and believed he 'couldn't do marketing'. He was becoming stressed because he needed more customers, but found that direct selling was extremely uncomfortable for him. He was not a natural 'salesman' and felt out of place at business networking events.

He was embarrassed that his website was not as well designed as it might be, especially because friends kept telling him that he needed a better one. Other friends and associates told him he should use social media more, especially Facebook and Twitter, because these were popular and effective.

Pete felt that marketing wasn't his strength and he needed help to sell his creations, so he started to read books about it, take courses and basically try to do all the things, from redesigning his website to running ads on Facebook to using search engine optimisation to appease our Lord: Google.

Pete found himself spending a lot of money and time on these things. He was exhausted much of the time, and disappointed that all this effort wasn't generating the sales he needed. He gradually became disillusioned with marketing and in despair about his business. In his mind, 'marketing' meant the painful process of trying to sell to somebody who simply wasn't interested. Marketing was bad news. The product of snake oil sellers.

Pete was nearly ready to throw in the towel when he finally resolved to ponder his existing customers, and look at things from their point of view. He thought about the customers he had sold to so far (even though there weren't as many as he would have liked) and how he had found them. He realised it was usually by word-of-mouth. Sales would happen almost randomly, through friends of friends and at unexpected events.

These friends of his friends were interested in his work and very much appreciated his creativity. They asked him about his inspiration, the materials he used, his techniques, and his workshop. Pete responded enthusiastically, telling them about every aspect of his creative endeavours.

He was in his element. He wasn't 'marketing'; he wasn't trying to sell anything. He was merely talking about his passion to people who were on his wavelength, and he loved it. Pete may be an introvert but he communicates brilliantly, authentically and enthusiastically when connected with the right customers, so much so that he doesn't feel he is selling at all.

Pete's problem was that he was trying to sell to the wrong kind of customers, showing up in the wrong places and with the wrong message.

No marketing strategies will work if you are using them to try to sell to the wrong kind of customer. Identifying the correct customer, or your Superfan is always the first step.

With Pete, the first step was identifying the correct market for his products – identifying the type of person who would be excited to buy his furniture. When he identified his Superfans, he could shape his strategy in a way that would get him in front of the right kind of potential customers which would allow him to be his authentic self.

Who is your Superfan?

- **Your Superfan has the problem you're solving**

If your Superfan doesn't have the problem you're solving, then they have no motivation to buy from you. There's also the danger of not being very clear on the problem you're solving and you aren't communicating what your Superfan needs to them. In any case, solving a pressing problem your Superfan has is a necessary requirement for anything you're offering.

- **Your Superfan has the same worldview as you**

When they see your product, your Superfan will experience the "That's the one! It was made just for me!" feeling. So not only does your product solve a problem they are deeply concerned about, this also needs to be communicated in a way that your Superfan understands. If your style and tone is crisp and professional, then your ideal customers will be crisp and professional. If on the other hand, your style is laid-back and irreverent, so too will your Superfan be.

- **Your Superfan has time and money to use what you sell**

A true Superfan won't complain that what you're offering is too expensive. Nor will they say they don't have the money right now. A true Superfan will recognise the value of your product or service and will agree with the price you ask for in exchange. In addition, they have the time to make use of what they buy from you. They understand that what you're selling can even save them time and money.

Here are the questions that will help you identify your (mysterious?) Superfan:

1) What does your Superfan really want?

Far more useful than standard demographics is the emotional drives behind your Superfan's drive to buy from you. Empathy is one of your introvert super powers and is going to give you the edge in defining your super fan's challenges and frustrations. By knowing what it's like walking in their shoes, you'll be able to create great products and services that address their specific pain points and problems.

Here are a few examples of challenges they might face:

"I suck at editing. I wish someone would teach me how to edit this video!"

"I need to find an unforgettable gift for my sister's 30th birthday."

"Ugh. I wish someone could just Tweet for me."

Your Superfan's challenges and frustrations impact you regardless of what you're offering.

If you offer services: The service you are offering has to cure a large enough pain point that your ideal customer will pay you to do it for them instead of doing it themselves.

If you make products, there's no difference. The products you make must solve your ideal customer's challenges or frustrations to be worth buying. And yes, art solves problems! If you've ever had to buy a birthday present for the person who has 'everything', you know what a problem that is.

2) What does your Superfan feel?

Still not sure about how your product or service is going to solve a problem for your Superfan? Let's talk about the limbic system.

The limbic system is the oldest part of the brain and is the part responsible for our emotions. Back in the 1940s–1950s, surgeons would often perform a lobotomy on patients to cure them of anxiety disorder. The operation involved severing the connection between their logical neocortex and the emotional limbic system. While this may have cured their anxiety, it also left the patient totally passive and devoid of all motivation. Not ideal.

Now, studies show that our purchasing decisions at the point of hitting 'Buy Now' or handing over our credit card, are made up to 95% in the subconscious mind and mostly depends on emotional factors.

When asked to explain why we made a purchase, as much as we might wish to, we cannot answer this question truthfully because we have no conscious awareness of how or why our limbic system chose to act the way it did. The best we can do is to rationalise our reasons after the behaviour has occurred.

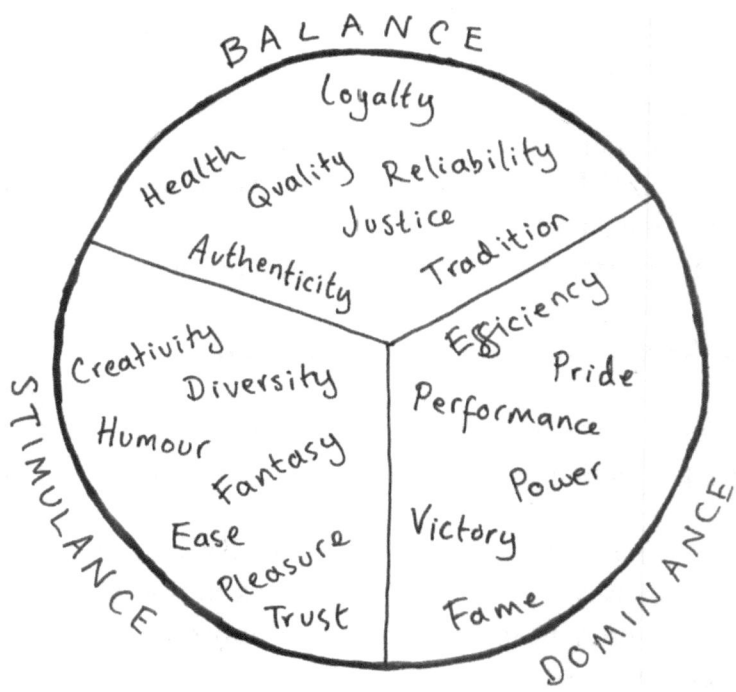

Looking at this mind map, it might very well trigger emotions both painful and pleasurable that could give you hints about your Superfan's desire to buy from you. It will help to really get yourself in the mindset of when you are making a purchasing decision. What are you feeling before you buy that thing? How do you want to feel after you have it? How do you feel when you use the product?

You can have a think (and a feel) about everything you decide, from what hairdresser you go to, where you buy books, clothes and food, what sites you browse and what brands you purchase over and over again.

Different types of people will be more drawn to certain feelings. For example, a person dominated by the Stimulance System is less motivated by a discount than by something new, limited edition, or rare. A person dominated by the Balance System, on the other hand, needs to know that they are making the right choice. This person is highly risk-averse, and really wants to be assured that a lot of people approve of the product before they invest in it. Rather than a discount, putting your best-reviewed products forward to showcase social proof would be a better tactic.

3) Where are your Superfans? Where do they get their information?

Knowing where your Superfans hang out influences everything from:

- Where you advertise (e.g. Facebook groups, niche forums, physical locations)
- Places you can go to listen and learn about your super fans
- The best blogs for submitting guest posts
- The best podcasts to be interviewed on

Have a think about the digital and physical spaces where your super fan hangs out. The more specific, the better.

"Hangs out on Facebook" is too general.
"Hangs out in the Wine Lovers of Atlanta Facebook group" is more precise and easier to reach.

"Likes the outdoors" is too general to mean anything insightful.
"Likes going to the park every Saturday morning with their kids" tells you their habits and what they value.

"Reads blogs" isn't targeted enough.
"Reads Lifehacker, Techcrunch, and Reddit" tells you not only what they're interested in, but where precisely you can reach them.

ACTION STEP:

Create an in-depth profile of your Superfan.

You might not have an existing customer or client to use as a starting point, which can make this exercise seem frustrating. But note that you're actually at an advantage: you're in the position to carve out the person you want to help, change and delight. This is an ongoing process; your Superfan will evolve with you.

The important step right now, is to get an idea of who this might be, then test that hypothesis over the coming chapters.

To add to the questions we went through in this chapter, here are some additional questions that can help you describe about your Superfan:

- What's a typical day like for them?
- If you had a look at their social media profile, what pages/accounts do the follow?
- What are their core values?
- What problems and challenges do they face?
- How painful is the problem you solve in their life?
- How much money do they have to solve this problem?
- How do they find you?
- How do they buy from you?
- What do they like about buying from you or working with you?

You'll find a template for surveying existing Superfans and potential Superfans in the Resources.

Chapter 4:
What Do You Want?

You've likely been asked before about your 'three year plan' or your 'five year plan' or beyond... And if you felt a surge of fear when you considered the answer, you're definitely not alone. Considering our future, for the most part, can fill us with fear because of the uncertainty any rational person knows the future holds. Or maybe you love answering this question and dreaming about your future self. Some people do: they could fantasise all day long... but when it comes to making moves towards it? They stall. It's much safer to be in imagination land than in the real world.

For folk like this, it's the daily grind that doesn't appeal. The gap between here and there is so vast, that they grow discouraged, and start to believe that future fantasy will never be theirs. Is there even any point in considering these distant futures, if they leave us feeling either filled with the fear of uncertainty or the discouragement of overwhelm?

Yes... AND no.

Yes to future plans:

The argument for having a future plan isn't because in doing so you'll create more certainty or make something happen, simply by stating it out loud. I'm all for vision boards, but not if you think that in the cutting and sticking of magazine and catalogue images that you'll magically bring them into your reality. That's a lot of pressure for some printed paper and glue.

But if you use methods like vision boards as a way to bring *clarity* to your desires and creative ideas, then I'm all for it. This is the single most valuable point of answering these three-year plan type questions: it brings clarity.

With clarity, you have something to set your sights on. You have something to get a grip on and something to work towards. Life can be just fine, swimming aimlessly at times, but at some point you'll want to swim towards the shore. But what shore? Where is it? What does it look like? What direction do you need to orient yourself?

Whether or not you make it to the exact spot of the exact shore you have in mind is not important. This is the part we miss when creating our grand plans. When we cling too tightly to the particulars of our plan, from getting that dream job to getting signed by that publisher: we end up feeling discouraged and disappointed. It then becomes much harder to re-orient ourselves and swim towards a new, more suitable shore.

No to future plans:

Enter my argument against making distant future plans: they can leave us feeling like we're attempting the impossible. Like anything we really want is too difficult or unlikely to achieve. Or because we know how likely we are to change our mind (a classic feature of a creative type.) We wonder: what's the point of getting so specific? We'll only go and change our mind along the way.

The result is that many of us end up over-thinking and trying to second guess our motives. Introverts are particularly good at overthinking, and whilst this can have it's benefits... it generally holds us back.

What's a creative introvert to do? What's an appropriate amount of time to spend considering the future? How detailed do we get in our grand plans? How GRAND do we get? How big can a dream be before it scares us off? Is it too small so it doesn't push us to expand and reach our full potential?

Enter... The Bridge

Regardless of whether you love or loathe long term planning, the answer to getting from where you are to where you want to be is the same: you have to **bridge the gap.** The gap is that abyss that seems impossible to cross. The gap that somehow, others have crossed... but then they must have had some paragliding skills you lack.

Wrong! Not everyone who has crossed the gap has had a special advantage. They just built a bridge. And building a bridge takes time, but you are totally capable of it.

To build a bridge (metaphorically speaking – I'm no engineer) you have to start small. You can work **backwards** from the grand plan, OR you can work **forward** from where you are today. The key is in getting the route that suits you.

If long term goals scare you, and you feel discouraged, start where you are and work forward. What would make tomorrow better? Then start thinking further beyond tomorrow, taking steps toward it. If taking baby steps is uninspiring and you love the big picture, start big and work backwards. What does that distant future look like? Then you can start breaking it down and making it happen.

Depending on what you prefer (or what scares you more!) you can pick ONE of the following options to use as your guide for building your Bridge. If you still aren't sure, read through both and pick one that feels right for you.

Option 1: Start from where you are

This is the option for you if you don't like answering the question 'where do you see yourself in X years from now?' You'll start with thinking about your daily life, and the small actions you can take that enrich your life now and set you up for the future.

Write out a typical day. Everything you can think of – no matter how mundane. What aspects are keepers? The things you wouldn't change for the world; the things that light you up and make you smile. If you have highlighters of felt tip pens, highlight these aspects. For the things that you don't enjoy, or want to change even a little bit, transfer these to another list. This is going to be the starting point of your Bridge.

Now for each of these less than ideal aspects, write down what you would prefer this to be or to feel like. For example, if getting dressed every morning is a pain, your desire might be to have a simple wardrobe full of clothes that you like and feel amazing wearing. Or if instead of waking up annoyed at the alarm or feeling unenthused about getting out of bed, you might want to feel well-rested and get out of bed with more enthusiasm.

For each of these desires, write down **one small step** you can take to move closer to them. For example, if it's the waking up scenario, then it might be going to bed 30 minutes earlier. It might be taking a magnesium supplement to help with sleep. It might be changing your alarm to a song you like.

Finally, think about your day in three months from now, if you were to continue taking action towards improving these things. Write about your day as you did before, but under the assumption that you did what you intended and things improve accordingly. These things may seem small, but these little improvements are what add up to a contented life.

Option 2: Start big, work backwards

This is the option for you if you love thinking big: the future doesn't scare you, it excites you... until you wonder how the heck you can make those plans happen.

Start with the end in mind. Write out a list of whatever it is you want for your future. It can help to pick a time frame, even if it isn't precise e.g. in three to five years time. Things to consider: where you live, what you do for work, what you do for fun, who you surround yourself with, how you feel most of the time.

For each of these desires, write out where you'd like to be with them in approximately half the time e.g. one year from now. Things might not be there yet, but you're making progress towards these aspects.

Now, half the time again, so you might be at six months from now. In each case, you want to try to make each aspect feel more attainable; less like a big, unrealistic dream, and more like something you can confidently work towards.

One more time! See yourself in three months from now. What would you be doing that would sow the seeds to each of these later visions? These are going to be small things, from browsing online for your dream flat and getting a clearer picture of what exists in your dream location, to researching clients that will allow you to do the work you dream of doing.

Congratulations! Regardless of which option you choose, you should be at roughly the same place: you, **three months from now**, taking daily action to bridge that 'gaping abyss', without feeling utterly overwhelmed.

ACTION STEP:

Pick ONE of the options above, depending on whether you love the daily steps (Option 1) or if big visions are your thing (Option 2.) Then start writing about your dream future. If you don't want to write, you can make this visual, using collage or Pinterest or any other artistic medium that helps you get clear on what you truly desire.

In any case, if you need some pointers to help imagine this dream future, try answering a handful of these:

- Imagine you just won the lottery – what would you do with your cash?
- Imagine you had no physical limits – what would you do with your body?
- Describe your dream day – what's different?
- What if you only had six months to live? How would you spend your time?
- What legacy would you like to leave?
- What would you want your tombstone to read?
- Describe the ideal version of yourself, with no limits – what does he/she have you don't?

TS: Making Difficult Decisions

Most of us are fully aware that we don't get our best work done when we're multitasking: we get distracted by the vibrations of our phone, the pings from social media, the 47 tabs open in the browser... It can feel pretty overwhelming to say the least!

However, just being aware of the 'evils of multitasking' doesn't make it any *easier* to actually find our one thing to focus on – and then stick with it. If the first step to focussing on one thing is actually deciding on what that one thing is, we've already got a problem on our hands.

How many of us can honestly feel assured that we've picked the one thing that's right for us? Maybe you're deciding over multiple layouts for an illustration project. Or you're deciding whether or not to take on this less-than-ideal client even though you could really use the cash. Even when we try to eliminate decision fatigue with our routine and 90-day plans, life can throw difficult decisions our way no matter what. The story that sums up this dilemma best is the one about the donkey. If you aren't familiar with our donkey friend, the tale of Buridan's Ass goes something like this:

An ass (as in, a donkey...) is standing halfway between a stack of hay and a pail of water. Unable to decide which to choose, the ass keels over and dies of hunger and thirst – and indecision.

I'm confident you're smarter than poor donkey. You can decide on your one thing by simply using a mix of logic and intuition to overcome our 'focus FOMO': the fear of choosing one thing will mean missing out on all other options you want to have.

There are two approaches I want to share, one for the more thinking-oriented introverts, and one for the more feeling-oriented introverts. Even though you might consider yourself one or the other, keep in mind it's worth switching up your expectations and trying the approach that seems less 'like you'. You might very well be surprised.

Option 1: The Thinking Approach

1. First, start with your aim.

Regardless of what choice you pick, what would be your dream desired outcome? This could be your 90-day push goal, or something less specific like your True North.

2. Next, create your hypotheses.

For each option you have, describe how it will give you the desired result. From this step alone, you might realise that some options stand out as 'safer bets', whilst others might be riskier but more exciting. You can use the classic 'Benefits vs. Risks' technique: drawing a line down a sheet of paper to create your plus/minus columns, listing the various aspects of your potential choice. Eliminate any options that aren't aligning with your aim.

3. Next, design your experiment.

For many options, it could be that you don't have to pick one or the other; you simply need to decide on one for now, and after you've had your fun with that, you can experiment with the next.

Your experiment could run for a set period of time (for example, when picking a social media platform to promote your work, start by giving yourself a time period like six weeks to trial it out), or budget (for example, running an advertising campaign until a set budget is used up). Whatever you choose: the idea is to measure the results at the end of the experiment.

After that period of committing fully, you can feel free to turn around and either stick with your one thing – or jump ship and try something else. The point is not to get so attached to the thing you pick and to chill out! Know that there is always the option to try something else if it's not working out.

If only our donkey friend picked either hay or water – he could always have come back for the other later!

4. Don't delay.

If it really is a now-or-never decision, and you don't have time or resources to experiment, then it's worth playing the worst-case-scenario game. Often, the reason for delaying making a decision is a psychological issue: fear of failure is the most common. The 'if this doesn't work then catastrophe will befall me' story.

If you can get clear about this possibility, taking the unknown into the known, you can start facing your fears and get a bit more comfortable with the possibility. You might even think of ways of reversing the worst case scenario, or at least mitigating the damage.

Then, ask yourself what the danger is in *not* taking action. Whatever decision you need to make, you're only burning time that could be used getting to your desired outcome. You might be able to pick a lane now you've come to terms with the risks, and feel more enthusiastic about the upside of taking action.

5. Last trick: set a deadline for deciding.

You still haven't picked?? Jeez. Not to worry: this will let you defer your decision to a date you might feel clearer or have more information, and stop you from ruminating over it whilst you decide. Get a 'decide-by date' in your calendar and remember that **no matter what you pick, commit!**

Remember: you're much more likely to regret what you didn't do, than what you did do.

Option 2: The Feeling Approach

The feeling approach is arguably quicker, but far less scientific!

1. Write your options on scraps of paper.
Roll them all up into little balls or fold them to hide the writing.

2. Pick one!
No explanation needed - this is a gut/heart choice, not a head choice!

3. Open it. Read it. Note how you feel.
Relief?
Excitement?
Dread?
... Want to pick again?

The idea here is that on some level: *you already know* what the decision you want to make is. By blindly picking, you can hit pause on the busy thinking mind, and defer to your inner intuitive self to tell you how you *really* feel.

I know many people who swear by this method, and whilst I tend to go through the thinking approach first, I always go to the scraps of paper when I simply reach my logical limit.

Option 3: Pick a card, any card

If you thought the last one was wacky, let me take this one step further. If you've come across the Tarot before, you'll either want to stop reading now, or already be nodding, pre-empting what my final tip is.

The Tarot is a deck of 78 cards, dating back to the 15th century. Originally used much like playing cards are used today, they are now mostly considered a divinatory tool: something we can use to communicate with something... supernatural.

Regardless of how they work, I've found that having an external, archetypal image to work with to be incredibly useful for giving me clarity about decisions that my rational mind fails at.

To play with this yourself, you can get a physical deck or an app, like Rider Waite Tarot (Android) Golden Thread Tarot (Android and iOS). Even drawing one card can reveal a wealth of insight you otherwise wouldn't have uncovered. Sometimes, there's something in the image that confirms a hunch I couldn't articulate before, or a word that pops out in the description (or correspondence) of the card, and that helps give you the solution you need.

So there you have it, three options for decision making, at different ends of the skeptic to seeker spectrum.

ACTION STEP:

Use one of the approaches above and use it to make a decision today. It might be that you're stuck over deciding what your Push Goal is for the next 90 days.

Or you can start small, practising on a decision that means relatively little to you, like what to eat for lunch. Then you can move onto bigger, hairier decisions like what to focus on for the next 90 days.

Resources mentioned:

Rider Waite Tarot app (Android) - https://play.google.com/store/apps/details?id=com.martarten.tarot.classic&hl=en

Golden Thread Tarot app (Android and iOS) - https://goldenthreadtarot.com/

Chapter 5:
What's Your 90-Day Goal?

So now you have an idea of what you want; some dream or ambition that's driving you. Somewhere you can see yourself being in the future, if you can align your actions with this vision. On that note... How do you get there? That's what you'll be figuring out in this chapter.

I recommend embarking on a 90-day journey towards your 'Push Goal.' This is the goal that matters: it's aligned with your True North, and on the path to building a business and life you love.

I won't leave you there though. On your 90-day journey, you'll set micro-goals: the baby steps that, if followed, will lead you to your Push Goal.

Note: Not all goals are created equal! I could spend the rest of the book gabbing on about smart goal setting, but before we go any further, the following two principles are going to be indispensable in setting a meaningful, achievable Push Goal.

Push Goal Principle 1: It's not an end point: It's a process

Scott Adams recommends taking a systems-based approach in his book *How to Fail At Everything And Still Win Big*. This is the idea of favouring systems over end-goals because it's a 'win-win' deal. Even if you don't hit your goal, you've benefited from the attempt to reach it. Then you can assess what you learned, maybe make some tweaks and start again. It's a system you create, like a science experiment, rather than taking a test you've got one shot at to pass or fail.

The way I turn a big, scary, distant goal into a system, is to start breaking it down into teeny tiny action steps. If I set a goal for three months from now, like speaking on a stage at a big venue in London, I start to break it down into micro-goals. These micro-goals are measurable and can start being achieved in days or even hours. When I hit one, I know I'm on track. It keeps me motivated. I can also estimate when I'm going to hit them, so if I find myself two months in and I haven't achieved any of my micro-goals, I know I need to pick up the pace or change my approach.

Ideally, I want to work out tiny actions I can take every day that will move me closer to this goal. The smaller the better. The first couple of weeks might mean I'm spending time every day researching venues to speak at. The next few weeks might mean I'm contacting a venue every day, as well as planning my talk. By the end of the three months, I'm practising my speech every day and visualising myself on the stage.

Push Goal 2: It's aligned with your True North

Your True North is going to be useful throughout the whole process from setting your goals to following through. If you haven't defined your True North yet, flip back to Part 1, chapter 5: What Is Your True North?

It will also help you decide what your Push Goal is. If you did the Bridge process from the previous chapter and have an idea of your ideal life in the future and even the next few months from now, you likely have multiple goals: maybe a few for every area of your life.

Choosing just one Push Goal that 'rules them all' is useful for keeping yourself truly focussed. It doesn't mean you aren't working away at other goals in the meantime, but having just one point of focus is going to help you achieve all the other goals on some level. Gary Keller describes this phenomenon in depth in the book *The ONE Thing*. It's why someone who is training for a marathon also finds themselves more productive at work: their energy and self-esteem is benefitting from their dedicated training, and it rubs off onto other areas of life.

For the sake of this book, it's going to serve you best to focus on your creative career. But even within the category of your creative career, you might have multiple goals, and you might be unsure what you desire most. Setting your Push Goal now will bring the beautiful sense of clarity and focus, that will push you through to measurable progress.

What's your Push Goal?

Examples of Push Goals:

- Getting one new client
- Complete a first draft of your novel
- Revamping your online portfolio
- Growing your Instagram followers by 25%

The important thing is that this push goal will in some way contribute to or align with your True North. This is key: whilst there will be other goals that will matter to you in life, the point here is to drive your creative career forward with such momentum that nothing can stop you from living the life of your dreams.

As discussed in Part 1, aligning your actions with your True North is going to make everything you do more enjoyable, and get you through the resistance when times are tough.

The first step is to sort your goals in order of priorities, by making a goals table.

MY GOALS	MY VALUES
lose 10 lbs	Health, Vitality
Start Etsy shop	Creativity, Abundance, Freedom
Learn Japanese	Travel, Learning

This maps out your goals as well as what values they align with. In your table of goals against your Values, put a checkmark against each value a goal fulfils for you. When you tally up the results, you should be able to illuminate the vast majority of your goals.

If you're still not sure and have some competing goals, try asking these questions:

- What effect will this goal have on the rest of my goals?
- What will happen if I don't achieve this goal?
- How would it make me FEEL to achieve this?

There's also a goal-setting checklist you can go through to ensure you've picked a smart goal - find it at the end of this chapter and in the Resources.

Now, write your Push Goal down!

You might be tempted to skip this step because, you know, of course you'll remember your goal... But regardless of your memory, I implore you to actually DO this one!

Writing your goal down gives you that first dopamine hit: the energy you need to pick up momentum. It also makes the goal feel more real and more achievable. Plus, you're less likely to forget it a few weeks from now.

When we start taking action, even the tiniest of baby steps, our confidence grows in response. It helps if you can make this as visual as possible: not just scrawled on a post-it on your desk. You could buy a postcard and write your goal on the back of that and fix it to your refrigerator door, or above your desk.

It also helps to re-write it regularly. If every day or every week feels like too much, try every month. This is also a great time to review your progress for that month - check off any micro-goals you've hit and reassess your alignment with your True North.

Enter the micro-goal...

In order to take on such a giant goal, you'll need to work out a plan that helps you know what to do, ideally daily, in order to accomplish it with ease. Micro-goals are the baby steps that add up to making your #1 goal a reality. It can feel overwhelming when we look at our dream day or even the one goal we're currently focussing on. But these micro-goals are the way you break a goal down into little, 'snackable' chunks that can be achieved in stages as you work towards the outcome.

Why micro-goals are so awesome:

Reason #1: They make starting easy

If each task is broken down into micro-goals, you can assign those to days of the week, and tackle them one day at a time. You know what you have to do today to make progress, which makes things easier to start.

A micro-goal should be small enough to fit in to a 60 minute session. If your task is looking too big to accomplish in that time period, break it down further. In some cases, a task will require a repetitive action, carried out over multiple days. This is also a great technique for a task, even a micro-goal, that feels a bit stressful.

For example, pitching podcast hosts was something I decided to do as part of my grand plan to get interviewed on more podcasts, and get a feel for the medium, before I started the Creative Introvert Podcast. It felt awful stressful, especially as I thought about the 'no's' and the 'why on earth would we have you on our prestigious podcast!?'

As ridiculous as my fantasies were, I found a way to accomplish the task by creating the following micro-goal: Email one podcast host every day of the week.

But when I first started, even that wasn't small enough for me. So I went even smaller: listen to one new podcast every day of the week. Then smaller: Follow one podcast host on Twitter every day of the week.

That was something that even I could do. It meant I only had to spend 15 minutes a day on the detested task, and over time... I started making connections with these podcasters. Because I wasn't stressed out or exhausted from the pressure I had put myself under, I soon found myself in a much better place to start emailing and asking to be on their shows. It didn't always work, **but I had momentum**, and as my baby steps added up, I got a lot of yeses.

Reason #2: Easier to stay motivated

Before I did my first long distance walk, a week on the South Downs Way in the south of England, I set myself the goal of walking 100 miles.

Each time I saw a signpost, I was relieved. But I noticed the ones that read '70 miles to Eastbourne' (my destination) were far less motivating than the in-between villages. These read things like' 41/2 Miles to Cocking' (a real place) and I would find my pace pick up and my spirits lift. This was because the smaller, more manageable miles were naturally more motivating because I knew I could get there.

Going back to the last chapter; bridging our hairy, scary goals with smaller, closer ones is a great way to take the fear out of our future. In addition, the reward we feel when we conquer a micro-goal is real - and kind of addictive. It will motivate you to keep going, one foot in front of the other.

Reason #3: Easier to keep on track

On the same walk, these signposts assured me I was heading in the right direction. When working on a long-term goal, it often isn't clear to see what progress you've made, without milestones; some marker to show you how far you've come and how far you have left.

Without milestones, we can be lead to flogging a horse long after it's dead OR giving up just before the end. Good goal setting needs to be broken down to micro-goals - easy to achieve, easy to keep track of and a great way of steering us in the right direction.

With micro-goals, I recommend making them small enough to do daily or weekly. Otherwise you may find yourself stagnating: it's much harder to pick up momentum again when you let yourself stop. These micro-goals can be as small as spending 10 minutes a day writing an email to someone you admire. Or it could be a one-time thing that removes a confidence block, such as deleting the Instagram app from your phone.

How to create your micro-goals

1) Chop up the bicycle

Did you know that a man once ate an entire bicycle? True story. And do you know how he did it? He chopped it up! Into tiny, pill-sized pieces. This is exactly what you can do for any overwhelming push goal.

The first step is taking a brain dump of every thing you can think of that will go into making this goal a reality. If the goal is getting a new client, brainstorm what needs to happen. This could include:

- Updating your Services page
- Getting some testimonials from old clients
- Adding some testimonials to your website
- Researching dream clients
- Creating a client contacts spreadsheet
- Write custom emails to each client
- Etc.

This might look like an overwhelming list now, but that's because you're looking at the whole bicycle. But when we don't consider all the steps it takes to reach our destination, we often become disheartened when we fail to get there.

Smashing a goal down into smaller, easier to achieve micro-goals gives us instant gratification. We can pick ourselves up and start small: one micro-goal at a time.

2) Bring order to chaos

The next step is sorting these micro-goals into some kind of order. It might feel like some tasks are equal in urgency and importance to another: that doesn't matter. It's really important to just decide on what comes first in order to move forward.

This is my tactic for avoiding decision fatigue. We'll get deeper into decision fatigue in part 3, but for now, know that the less decisions you have to make on a daily basis, the less resistance you'll have to doing the work.

Consider:
- Urgency - is the micro-goal time bound?
- Importance - will this goal have a direct effect on my Push Goal?
- Frequency - is this a one-off, or something I will do daily or weekly or monthly?

- Time required - is this quick (60 minutes or less) or more time consuming?

Note: If your micro-goal is longer than a couple of hours, I recommend breaking it down further. Make it micro, not just small!

3) Get your micro-goals in your calendar

Next is adding these micro goals into your calendar. It doesn't matter how you do this; whether you use a wall calendar, a pretty planner or a digital tool like Trello or Asana.

Personally I like to use a mixture: Asana is where all my projects go and I can look at my month in a glance. But each morning, I use a paper planner to map my day out, hour-by-hour. It doesn't matter what you pick, just make sure each item on your list is in your calendar, ideally with a time and day to tackle it added too.

Want to geek out on time management? Here we go:

3a) Map your plan out

I start with Asana, a great free app you can run in your browser or on your phone. I've come to adore it's interface, but all you really need is some way to add tasks and see them on a calendar. An advantage of Asana and similar tools, is that you can add subtasks to an individual task. You can also sort tasks into Projects, which each have neat little 'boards' and allows you to have a colour coded system.

It might take some practise to work out how much you can reasonably schedule and do in a given time period. When you have lots of things on the go, it's easy to over-book yourself and end up on the wrong side of overwhelmed.

To start with, try to under-schedule. If this means something will take longer than you expect: that's OK. Roll with it. You can always adjust as you go along.

3b) Set to-do dates

Having a deadline is one thing, but having a 'do date' is much more powerful. It means you're much less likely to forget or push back a less-than-sexy task. You can go one more step and assign a 'do time', which also removes indecision on the day itself. Then, when it comes to the day, all you have to do is look at your calendar in the morning and you know what's on your plate.

I can't stress the impact this simple change has made, compared to when I just used deadlines. With a looming deadline, it's easy to let other external factors take the reigns. Before you know it, the deadline comes and you've made zero progress on your micro-goal.

Scheduling in your tasks might mean saying no to spontaneous requests that comes your way. If I'm honest, for this introvert: that's a blessing. Too many creatives are putting others needs before their own, which may sound altruistic, but it's only hurting yourself and others when you grow resentful and have blocked your artistic drive.

4) Schedule reviews

There are a few extra dates I suggest you schedule. One is weekly review time. This doesn't have to take more than 15 minutes: it's just a way to reflect on your progress, and make adjustments for the following week. My reviews involve me looking back at my completed tasks, and the ones that are still to do. I also note any changes I'd like to make e.g. 'Do emails at lunchtime, not first thing in the morning' as well as things that have gone particularly well, or serendipitous events that have occurred (purely for a little motivational boost!)

I also schedule a quarterly review, which I allow a bit more time for. This is ideal because it coincides with my 90-day Push Goal. It means you can look at the goal you set out at the start of the quarter, and flick through your weekly reviews to see if you spot any patterns. Are there any tasks that consistently took longer than planned? Are there any tasks you avoided altogether? Do some digging to find out why this might be happening, and what impact it is having/had on your goal.

So what if you get to day 90 and you still haven't achieved your big goal? Not to worry: there's another 90 days to come! I'll be going through the process of Pivoting in Part 4. For now, focus on the first 90 days.

ACTION STEPS:

1) Decide on your 90-day push goal. Write it down. Make it pretty. Keep it somewhere visible and safe. You can use the Goal Setting Worksheet in the Resources.

2) Break it down into micro-goals.

3) Set deadlines for each micro goal and get them in your calendar.

4) Set a date to regularly review your goal progress.

5) When you achieve that goal, how will you celebrate? Who will you tell?

BONUS: Go through your goal setting checklist.

——

GOAL SETTING CHECKLIST

Setting the wrong goals is kind of like deciding to bake a chocolate cake, then going to the supermarket and buying some bananas and cabbage. Then throwing the bananas and cabbage in the oven and hoping a chocolate cake manifests.

No: this isn't a new recipe for a banana-cabbage-cake (although now you mention it, that could... NO!) This is a reminder, partly to myself, that there is such a thing as shitty goal setting.

I'm a goal setting addict, quite honestly. Sometimes I'm amazed at what I can get done when I set a good goal. I've been baffled in the past as to why I didn't hit the goal. It turns out, it's not for lack of effort. It's because I've been setting the wrong goals. Or, there's something screwy in my approach to achieving the goal.

So, after trial, error, reading and listening to all the goal-getting pros, I feel like I'm in a good place to share my Goal-Setting Checklist that I go through to make sure I set the RIGHT goals.

1. Is the goal specific?
It's tempting to set vague, blurry goals because they feel more attainable than going specific. For example 'lose weight' sounds easier than 'lose 10 pounds' because when we set the latter: we'll know damn well if we've failed or not. But when you set a vague goal, you end up with vague – or non-existent – results. Be brave: go specific.

2. Is the goal realistic?

I'm all for dreaming big, but then there's dreaming stupid. If we don't believe we can achieve what we set out to do: it won't happen.

"Whether you think you can, or you think you can't: you're right."
~ Henry Ford

The hackneyed quotes are the best, aren't they? Challenge yourself, but make sure there's a shred of hope in attaining your goal.

3. Did you set a hard deadline?

Having a time scale is key to getting anything done. I'm great at checking things off a to-do list: but only when I've set a date to get them done by, or do them on. I've noticed that when a task doesn't have a due date/to-do date attached: it stays undone. Set deadlines, and if you need to: set a load of reminders, whether it's on your phone, on your calendar, on your wall, on your roommates forehead...

4. Is it measurable?

This is another reason our goals need to be specific. When we have a way of measuring our progress, and the end goal, we can see clearly how close to the mark we are. Goals like 'get a better job' might be tricky because we don't have a measurement set. If the measurement unit is cash, then make it so. If it's time flexibility, measure the hours.

Bonus tip: When you have your measurement unit, measure regularly! Set an interval if you can, so you are tracking your progress as you go.

5. Did you set mini-rewards?

Other than the goal itself, which I suppose is the ultimate reward, it helps motivation to set mini-rewards. I like to set my goals for the week on a Sunday night. I also like to do some online window-shopping on a Sunday night... I tell myself that I'm 100% entitled to buy the thing I'm drooling over, so long as I hit my goal for that week. It's amazingly effective – especially when it's getting colder and you really want that new winter coat...

7. Is it risky?

If your rewards are the carrot, what's the stick? Naturally, our aversion to loss is a powerful driving force, and one we can take advantage of every once in a while (Lord knows it does the same to us often enough...) If you can, think of something you risk losing if you don't achieve the goal.

8. Do you identify with it?

This is a total brain-trip but it really works. The more we identify ourselves as the kind of person who does the thing we're trying to do/be/have: the more we're likely to follow through. So, if your goal is to go to the gym five times a week, tell yourself repeatedly: "I am the type of person who goes to the gym five times a week." It takes some time, but if you repeat this often enough (with emotion) then you'll believe it and act accordingly.

9. Have you set some margin for error?

Have you ever tried to do something daily, failed once, then given up entirely? Er... if you haven't, WHO ARE YOU?! I'm a sucker for this: I'm naturally an all-or-nothing type, so this goal setting adjustment has made all the difference for me and my perfectionistic tendencies. For example, your goal might be to cut out all refined sugar from your diet. If you tell yourself instead "My goal is to eat no refined sugar at least six days a week" you've built in margin for error. If you hit seven days, you rock! If you hit six, you still rock! Heck, if you hit two, you still rock: as long as you pick it up again when you're done on the sugar binge.

"Never confuse a single defeat with a final defeat."
~ F. Scott Fitzgerald

10. Did you set a time to you reflect?

I have a habit to set aside some time and reflect on the past week's goals. I ask myself whether I achieved them, sure. But more interesting to me is thinking of why I did or didn't manage to. This is the real point in any goal setting: we're setting the goal in the first place to GROW. To improve some area of our life.

Even if you missed the mark by a mile, you can still learn from what happened, and where possible: course-correct. That's the real benefit from goal setting. Otherwise I'd set goals like "make sure to drink coffee every day" – I know that isn't hard and I know that I won't exactly be growing from setting that goal. Reflecting on our goals also motivates us to keep going, and push past failed attempts. Failure gives us a choice: stop learning and stop growing by giving up OR learn, try again and ultimately: succeed.

Chapter 6:
What's Your Business Plan?

If you're a good business plan writer, you've probably got a good career in science fiction too. Sorry... My problem with business plans is that for most of us (especially in the creative industries) is that there are simply too many unknowns in our business. Coming up with answers in order to write a plausible business plan feels a lot like writing a science fiction novel: we usually don't feel grounded in reality.

When I was accepted onto the Princes Trust Enterprise program, the first thing they had us do was get us to write a very old school business plan. I slaved away at it, plucking numbers from the air and hoping for the best. It passed the test alright, but that thing was looked over once and never again saw the light of day.

That said, I'm not against the idea of business plans: my problem is in the old-school format many still adopt.

Enter... The Creative Introvert Business Model!

Fortunately, I've since been introduced to the Business Model Canvas: a dynamic, straightforward, BS free, actually very useful tool for mapping out your business and sharing it with other people.

It's a one-pager, divided up into sections. I've adapted the classic version to make the Creative Introvert Business Model, a more suitable version for the people I tend to work with, whether you're a freelancer or an entrepreneur.

1. Who are you creating for?	2. How will you communicate with your customer?
3. What problem/s will you solve?	4. What metrics will indicate your success?

5. Who do you need to collaborate with? Who are your suppliers?	6. What are your costs?	7. What will you charge for your work?

The important part is the questions it asks; all of which a regular business plan covers, just in a more concise and useful fashion.

Let's look at each of the sections in depth:

1) Who is this for?

If you only filled out one section, let it be this one! This is your Superfan (more on that in the next chapter.) This is the person who has no doubt about buying your product or hiring you: they simply love what you do and know it's for them. They'll be your most loyal returning customers: the ones who recommend you to their friends.

Of course, not everyone who buys from you will be your Superfan, and that's perfectly natural. But when you focus solely on your Superfan, the other lesser fans will jump on the bandwagon in time. Your Superfan is your ambassador: who does the marketing work *for* you.

A great example comes from Tim Ferriss, who after failing multiple times to find a tone for his first book, *The 4-Hour Work Week*, decided to write it as he would an email to his friend. The result? A book that reached not only Superfans (people like his friend) but over time, spread worldwide to people from a variety of backgrounds because it had enough momentum from the early adopters (people first to take on a new idea.)

When you get clear on your Superfan, and concern yourself only with their needs, the others will follow.

2) How will I look after my customers?

Once you know who you're creating for, it's time to think about keeping them happy. Whether you are creating a digital product, physical products or serving a client one-to-one, your top priority as soon as they become customers is to treat them like royalty.

There are some tried-and-true techniques that people adopt to offer high quality customer support. A supplement company might offer 100% money back guarantee, no questions asked. A web designer might offer six months free support after their client's site goes live. An Etsy seller might throw in some cute stickers alongside the print they shipped.

The important question to ask is whether or not it appeals specifically to your Superfan. If they're concerned about something before buying, no doubt they'll have the same concerns after. You have the opportunity to get in there and reassure them before they even make a purchase, so that they have no doubt whether what you're offering is for them. You might also have the opportunity to keep delighting them after the sale; surprising them with fun packaging, checking in weeks later to make sure everything is running smoothly with the new website.

3) What problem do you solve?

Just as with the concerns someone might have about buying, you have to be a bit of a mind-reader here about what your Superfan is struggling with. You'll go more in depth with this in the next chapter, but for now, have a think about all the problems your existing product or service might solve.

People aren't usually buying something for fun (even if it sometimes appears that way) but to solve a deeper problem. Some problems may seem a lot more urgent and important than others, but don't let this put you off. Have a think about some of your recent purchases, from toothpaste to sneakers to candles to toilet paper. All of these are solving some sense of lack or need you feel you have, even at a subconscious level.

4) What needs to happen to deliver my promise?

This is a helpful way to think about all the day-to-day tasks that go into making your business happen. For example, someone who crochets cardigans might need to spend time making the products, taking photos and listing them on their online store, promoting and posting on social media, reaching out to stockists and press, as well as answering emails from customers. It might help to think about this in terms similar to the parts used in this book: preparation, planning, producing, promoting, progress and people.

5) Who are my suppliers, collaborators, investors?

These are the people and resources you have at your fingertips, as well the people you'll likely be needing in the near future. This could be a very small list, particularly if you're a one-stop shop service based business, but I encourage you to add as much as you can to the list. There will be more examples and ideas for this in part 6.

6) What are my costs?

Costs are pretty straight forward, but it's also something many of us creatives tend to put off thinking about. Spend a good amount of time thinking about all the costs from hosting your website to buying supplies, postage and packaging and coffees with potential clients.

7) What will my customer pay?

Similar to considering your costs, it's very helpful to list out all your price points here and really see where your cash flow (the cash that flows in to your business) is coming from. More on pricing in the next chapter.

See? It's not so bad! I promise this will help clarify your ideas and will serve you very well if you're looking to get funding for your ventures now or in the future.

ACTION STEP:

Download your free Creative Introvert Business Model from the Resources. Don't worry if you can't fill it all out in depth right now, just start to get familiar with it and the questions it asks.

Troubleshoot: Finding Your Focus

F.O.C.U.S. = 'Follow One Course Until Success'

Ok, I totally nabbed that one from John Lee Dumas. It really resonates with me – a self-professed 'Multipotentialite,' which Emilie Wapnick describes as "someone with many interests and creative pursuits."

I know I'm not the only one that struggles with how to stay focused on my goals. I also know I'm not the only one that struggles with 'shiny object syndrome', which is the frustrating habit of starting one thing and then getting distracted by the next shiny project that comes your way. Ultimately, this disrupts your flow and leaving you with a lot of unfinished business. Sound familiar?

Think about it. You want <insert your Push Goal> and you want it accomplished by <insert your deadline> BUT, to get that done, you first need to tackle the other 1,482 things on your ever growing to-do list.

Enter... Overwhelm. The truth is, trying to do everything all at once is the quickest path to procrastination, stress, exhaustion and ultimately: burnout. Where creative introverts go to die!

To find your focus, you don't need years of mindfulness meditation, certifiable skills, weeks of planning, or days of decision making. A large part of overcoming your struggle with focus is simply addressing your fears. Fears like...

"What if I do this all wrong and have to start over again?"

"What if something better comes along but I miss it because I already got it done?"

"Maybe I should sit on this decision longer, because I'm just not ready!"

To help you bask in your productivity (and keep those fears in check), here are four ways to help you stay focused on your goals, so you can find your focus and actually get stuff done.

1) The Domino Test

One of the most satisfying visual feasts on earth is the collapse of a lengthy line of dominos. (Unless it's your younger sibling who set it off, of course.) Your Push Goal is a goal that acts much like that first domino, helping to knock down everything else that follows it. A goal that "if achieved would make all (or most) of your other goals possible", as Gary Keller, co-author of *The One Thing* would say.

This is a great technique to quickly figure out whether something is truly worth your full attention right now, or if it's just something you should let go of. For example, is writing a blog post every week something that will directly result in making any or all of your other goals more attainable?

Will it help you reach any of your other goals such as:

- Developing a creative style
- Growing an audience
- Building an email list
- Gaining industry experience

If you can say "yes, it does!", it passes the Domino Test. Go through the Domino Test with the tasks currently overwhelming you, or crowding your week and distracting you from your Push Goal.

2) Set up an experiment

Now it's time for an experiment, so put your lab coat on! Approaching a task in a scientific way can take a lot of self-sabotaging emotion out of picture. After all, if it's an 'experiment', you can't fail. You just observe, test and test again and again until you get the result you were looking for.

If you're feeling fear around the outcome of a project or task, try approaching it as an experiment. Setting your experiment is simply a matter of:

- Setting a measurable goal/outcome
- Setting a realistic deadline to make your measurement

- Taking your measurement and reflecting on what you learned

For example:

My measurable goal: finishing the illustrations for my comic book
My deadline for measurement: 12th January
...
12th Jan: I did it! It still has some typos and I need to rework some frames, but I'm super happy I got it done. It wasn't so painful after all!

Bonus tip: Create a visual reminder to keep your goal and outcome at the forefront of your mind. That may come in the form of making a vision board, sticking a post-it to the fridge, or setting a wallpaper on your home-screen or desktop. Do whatever method works best for you. It's all about eating, breathing and sleeping your one super focused goal at a time.

3) Take a 20 minute walk

Walking away and getting your heart rate up is the best free tool you have in the quest for focus. I know it might seem counterintuitive to take a break right when you're at your busiest, and especially when you're drowning in your massive to-do list, but the effects it will have on your clarity and ability to focus are undeniable.

Walking is physiologically proven to relieve stress and clear your mind. In fact, most of my most brilliant ideas (ok, and some pretty terrible ones too) have occurred on my daily walks.

If you give this technique a try, you'll likely find that you're **much more productive** than before you took a breather. Over time, if you do these walks daily, you'll quickly find that your to-do list starts to feel a lot less significant, and a lot more doable. It's all about keeping your cool, finding your focus, and that's what short daily walks will allow you to do.

4) No self-imposed restrictions

If lack of self control is something you struggle with (and chances are, if you consider yourself human, you'll probably admit to this) then I have some good news for you... There are apps for that!

There are plenty of clever apps and online tools that allow you to physically restrain yourself from procrastinating or losing your focus on the important things.

For example, Self Control is a favourite of mine that I've been playing with for some time. I love it because (1) it's super simple (2) it's free. Simply download the desktop app or install the Chrome plugin, and it will let you restrain yourself from certain distractions online: you tell it what websites are sucking up your time, and it does the rest.

Other great apps for focusing are Rescue Time and Hey Focus. Don't feel like you have to do this alone. Let these apps help you find and bask in your focus. That's exactly what they are there for!

5) Mindfulness

Finally, remember that focus is a practise, and one you can work on over time. There will be times when focus will come easy to you, and times when your creative mind will be fighting to break free like a wild horse. The key is to go easy on yourself.

Again, there's an app for this too! There are many, but I recommend Insight Timer for the sheer range of guided meditations you can listen to, or Meditation.Live for the interaction with real teachers.

Similarly to walking breaks, you may feel at first you don't have time for meditation. But I'll have to quote the classic: 'You don't have time to NOT meditate!' This theory has always proved true in my most busy, hectic and unfocused times. When I can dedicate even 10 minutes of quiet time to myself in a day (usually easiest in the morning), it's never long before I start re-focusing and feeling like me again.

ACTION STEPS:

1) Make a list of your most common distractions.

2) Pick one of the above tools or strategies to help manage your focus for the next week, and check in with yourself in a week from today. You might find that simply noticing that you get distracted is enough to reign yourself in, and find your focus again.

Resources mentioned:

Self Control - https://selfcontrolapp.com
Rescue Time - https://www.rescuetime.com
Hey Focus - https://heyfocus.com/

Chapter 7:
How Much Will You Charge?

How much does that cost?

Did you cringe? I don't blame you. Most creatives shy away from the money question – especially introverts. It's understandable, given the battle we face: charging so much that we get rejected by our potential buyers, versus charging so little that we can barely afford to feed ourselves. One of the problems that makes pricing our creative work so difficult, is how we conflate the number on the price tag with our own personal worth.

The result? Charging too little will reflect our low self-esteem, and if that's all we believe our work is worth, we start to believe it's all *we're* worth. Charging too much and being rejected? We tell ourselves *we've* been rejected.

The first tweak in your Mindsettings in this chapter is that: **your pricing should make you feel good.** That you are NOT your work; nor your work's worth. It should scare you a little, but not so much that you feel like a crook. There is a sweet spot, and this chapter will help you find it.

How to price your services

I used to start every conversation with a potential client with price. I knew (or thought I knew) that their first question would be 'how much will it cost?' So I figured I'd get it out of the way as soon as I could. And because I was assuming the worst, I pitched as low as I could reasonably go, my hourly rate of around £30. It usually went down well with them. Until the next question. Which would undoubtedly be... how long will it take?

My answer was always an apologetic: *it depends*. That's when a silence would fall and my potential client started to get that uneasy look, as if the waiter just told them that fish they'd eaten might have been a few days old. Whoops.

What I was doing was focussing on my concerns, not on my clients. I was worried sick about that nightmare client who is simply never satisfied, long after the brief is met. The problem I had was that I didn't even know what my client wanted, which comes as no surprise because... I hadn't asked them yet.

Without knowing your clients needs at a deep level, you can't possibly price appropriately. In addition, when you talk about price *before* exploring what your client is trying to achieve, you risk creating a solution that isn't even right for them. Can you blame them from becoming a nightmare client then?

When this finally clicked, I started to tell them I needed to understand what they wanted, *before* I gave a price. Most people are fine with that. If they're desperate to know a 'ballpark' figure, you can give them a range, but do your best to avoid that. As a rule of thumb: the person who gives a number first, loses! In addition, if your prospect is someone who focuses on the price before anything else, you're better off fishing elsewhere anyway.

You want to find out whether this person is one of your Superfans, or close to it. You want to know the pain they might be experiencing, the problems they want to solve, what their dreams are, what their big goals are.

If they aren't clear about their needs, then pricing becomes guesswork, and the project probably won't run smoothly. In order for you to do your best work, and for the client to get what they pay for, both of you need to know that the work you deliver can meet the specific needs of the client and generate a return on their investment. You'll sleep better when you know that too.

How to help a client express what they want

Ideally, your client can express what they're trying to achieve in a monetary amount; how much they can make or how much they can save. A website to 'raise brand awareness' is tricky to price, but a website that generates approximately £10,000 per month gives you something to work with. Sometimes, you have to use your own imagination to work out what measurable value you can bring your client, and explain that to them.

For example, you might have a client who says they'll know the project is successful if people think the resulting website is 'beautiful.' Beauty isn't exactly easy to measure, but you could run before and after surveys on your client's audience, asking how beautiful they deem it to be. If the survey shows the percentage of people who love the new website goes from 25% to 75%, that might be valuable enough to them. You could ask what would they be willing to pay to see that kind of result.

Why value-based pricing is great for awkward introverts

What I love most about value-based pricing is the more you practise this approach over the hourly/daily-rate approach, the more confident you'll get in sending your invoices. I've seen this happen myself as well as to countless other freelancers. When you know that what you're doing is backed up with real value, you free up your time and stop being a slave to the clock. You'll take pride in your work, knowing the higher purpose for each job. In addition, you'll be motivated to level up your skills, knowing that the more value you can add, the more you can get paid.

Two pricing strategies for services:

Services Sample Pricing Strategy #1

Use this when you don't know how long the project will take, and/or if you think your client has other good options.

1) Identify your customer's 'second-best option'; your competition. If your customer can't buy your product or service, then what would he or she choose?

2) Find out the price of that second-best option.

3) List all of the ways that your offering is better. Estimate how much you think these differences are worth to your customers.

4) List all the ways that the second-best offering is better. What can they offer that you cannot? Be very honest here.

How much do you think these benefits are worth to your customers?

5) To calculate the best price:
- Take the price of the second-best option;
- Add the value of your advantages;
- Subtract the value of the second-best option's advantages.
-

Your final number is your quote!

Services Sample Pricing Strategy #2

Use this when you have a good idea of project scope - time required, resources, the nature of the client and so on.

1) What's your hourly rate (your 'wouldn't get out of bed for less' rate)?

2) How many hours do you think the project will take?

3) Multiply the two numbers above, then go through the following, adjusting that figure as you go:

4) Who's the client?
- Private Client Private Client - The Client is paying for the project from his personal money - change nothing
- Small / Medium Business Small / Medium Business - The business is already making some money or funded - multiply by 1.1
- Large Corp Large Corp - A company with lots of employees that's making lots of money - multiply by 1.2

5) Is the project interesting?
- Boring - multiply by 1.2
- Not bad - multiply by 1.1
- Dream Project - change nothing

6) After the project...
- I will hate myself a little - multiply by 1.2
- Not much/will look good on my portfolio - multiply by 1.1
- My life might change - change nothing

Your final number is your quote!

There's also an online version of this that does the maths all for you. Take the test: http://thenuschool.com/how-much/#/client

How to price your products

Products are somewhat more simple to price than services, because we often have a guide to work with due to material expenses. That said, you still need to factor in time and skill: two valuable but ineffable variables that only you can gauge accurately.

1) Calculate your cost of goods sold (COGS)

The first step is working out a cost price: what it takes you to make your product, your raw materials and so on. Things to calculate and add up:

- Raw materials/variable costs

List absolutely everything you use to make each item, from canvases right down to the tiniest scrap of ribbon.

- Your labour costs and experience level

How long does it take you to make one item and how much are you going to charge for your time? For example, if you can make two necklaces in an hour and you want to pay yourself £15 an hour, then the labour cost for each necklace is £7.50. Also keep in mind your experience level, when you think about how much you want to earn per hour. This is the thing that crafters and makers seem to struggle with most, but let's just say you're probably worth more than you think!

- Overheads/fixed costs

Your overheads are things like rent on your workshop or studio, any equipment you need, phone and internet, the cost of electricity and other utilities, insurance, marketing materials, labelling and packaging and so on. You need to cover all these costs to ensure that you are not operating at a loss. These are known as 'fixed costs' because they remain the same, no matter how many or how few items you sell. You may find it easiest to calculate these as a monthly amount.

Remember, all the above can go up (or down) with time. It's worth keeping track of this in a spreadsheet, and making a point to regularly re-calculate them. Find your COGS spreadsheet in the Resources.

2) Next, it's time to get your calculator

Once you've got a number for your raw materials and labour costs per item, have a think about how many items you can make and sell per month. Then divide your fixed costs for that month by the number of items you expect to create and sell over the same period. Add that figure to your variable costs, and you know the true cost price for one item.

For example, say your raw materials and labour costs for one item come to £5.70 and you think you can make and sell 300 items in one month. Your fixed costs come to £800 per month. Divide £800 by 300 and you get £2.66. Add £5.70 to £2.66 – this comes to £8.36.

This covers all your costs (assuming you sell all 300 items) – but all you've done is break even. To make a profit you have to add a mark-up to each item.

3) It's time to set a price

Generally, you should aim for at least a 100% mark-up – that is, double the cost price. Ideally, multiply the cost price by 2.4 or 2.5. Most shops for example will work on this principle of a x 2.4 or x 2.5 mark-up on what they pay you – so if you sell to them at £10 per item, they will sell the item at £24 or £25. (Bear in mind that the extra £14 or £15 is not pure profit for the shop: they have their own overheads to cover.)

Allowing shops to order from you in bulk means you may sell more but at a slightly lower price per unit. Weigh up how much profit you're set to make and look at setting up a minimum order, whether it's for ten items or 100.

Don't be afraid to negotiate with the buyer. Larger stores with a more established reputation may wish to place a small, introductory order to test the waters – if you're happy with this and feel it will benefit your business, give it a go, but nor should you feel pressured into saying yes to something if you feel you're being taken advantage of.

Sample pricing formulas

Here are the pricing formulas commonly used by creatives with physical products who want to determine a price for wholesale and/or retailers:

- Raw materials + Your time = Item cost (COGS)
- Item cost x 2.2 (up to 2.5, depending on how much you want to mark up) = Wholesale price
- Wholesale price x 2.2 = Retail price

Other pricing factors

You could also work out what the market-value of the product you make is (for example, a knitwear designer may look at other designs for sale to get an idea of costs) and work backwards to see whether that gives you the profit margin you need – but you still need to know your costs in order to work out if you're making enough.

Looking at what your competitors charge is a really useful exercise to see where your offering sits in the wider world. You don't want to pitch your price too high and price yourself out of the market; equally, there's no benefit in undercutting a competitor's price if you end up selling more but making less profit.

Much of this comes back to your original market research and **what you know your Superfan will pay.** Remember there's just as much risk in pricing your product too low as too high: customers who buy original art or handmade products, for example, expect quality and this should be reflected in your prices. We expect a premium product to come with a premium price tag. Price something too low, and your customers might assume that it's not of the best quality or craftsmanship, and shop elsewhere.

ACTION STEP:

Select one service or product that you offer or plan to offer, and work out the cost price. How much are you currently selling it for? Do you need to up your prices, according to your new formula?If so, start updating anywhere your work is listed, stat!

If you're a service-based business with retainer clients or clients likely to return for more, consider sending an email to update them on your new prices. This is very common, and something I urge you not to shy away from. Employees have raises, usually yearly to reflect inflation, and no doubt you're overdue a personal raise.

Find an email template for raising your prices in the Resources.

Troubleshoot: The Starving Artist

What happens when you've done the work? When you've birthed your creative project and it's out in the world, kicking and screaming and making a fuss? What next?

How do you actually send your creative work 'out there' so that it doesn't fall flat on its face; so that it gets noticed by the cool kids and (hopefully) not bullied? These are the questions that marketing answers.

Oh jeez. I wrote the 'm' word already... Marketing.

How about this one: 'self-promotion?'

Or 'personal brand?'

If you're still reading, I applaud you. These are terms that send many creative introverts running for the hills – or better, a nice warm bed far, far away from the land of advertising and showy sales pitches.

Can't we just do as Steve Martin says and "be so good they can't ignore you?" Well, not unless you're Steve Martin. Not unless you're willing to wait until it's too late to be 'discovered' by your knight in shining armour.

"In order to be found, you have to be findable."
~ Austin Kleon

Being 'findable' means:
- Sharing new work, regularly with your audience
- Knowing what you do and why you do it and being able to explain that to someone in a clear, concise way
- Having a specific idea of your Superfan - specific enough that you could write them a friendly email about a subject that interests them
- Making it a no-brainer for your audience to tell their friends about your work

It does not (have to) mean:
- Schmoozing with journalists at glitzy networking events
- Spending multiple hours a day on all the social media platforms yelling about your stuff for sale
- Buying likes or followers
- Pretending to be something you're not
- Selling your soul to the devil
- Becoming an extrovert

It's quite simple really: in order to make a living that involves doing what you love (for the most part)... you need to get paid. To attract a group of people who appreciate what you do and want to support you so that you can keep doing it (and they can continue to benefit from it). No 'extroverting' required.

"We don't make movies to make money. We make money to make movies."
~ Walt Disney

Jeff Goins in *Real Artists Don't Starve* enlightened me about the 'real' Michelangelo. The myth that he was simply a poor servant of others, a slave to his art. It surprised me to learn that Michelangelo was, in fact very wealthy. His net worth after finishing the ceiling of the Sistine Chapel, was roughly $47 million in today's money.

I won't lie: this little factoid didn't make me warm to the artist nearly as much as being told about Vincent Van Gogh's woes; the starving, troubled artist who never got his fair dues in his lifetime. I was in love with the romance of the starving artist.

Until I realised: that's not the life I wanted. I didn't want to live a life of misery because no one values my art. I decided I'd make a living – a good one – doing what I loved, at least most of the time. Similarly, the archetype of the extroverted salesman with slicked back hair and shifty eyes is also one I knew I wanted to avoid, and I imagine you do too.

The danger of fearing these archetypal characters is the risk of you losing your power to choose something better; a life on your terms. When you lose this power, you get lawyers who dreamed of painting, accountants too scared to pursue ballet. Worse, you get the miserable artist; who grows old and cranky with resentment, struggling to make rent because it isn't honourable to get paid for their work.

The internet is supplying us with more opportunities than ever to find support in communities, both financially and emotionally. You don't need an expensive PR team, a degree in Marketing, to go to every networking event under the sun... You don't even need a rich Italian family supporting you like ol' Mickey A.

Creatives can step up, take risks and go for opportunities they never had before, and reap the rewards; all without becoming something they're not. Creative introverts can do what they love, get the recognition they deserve AND make a very good living doing it... If they're prepared to take matters into their own hands.

This isn't the easy path, I'll grant you. In fact this part of the book might make you push your comfort zone more than any other. But: my promise to you is that you will be given the tactics and tools to craft your very own promotional plan that feels right for you – and that actually works.

How to drop the starving artist myth

This starving artist stuff is a lot more complex than I've described it so far. Lifelong, inherited issues surrounding money, self-worth and our place in society plague many of us, not just those trying to pursue a career in the creative industries.

I wish I could tell you that removing these 'money blocks' is as simple as unclogging a drain with bicarb soda and vinegar (works a treat, by the way.) But the truth is it can take years to uncover our true sense of value, and develop our ability to ask for what we have earned through our hard work. This is an ongoing process, something that you can master over time, with patience and willing.

The good news is: there are a few simple, practical steps you can take, starting today, to make a start on unclogging this financial blockage:

1) Start surrounding yourself with folk who don't moan about money

They certainly don't have to be millionaires, but they do have to have a positive outlook about financial success, and might have even made a fair penny from their own creative pursuits. If you can't find them in person (or don't want to) have a quick look online and join some groups on Facebook. Who are the professionals in your chosen industry?

Whose success would you like to emulate? Is there someone you can ask the question, "how did you get to where you are?" This is partly why I began The Creative Introvert Podcast: to have these very conversations! Having conversations with people who have a healthy relationship with money or at least have little to no resistance around earning money, will ultimately rub off on you.

It's said that you're the average of the five people you spend the most time with. I've come to believe this one. Who are the five people you hang around most? Are those five people helping or hindering your money mindset? Even if you don't want to hang around with anyone new, you can still go on a 'junk conversation' diet. No more moaning about money, lack of money or people who make money.

2) Identify your starving artist myth

Something that has accelerated me healing my relationship with money was getting clear on what my money blocks were. Get a pen and a piece of paper and answer questions like:

- What thoughts do I have around my ability to make more money?
- What do I think about people with a lot of money?

- What do I think my work is worth?
- What have others told me about making money from creative pursuits?

Write out all of your money beliefs and thoughts – and don't censor yourself! Like I said, this is an ongoing process for many of us, and I often return to this exercise when I reach new financial goal and feel the resistance creep in.

3) List the ways you could be letting more money in

This could range from going for a promotion at work (all the more cash to fund your creative work) to raising your rates for your services work to adding higher priced products to your online store.

You don't have to act on these straight away, but notice the opportunities you already have. The more often you do this exercise, the more readily you'll spot new opportunities for creating income, and the more comfortable you'll feel with asking for fair prices for your work.

ACTION STEP:

Work through the worksheet, 'My New Thriving Artist Story' in the workbook.

Chpater8:
Who Do You Need To Be?

"Before you can do something, you first must be something."
~ Goethe

Confession time. My name isn't really Cat Rose. It's Catherine Rose Anne Neligan. I know there isn't anything wrong with the name I was born with (especially when my aim in life is to marry someone with a last name starting with a 'P', for the comedy initials I'd get.) But when I went to art college, I decided my name would no longer be Catherine: I would introduce myself as Cat.

At first, this was a way to escape the uncomfortably long, multisyllabic name I was given (which I also associated with being told-off) and replace it with an easier option, also a nod to my favourite animal species on the planet. But I soon discovered it was much more than a simple drop of six letters. I found a new kind of confidence in my name. When I started art school, introducing myself as Cat, even if it felt uncomfortable at first, started to make me feel like a different person. Like I might actually fit in with all these cool, artsy hipster kids, with names like Poppy and Hudson.

There's nothing wrong with my family name either (despite the countless mispronunciations by admin staff over the years) but 'Rose' is a pretty good middle name, one most people can pronounce, so I upgraded it to my last name. With that, Cat Rose my Alter Ego, was born.

Over the years, she's really come into her own. She has determined the clothes I wear, the words I use, the places I go for fun and - through no conscious effort - the people who are drawn to or repelled by me.

She's the one I call on when I need to step on a stage and talk to a room full of unknown, expectant faces. She's the one who speaks my pre-planned words on each podcast; who selects the cadence and emphasis and slips in a cheeky swear. Is she a parasite? Something that lives inside me and I let out on occasion? Heck no! She's my Alter Ego, or what Carl Jung would refer to as my Persona.

The Persona, as Jung defines, is what we would like to be and how we wish to be seen by the world. The word 'persona' comes from a Latin word that literally means 'mask'. In this sense, the word can be applied metaphorically, representing all of the different social masks that we wear for different groups of people and situations.

I don't recommend over-identifying with your Persona or Alter Ego, as this is not your *whole* Self. Instead, seeing it as your translator, your bodyguard, your sexy frontman: the one who helps you stand your ground and do what you need in society. If someone doesn't like it? Big deal. It isn't your *whole* Self. It's just a carefully chosen sliver of Self.

Am I suggesting you change your name? Start dressing differently? Adopt an accent? Whilst all of that could be great fun, it really isn't necessary. Your Alter Ego could be as simple as a picture you hold in your minds eye as someone who stands up tall, and meets people with a smile. When you step into this imagined state – and practise it – magic happens. You become that version of you.

Keep it real(ish)

Creating an Alter Ego in this book, does not mean faking anything. This is part of my ongoing war against 'fake it till ya make it.' There's a good chance you've heard or read this common piece of advice at some point. That all we have to do to appear more confident, appropriate or successful is to just... FAKE IT!

Whilst acting 'as if' might work for some, for the majority of creative introverts I've encountered, feeling like we're faking something doesn't breed confidence: if anything, it just increases imposter syndrome.

What is imposter syndrome?

One of the reasons you might lack confidence in a situation is feeling like an imposter. Like you're a total fake: just waiting to be found out. I've experienced this throughout my life, whether it was in my first job (junior web designer), with no real experience in web design other than my own experiments in Dreamweaver (more like Nightmare weaver...) to starting my freelance design career and wondering if I was even invoicing correctly.

I haven't found hard evidence to support why imposter syndrome is so common in creative introverts, but Laura Woods offers a plausible answer:

"Introverts tend to be highly, perhaps overly, analytical and self-aware. It could be that the root of Imposter Syndrome is really just self-absorption: spending too much time worrying about yourself and how others see you."

However, there are plenty of outwardly confident people who are struck by this fraudulent feeling too. Celebrities such as Natalie Portman have openly admitted to feeling insecure about their abilities.

She reported "I felt like there had been some mistake, that I wasn't smart enough to be in this company, and that every time I opened my mouth I would have to prove that I wasn't just a dumb actress," when arriving at Harvard as a freshman. Basically: no one is safe from feeling like a fraud – regardless of achievement or fame.

Hopefully this news won't destroy your hopes of 'growing out' of imposter syndrome, but will illustrate the point that imposter syndrome has nothing to do with your level of talent or skills. The problem comes from feeling like we're 'faking' something, which inherently makes us feel guilty. Insincere. Like we're going to be found out.

The reason I bring this up is to emphasise why finding an Alter Ego that aligns with your most authentic, true Self is so important. When your Alter Ego is working for you, you won't feel like you're going to be 'found out' or that you can't step up to the plate, in case you let someone down. Your Alter Ego will carry you through: it's hardy, capable and still true to you. After all, you created it.

Your Alter Ego is always evolving

Do you start learning to drive a car already feeling like a qualified driver? Not likely. Instead, you go through the learning process, which feels more like 'becoming' than being there. The process of learning to drive is really about learning to feel what driving a car is like. So much so, that your body intuitively knows what to do when you're out on the road. Calling yourself a 'Driver in training' or a 'Learner' is a way of bridging the gap: it feels authentic. It gives us the permission to get behind a wheel with our teacher, and enough confidence to know that at some point we'll be licensed to drive solo.

Virtually any new experience could be seen in this light. It isn't a black and white distinction, between being a total newbie to being a pro. As soon as we say yes to something new: our Alter Ego adapts to fit the new identity. We are always Creatives in the making. No one can stop us. They might be able to delay our journey, but only for a little while. It's up to us to keep up with our momentum.

If you find someone who truly believes they've 'made it', that just means they've stopped growing. The function of a creative is to always be creating on some level. It feels pretty terrible when we're not moving forward... it feels a lot like depression. Conversely, moving forward too fast without keeping up with our own creative momentum can feel intensely stressful... it feels a lot like anxiety.

Your Alter Ego is a way of encapsulating a sense of self, a cluster of feelings that adapts when you need to take on something new, enabling you to move in the right direction at the right speed.

How to Find Your Alter Ego

This starts with the simple question: who do I need to be to make this happen? You might have seen the What Would Jesus Do wristbands. How about asking yourself, What Would <INSERT YOUR ALTER EGO NAME> Do? More importantly, how would they *feel*?

In preparing to speak on stage, I don't expect to feel free from nerves. I wouldn't want that for my audience: I know a little bit of adrenaline will help me bring the energy I need for an engaging talk. Nor do I spend my time freaking out about making a mistake.

Instead, I ask myself what my Alter Ego would be doing and feeling in that moment. She might be remembering to take deep breaths. Standing up tall with her shoulders back. Feeling excited – maybe a bit giddy – to share her message and get to her favourite part: questions from the audience.

Just running through this helps me align with a believable version of myself: this Cat Rose character is not Lady Gaga on stage; she has her own style. It's close enough to my true Self that it feels attainable: but not so far beyond my lesser self that I feel like a faker. It's like having someone just one step in front of you, who holds your hand and helps pull you in the right direction.

ACTION STEPS:

You can do one, two or all of these exercises. They're really just fun ways to start clarifying who your Alter Ego is and ways to call on them when you need an extra boost of confidence or anything else for that matter.

1) Your Alter Ego's Lucky Socks

You don't need to power dress to make use of your Alter Ego. But I do believe in the power of a good outfit or item of clothing that helps you feel like a badass.

This is very individual, but consider how you like your clothes to make you feel. You might simply want to feel comfortable. This is partly why I refuse to wear stiletto heels. That would be both uncomfortable and a safety hazard. You might want to keep it subtle: maybe it really is a pair of socks that make you giggle, but no one else needs to see them. You could wear them to a dull meeting at work, to bring a bit of creativity and play to your Monday morning.

Try on lots of options. Go through your wardrobe and ask yourself on a scale of 1–10 how those outfits make you feel. If you're getting mostly 1–5s, consider going shopping for a new item of clothing. It's easy for us to get stuck in wardrobe ruts, and sometimes it means buying something totally new and 'unlike' ourselves, in order to shake it up and feel like someone new.

2) Your Alter Ego's Day in the Life

Walking through your ideal day is a wonderful way of imagining what your Alter Ego would do, feel and create. When you have this roadmap, you can work out ways of bringing more of this character into your own life. Ask yourself:

- What would your Alter Ego do in the morning?
- What time would they wake up?
- What would they eat for breakfast?
- Would they work out? What exercise would they do?
- How much time would your Alter Ego dedicate to creativity?
- Who would your Alter Ego spend time with?

Finally, ask yourself which of these you could adopt in your own life. This really is remarkable in that when you start making slight tweaks to your everyday routine, you can over time, start feeling like a different person.

3) Your Alter Ego's Mascot

This is a fun, quick addition you can take with you wherever you go. For example, is there a lucky charm you've used in the past? Or is there something new you can use to mark your creation of this Alter Ego: maybe it's a little illustrated character you keep on a card in your wallet.

Anything that reminds you that you have this ability to tap into a next-level version of you. Again, this Alter Ego isn't a different person: it is simply an extension of you, a juiced-up version that you can use to take on just about anything you dream of.

Part 3:
Promote

Chapter 1:
Authentic Promotion

"You need to stop wishing that one day you'll be discovered, or there will be a sudden surge in interest in your work, or that a wealthy patron will drop large and regular cheques through your letterbox. Yep, it happens now and again, but not to most common mortals."
~ Pete Mosley

It's likely you've been exposed to the kind of sales techniques that make you feel queasy. Our TV screens, laptops, and phones are full of them, after all. The 'hard sell' that makes you feel pressured into buying something you don't need and don't even want. No wonder we don't want to talk about our work; God forbid anyone think we're trying to do the sleazy car salesman on them.

When I had my first go at business, which was in selling my designs on t-shirts and prints, I absorbed a wide range of information about sales and marketing. Some of it was wise, and responsible for many successes that I still benefit from today. Some of these approaches might have worked for some, but when I tried them, I just felt gross.

I noticed a pattern. The stuff I tried that didn't feel good, was the stuff that didn't work. It's like my audience could sense my discomfort; that I wasn't being true to myself. When the methods you use to share your work feel wrong, the results will be lacklustre.

What I did find was that by adapting little things, tweaking someone else's advice to suit my own personality type and preferences... I started seeing results.

It takes confidence to show your work and talk about what you do, but this becomes much easier when you **believe in what you're saying**; when you trust your feelings about it, who you're presenting it to, and where you're presenting it.

Common objections to sharing our work:

"I'm afraid if I share my ideas and get rejected, it will confirm that I have nothing of significance to offer anyone." (Judgement)

"When I share my work and get no views or likes or comments, it feels terrible. I hate the feeling of being invisible." (Insignificance)

"My work isn't unique enough." (Originality)

"It's not developed enough, it isn't ready to communicate what I want it to." (Perfectionism)

"My work says so much about myself. Showing it to others makes me feel naked." (Vulnerability)

"Fear of success. Getting overwhelmed by it." (Responsibility)

"I don't want to give away great concepts for free." (Greed)

"My technology blows, and I can't quite achieve a look like the pros achieve." (Comparison)

The truth is that all of these fears comes down to **self-doubt**. Do you doubt your ability to deliver what you promise? Do you doubt the quality of your work? A good way to test this out is in your elevator pitch.

"The worst enemy to creativity is self doubt."
~ Sylvia Plath

In this part, you'll find the tools, techniques and self-talk I've learned over the years from my own struggles with confidence to get my creative work out there, and what I've seen work with the creative introverts I coach.

1) Why Do You Struggle With Self-Promotion?

If you think marketing isn't for you because you're an introvert – sorry! No excuses any more: I'll reveal why introverts are actually excellently equipped to market and sell – all without selling their soul to the devil and uncover how to think differently about making a fantastic living from your creative work.

2) How Does Content Marketing Work?

Next I'll bring out the big guns: content marketing – a way that you can give your audience tonnes of value, attract and connect with your Super Fans and make it a no-brainer for them to hire you or buy your stuff.

3) How Do You Build Your Online Home?

If you still don't have somewhere to share your work online, this is a chapter to bookmark. It lays out my entire step-by-step process for building your very own online home.

4) What the Heck Do You Say?

In case you still have doubts about your ability to create content that connects with your Superfans and showcases your work, I'll be answering all your concerns here.

5) How Do You Plan Your Promo?

By the end of this chapter, you'll have the ability to go out there and promote your work better than many people who get paid to do this. The best part? You'll be able to do it in a way that suits you down to a Tweet.

6) How Do You Grow Your Audience?

This is where you get a LOT of bang for your buck in getting eyes and ears on your work. Getting yourself in front of other people's audiences is key for leveraging your marketing efforts. Don't worry – this isn't as stressful or complicated as it sounds. And you might be happy to know creative introverts are better at this than the average bear.

7) How Do You Collaborate (and Why Would You?)

My secret weapon! And the one I was loathe to use for the longest time. This is everything I know about working collaboratively with someone, without driving each other insane and rueing the day you ever considered sharing the load.

8) How Do You Network?

Networking is still a word that sends shivers down my spine; I only use it because I think you know what I'm talking about. I prefer to think of it as 'bulk connecting' because that takes the pressure off this massive 'network' I'm meant to be building, plus it describes more accurately what I feel like I'm doing. I'll share the ways in which I turn nearly any event into a connecting opportunity - no networking required.

9) How Do You Speak in Public?

One of the most useful life skills a creative can have, regardless of how introverted they are is... public speaking. I don't know if this is scarier than death, but let's just say I've been through it and come out the other side relatively unscathed (public speaking, as opposed to death.)

There are Action Steps at the end of each chapter so be sure to have a pen and paper next to you! You can also download your accompanying Creative Introvert workbook and all the resources mentioned throughout the book at: www.thecreativeintrovert.com/book

You will also find Troubleshooting chapters peppered throughout the book, to help you overcome any challenges that may arise in working through the exercises. And if you have any questions for me at any point, don't hesitate to email: hello@thecreativeintrovert.com

Chapter 2:
Why Do You Struggle With Self-Promotion?

What if everything we thought about our self-promotion abilities was just plain fantasy? A miserable one at that. You might think you're not wired for talking to the masses about what you do and you might think you're a walking disaster when it comes to selling. But what if that's all... hooey?

I'll be the first to admit, as a hardcore introvert: many of the tactics and skills preached by typical marketing and sales 'gurus' rub me up the wrong way. I know how difficult it is to blow our own trumpet, and I'm certainly not recommending you do something that makes you feel slimy and inauthentic.

But what if our introvert Superpowers (see Part 1, chapter 4) **actually give us an advantage** over our extroverted counterparts? Let's have a look at what we know about the gifts of introversion, and how they apply to see-promotion:

1) Empathy

I don't believe this or any other skill I'll mention is reserved for introverts alone, but there is research to suggest that innies are naturals at accessing empathy.

How does empathy fit into marketing your creative work? Well for one, it's the ability to tailor your pitch specifically for the recipient; making it all about them, and less about you. The result is that our pitch, whether it's in an email or on a blog post or in-person, expresses how much we care. And that goes a long way when it comes to someone liking and trusting us enough to fork over their cash.

So how does one apply these innate empathy skills? To start, work out exactly what your audience needs, wants, desires and how you can make it happen for them. For example, I worked out that helping the big community of health and wellness professionals in my city would be a great way to make a name for myself when I was starting out from scratch as a freelancer. Why them? I understood their niche because I spent three years as a healthy lifestyle blogger myself, I knew their audience, and how to reach them. Plus my design and marketing skills meant I could create a package really tailored to their reeds.

So when it came to reaching out to local businesses, I didn't just say "Hey stranger, I do this and I'm amazing at this and I've worked with them and oooh don't you want to work with me??" No. Instead, I matched their needs to my skillset and customised my approach, after doing my research on each and every potential new client.

It worked rather well, with a 40% reply rate and 25% becoming new, loyal clients for my design and marketing services. Considering these were 'cold' pitches (I was new in town after all), these are pretty great results.

You've already put your empathy skills into place if you took action from Part 2, chapter 2, where you identified your Superfan. Kudos! The next step is listening to them.

2) Listening

Now this is the biggie. Yes, it can certainly help to have the gift of the gab as a creative: you can spread your ideas to others, negotiate when you need something and talk endlessly about your latest, greatest project. But listening is a skill that can strengthen a relationship and is required to connect on a deep and meaningful level with others.

For example, a study by Adam Grant revealed that employees were more likely to be proactive and productive under introverted leadership, as they felt more encouraged and listened to. He found that extroverted leaders are more likely to feel threatened by employee proactivity, and less likely to listen to suggestions from staff.

You may not feel like a leonine leader, but you become one as soon as you decide to take matters into your own hands and reach a wider audience in order to make a living from your creative work.

An introverted creative can go far, simply by using their natural skills to do more listening than speaking, because people want to be heard. Listening to your customers or even potential customers will dramatically change your relationship with them, founding it on trust and their faith that you are the one they want to support or hire.

Listening could be asking people what they like about something that already exists, and what bugs them about it. You could also listen to conversations in cafes that your potential Superfans might hang out at. It's surprising what you can learn from over a cheeky cuppa.

Then there's listening to your existing or past clients and customers, letting them share what they really think about your work or what they need now.

The next step is using what you hear. This means playing back what you hear but in your own words. Rather than continue to ask more questions, you make statements. You check that what you heard means what you think. Then you can take what you heard and make it the foundation for your next idea and how you present it, whether it's in an item description, sales pitch or new product.

What to listen out for:

- Strong opinions, positive or negative
- Pain points, problems
- Irrational loves, obsessions
- Comparisons to existing ideas, products, brands
- Anything that brings up an emotional response

Places to listen:

- Cafes, coffee shops
- On social media (try searching a hashtag related to your niche)
- In your client/customer testimonials
- Send surveys (see resources for templates)

What to do with what you hear:

- Use it in website copy
- Use it in email copy
- Use it in a product listing
- Use it when pitching an idea

3) Introspection

Let's say you've used your empathy Superpowers, you've used your profound listening skills on your Superfans... what then? Now it's time to listen to yourself.

Despite the introspective habits of great philosophers to modern day neuroscientists: the majority of people today spend little to no time really investigating themselves in a meaningful way. This doesn't mean navel gazing and thinking about what house at Hogwarts you'd best be suited to (though that is fun...) it's about using what you know about yourself to **inform what you know about others**, and working out ways to act on those insights.

Whether you're assessing the results of a survey you sent out, or thinking about copy for your latest product listing; a good dose of introspection will go far. It's the ability to reflect on what you've done in the past, what worked, what didn't work, as well as weigh up your future choices. It's reflecting on what specifically worked for your personality type and preferences.

Without this ability, your market research and marketing efforts will be wasted, unless you strike it very lucky. Chances are, the reason those overnight successes that you never hear of again failed is because of a lack of introspection.

How to turn around self-doubt

If there are any remaining ghosts of self-doubt, I'm going to let you in on my favourite exercise for turning doubt around.

This exercise is based on the work of Byron Katie. It's a simple (though not necessarily easy) process that takes you through any thought you keep thinking that is holding you back or making you miserable in some way.

It might feel a bit odd at first, but be patient. It's never failed me for uncovering hidden gems in my flawed thinking.

Step 1) Answer these four questions:

1. Is your thought true? (Yes or No. If No, move to 3.)
2. Can you absolutely know that it's true? (Yes or No.)
3. How do you react when you think that thought is true?
4. Who would you be without the thought?

Using those four questions, let's explore the statement: 'I suck at marketing my art.'

1. Is it true?

Is it true that you suck at marketing your art, 100% of the time?

Yes! I suck at marketing and it's never worked for me.

2. Can you absolutely know that it's true?

Do you know for sure what good or bad marketing even is? Can you absolutely know what you're capable of is only sucky marketing?

Well, I suppose I've only sucked in the past. I suppose I could be better at it in the future.

3. How do you react, what happens, when you believe that thought?

What happens when you believe 'I suck at marketing my art' and you're getting no responses from your latest post or no sales of your work? Do you experience anger, stress, or frustration? Does this prevent you from taking more action to try different marketing approaches? Does that thought bring stress or peace into your life?

Yes! All the above. I feel hopeless. I get a sinking feeling in my belly.

4. Who would you be without the thought?
Close your eyes. Picture yourself as someone who you follow online, some creative you admire and who doesn't seem to have any trouble in marketing their work. What do you see? What would your life look like without that thought?

Wow. I would feel amazing if I was that person. I would feel free, powerful and like I could actually make a difference with my art.

Step 2) Turn it around

We're not done yet! Virtually any statement can be turned around to yourself, to someone else, and to the opposite.

For example, 'I suck at marketing my art.' turns around to:
- I suck at marketing myself (to the self)
- My art sucks at marketing me (to the other)
- I'm brilliant at marketing my art (to the opposite)

As odd as they may sound at first, give yourself a chance to really experience the turnarounds. For each one, find at least one specific, genuine examples where the turnaround holds true. This isn't about forcing yourself to believe something you don't, **it's about making discoveries,** generating potential solutions to problems and finding alternatives that can bring you peace.

For example, each of these new statements could lead to some significant changes in your behaviours and ways of approaching marketing:

- I suck at marketing myself (to myself)

This could be true for many creatives who prefer to keep a sense of privacy and protect themselves from criticism. Of course, the danger is thinking that marketing ourselves and marketing our art are the same thing. This turnaround might help you remember that the two are distinct, and when you're marketing your art, you're not putting yourself on the line for criticism, just your work.

- My art sucks at marketing me (to the other)

Again, this could be true for you. While we're not the same as our art, part of us may want to be recognised as the creator and acknowledged for that. You don't have to be visible for people to know your art: think about Banksy who is still mysterious as a person, but whose work is easily recognisable worldwide. Having a solid body of work with a recognisable style or theme is one way your art can market you, without you ever revealing your name or face.

- I'm brilliant at marketing my art (to the opposite)

Even this statement, the opposite, likely holds true for you - even if it was only once. Sometimes we don't realise how well we're doing, until we look back at the real evidence. How did you get your first job, client or customer? Marketing was likely in some way involved, even if it was posting a few pieces of work on a jobs board. If you've ever had a returning client or customer, then you did something to make that happen - and that was marketing.

Or maybe it's revealing a hidden talent you have yet to discover. Even if you're totally new to sharing your work, then it's possible that you are brilliant at marketing - you just don't know it yet.

The point of this exercise is to show you how malleable our beliefs are. We can look at them like a kaleidoscope, switching our grip to change what we see - and often, this results in our original beliefs falling away entirely.

Hopefully that's given you a bit of a pep to make a go at this marketing stuff. Remember that it isn't necessarily an overnight change: your only job is to find a groove that works for you, and you'll only find that groove through a fair bit of trial and error. The hardest part? Starting.

ACTION STEP:

Make a start by taking a limiting belief you have around marketing or selling your work, and try out the Turn it Around exercise.

Chapter 3:
How Does Content Marketing Work?

Marketing isn't all about shouting at people with a megaphone, 'Come buy my thing!' It isn't complicated either, as much as some people will have you think. The way I see it, marketing can be approached in an incredibly creative way, which also happens to be the way it actually works.

Content marketing is a term you might have come across before. If not, here's a quick primer:

In its simplest form, content marketing is simply a way of communicating, with the hope of building an audience's awareness, trust and desire for a brand's product or service. That also means it has to be of some value to the right audience, and relevant to whatever the thing is that brand is pitching.

If you're thinking: "Cant' I just... make my art?" Don't worry! I get you. I've been there. I have good news... and bad news.

The good news is, yes, to an extent you can just make your art. But you also need to give it some context. The bad news it, just one great work of art is seriously unlikely to make you any cash if all someone ever sees of you is that piece. The same is true for one great song or one great poem: audiences need a reason to stick around to see your body of work.

"Good Content Marketing is storytelling. It's NOT churning out crappy articles and blog posts just to get search engine attention. It's NOT spamming your followers on Facebook and Twitter. Learning to tell your story in a compelling way, across multiple mediums, is the key to good content marketing."
~ Corey Huff

One of the reasons many of the creatives I speak to find marketing such a slog is that they don't feel like they have anything to say. As Thumper's mum told him, 'if you can't say something nice, don't say anything at all.'

Replace 'nice' with 'valuable' or 'worthwhile' and you get an idea of the problem. But unless you're someone who *doesn't* have any hobbies, read any books, magazines, blogs, or watch TV, Netflix or Youtube, or scroll through Facebook, Twitter or Instagram... You do know what kind of content interests you. You do know it's out there: it does exist, people are churning the stuff out (not all of it is worth a glance, I'll grant you) and some of it is actually useful, creative and inspiring. Hopefully you also know (now) that you could be producing great content too.

Don't worry, I won't leave you with 'just create great content' without some practical steps.

Good content marketing is answering the questions:

- Why should I (the audience member) care?
- What does this tell me about you (the creative)?
- What's the call to action (and is it relevant)?

Let's look at each in depth:

'Why should I care?'

The first question, 'Why should I care?' relates to what you can post that will classify as worthy of your audience's attention.

1) Does it entertain? e.g. Cat videos
2) Does it educate? e.g. Advice articles
3) Does it emote? e.g. Personal stories

If you can get an answer to at least two of the above, your idea is likely to fly well as a piece of content marketing. Ultimately, it's these characteristics of something that make us willing to share it with others.

When you can produce content that's 'share worthy', you won't have to worry about being the one tooting your own horn - your audience will be doing it for you.

'What does this tell me about you?'

The next question, 'What does this tell them about you (the creative)?' relates to what someone is really buying when they hire you or buy an album or a book. A great deal of that decision is in their perception of you. Again, I'm not saying you have to have your face plastered all over your website or take photos of your most intimate moments for Instagram; but I am saying you need to give some kind of evidence to let someone know you're a real person, with a story and a motivation for creating this work.

You can read my actual story on my About page of my website, but it also crops up in nearly every podcast I record or email I write. I'm letting my audience know about my past;

how I came to do the work I do, as well as some of my beliefs, regarding topics we discuss like personality type theories. Finally, I let you in on my struggles, and what I learn along the way.

Of course, some of this will and some of this won't apply to you. But hopefully you can imagine what an artist who paints exotic places she visits could reveal about herself and her work; from finding a love for painting to preferences for painting mediums to stories about places she visits. All of this is wonderful fodder for content, that not only puts your work into context, but also helps connect you with your audience in a meaningful way.

My About page for reference:
http://thecreativeintrovert.com/about-cat-rose

'What's the call to action?'

Finally, add an easy way for your audience to take action. This isn't just an attempt to capture a credit card number; this serves as a reminder for you to make sure that the content you produce is relevant to your end goal. It's tempting to see someone else's popular blog post or look at what they're posting on social media that's getting so many views or likes, but unless you're just doing this purely for fun, I encourage you to think about the purpose of each piece of content you produce.

Sometimes you may create content that doesn't have a direct call to action, but it still serves the purpose of educating your audience about something that may ultimately bring them closer to you or your work. It's worth paying attention to what some of the creatives you follow are doing and trying to spot how and where they are using content marketing effectively.

Now you have some ideas for what a piece of content marketing should contain, it's time to figure out: how do you communicate best?

There are a few options for you to consider:

1) Written content

This suits most introverts in particular, because the written word is our loyal friend who gives us time to think. It removes some of the pressure that speaking out loud does, and clarifies our ideas in a way that thinking alone cannot.

In addition, we can put to use our skills of listening and empathy when we get to express ourselves through writing. All the nuances we pick up on in daily life get to crystallise on the page, and we have a chance to process everything from the small details to the big ideas that have come to our attention.

Not everyone enjoys writing, of course, it can feel like a slog to many – and just because introverts are stereotypically seen as natural writers, doesn't mean you have to be lumped in with that assumption.

Ask yourself if you ever write for fun, or feel better once you've had time to write about what you've experienced or thinking about. Have you ever kept a journal? Did you enjoy creative writing at school? Just because you don't do much of it now doesn't mean it's not something you can start.

2) Visual content

Whilst this book isn't just intended for visual creatives, I'm going out on a limb and saying that most folk reading are visually inclined, and whether or not it's your primary creative outlet, you've doodled on a notepad in a class or a meeting, or taken a picture with your phone.

Every social media platform, website and even emails now, for the most part, benefit from a visual element. I've also seen a strong bond between the audio and visual world, whether it's through album artwork, music videos or merchandise.

When it comes to communicating with your audience, having a visual style, something that can be identified as part of a whole that points to you or your brand, will help people make sense of what you're about; what you can offer them. If I see a social media account with no consistency across messaging or visual style, I might feel confused on some level, and leave because I don't know what to expect from them. The truth is: we like predictability. We like to be sure that something is for us, or not for us. This is exactly what great – or even just good, as long as they're consistent – visuals will do.

3) Audio content

Before you write this off as not-introvert friendly and remain firmly in your comfort zones of writing or images, give the spoken word a chance!

It only occurred to me after I'd been listening to podcasts for over two years virtually daily, that starting my own might just be a good idea. If I looked at my situation rationally, I might have seen the obvious sooner. My line of thought went something like:

I need to create content for my ideal audience...
My ideal audience is a lot like me...
I get nearly all my info education and entertainment and enrichment from podcasts (previously it had been blogs) ...

If my audience are doing the same (and if they're like me, they likely are) I should probably give podcasting a go!

So that was it. I began the scariest experiment I'd ever run in my business... and without a doubt, the best decision to date.

The spoken word doesn't require you having the gift of the gab. It doesn't mean you have to get on camera (though, if you're interested in it, video is worth considering.) It doesn't require having elite speaking skills.

Particularly in the first year of The Creative Introvert Podcast, I wrote out my script for each solo episode, word for word. Luckily, I write exactly how I hear the voice in my head, so when I read it out aloud, I've been told it sounds relatively spontaneous and not too robotic. If you're already dabbling in blogging, or have an established blog, I see no reason why you wouldn't try turning those posts into a podcast.

That said, I'm not trying to encourage you to start a podcast if you have no interest in the medium yourself. Rather, I'm trying to encourage you to produce content in the form that YOU personally consume. This will make content marketing feel more like a creative outlet, rather than a dull school project you see no purpose in.

Now that you have an idea of why to share, what to share and how to share it, it's time to learn the most powerful way to **distribute your content** in a way that leads your audience directly to the door of your gingerbread house. Let me explain...

The Breadcrumb Trail

A lot of advice you'll find on content marketing will stop before you get here. You'll be told 'start a blog, make it good, and just wait for the sales to roll in.' Unfortunately, this is NOT what generally happens.

The real brilliance of content marketing, and the only reason I'm still going with the Creative Introvert as a business, is because I learned about the Breadcrumb Trail. This is my way of explaining the journey you're taking your audience on... the one that takes them from curious visitor to your most hardcore Superfan.

There's an awful lot of people throwing as much spaghetti at the wall as they can, before something sticks. It's true, some will indeed stick. But I know from past experience that hurling spaghetti gets tiring... and messy.

That's why I'm encouraging you to carefully select your spaghetti before slinging it. You want to pick the most sticky-looking spaghetti before hurling it at the wall, but be prepared to sling quite a few.

I'll stop with the spaghetti analogy: all I want is for you to provide the universe with enough routes to your door as possible, so that clients, customers or anyone else you want to come knocking knows exactly how to find you.

Enter, the breadcrumb trail...

The breadcrumb trail is the way you get discovered. It's a route for someone to follow so that the chances of them finding you – and wanting what you have when they get there – are as likely as possible.

Of course, nothing is a sure thing. This is why having several Breadcrumb Trails set up is so important for maximising your chances.

Let's look at an example of the Breadcrumb Trail in action. Tara Swiger is someone you might already be familiar with, especially if you're in the craft world. I personally came across her in Gary Vaynerchuck's book, *Jab, Jab, Jab, Right Hook*.

I remember clearly reading this on a stuffy train when I was commuting to another thankless client, not long before I swore off in-house design work for all eternity. I figured this Swiger woman was someone I could learn a thing or a dozen from, and when I googled her name, I was delighted to find reams of content - freely available - from a podcast to an excellent blog to some great downloadable guides and courses. From there, I became a Superfan. I was on her Breadcrumb Trail.

From there, Tara could keep dripping me more breadcrumbs, from podcast episodes (I was subscribed so each episode would reach me without her doing a thing), email updates (usually based on that week's podcast topic – she didn't have to worry about creating new content for each platform) and social media posts. Her Instagram stories alone are amongst the cream of the crop, in that they're uplifting, educational and adorable – especially when her pups make guest appearances. When it comes to Tara making an offer, I'm all ears, because I've been nibbling on these breadcrumbs for all this time.

This may sound like a long, lengthy trail, but it's reality. It probably will come as no surprise that overnight successes are few and far between, and expecting someone who has literally just found your Instagram account from a hashtag search to go and visit your shop and buy immediately, is incredibly unlikely. It takes time, and multiple breadcrumbs to lead someone to your gingerbread house (an imperfect analogy, I'm certainly not comparing you to a wicked witch!)

Ok so now you know how the Breadcrumb Trail works, it's time to figure out how you might map your own trail out. This breaks down to the following:

The first crumb

This gets placed strategically somewhere your potential Superfans are likely to find it:

- Guest posts on other people's blogs
- Interviews on other people's podcasts
- Magazine/press coverage
- Events/craft fairs
- Flyers in local businesses
- Paid advertising on Facebook/Instragram
- Hashtags (Instagram, Twitter)
- Pinterest posts on group boards
- Blog posts on your own blog (more difficult than it used to be)

There's more tips waiting for you in part 6, for pitching some of the people who will get you featured in some of these outlets, but for now, just have a think back to where you find new creatives, and what your potential Superfans are likely paying attention to.

The second crumb

In order to keep these folk who find your first crumb on your trail, you'll need a tasty looking second crumb not far off. Why would someone hang around? Well, the promise of more great content from you. Your best bet here is: getting them on your email list.

Email list? Yes, your email list. You've likely seen plenty of annoying pop ups (including on theCreativeIntrovert.com) offering you some kind of free goody or discount code in return for your precious email address. This gives someone permission to keep you on their breadcrumb trail, while you get to enjoy your second crumb.

It's easier than you think to get this set up. I recommend Mailchimp.com, particularly now they offer a landing page style form to grab email addresses. Deciding what to offer as your second crumb, or your 'opt in' in marketing speak, doesn't have to be brain surgery either.

Ideas:
- A discount code for use on your products
- A free guide that educates someone on how to use your product
- A free sample chapter
- A free sample track
- A free digital wallpaper
- A free digital zine

If none of these appeal to you in the slightest, no worries. You can simply say that this is a way to keep in touch with your visitors who find your site. That's been enough for me many times, particularly with artists who run events or have a store with products I'm not quite ready to purchase, but will be one day soon. I don't trust my memory as far as I can throw it, so email is a great way to keep a note of creatives I find.

Your third crumb and beyond

Now it's your job to keep the crumbs coming, and this should be a no-brainer now you know about content marketing and have found a format you can communicate to your Superfans in.

Consistency is everything here, if you plan on making any kind of profit from your free content. I can't tell you how many times I've signed up for an email list and haven't heard a peep from someone until months pass. Then, an email asking for a sale pops up and I wonder, "who the heck is this person and why should I give them my moneys?!" Had they stayed in touch and kept dropping crumbs for me, this could have been a sale for them.

Your gingerbread house

At some point, you'll be ready to give your Superfans a peek at the gingerbread house: your BIG OFFER. Depending on what this is, it's worth having a think about your 'big reveal' – how you can best communicate your offer. This could be a new product launch, a special sale on your Etsy store, a new package of your services, a new book or album... Pick one to focus on for now, and have a think about how you want to tell your Superfans about it.

ACTION STEP:

Plan out your Breadcrumb Trail. You can download the workbook to find a template for working through this in the Resources.

Chapter 4:
How Do You Build Your Online Home?

Ever heard the advice to buy, don't rent? Personally, the thought of buying in my city is laughable, so the property market is not the best example for this point.

But in terms of online real estate, you undeniably need your own turf. Social networks are great, but we can't depend on them. Building your entire fanbase on Myspace sounded like a great idea in 2002. Algorithm changes mean our 'smart feed' (what we see first when we scroll through Facebook, Instagram and others) is not showing updates from accounts we like or follow – unless they pay to advertise. Increasingly, it is becoming more difficult to reach our audience in the cacophony of social media. Plus, at any moment one of the social media bigwigs can decide to close up shop, or take away our years of accumulated data.

Having your own website however, means you own every pixel and cannot turfed out if your landlord changes their mind.

My first site consisted of my logo, and four grotesque cats, serving as a semi-functioning navigation. It was hopeless, but it was a start.

Now, it's easier than ever to build your own online space: one that you own, have full control over and showcase your work - without the interference of ads or trolls.

Wordpress, Squarespace, Wix and others are putting the power in your hands. I started talking myself out of web design jobs for this very reason: I know for the majority of creatives out there, with more time on their hands than cash in the bank building their own site using one of these platforms is 100% within reach.

What I can do is give some points about what your website should contain, and a few pointers should you want to take matters into your own hands.

Your website isn't a dumping ground for all the work you ever created. Nor is it just a storefront. It's a reflection of who and what you aspire to be. The best sites evolve over time, along with you and your goals. They're a way of exhibiting you at your best: and an irresistible calling card for the right client who lands there.

Part 1: The Tech Set Up

The Options

All-in-one solutions are better than ever (Wix, Weebly, Squarespace) BUT are still either limited, or quite expensive.

- Less customisable
- Less future-proof
- Issues with SEO

+ Easy as pie

\+ Good support
\+ Did I mention they're easy as PIE?

My preference is still a self-hosted Wordpress.org setup.

\- Tricky initial learning curb
\+ Customisation is almost unlimited
\+ Lots of support online
\+ You own it
\+ Slightly cheaper

Quick Start To Wordpress.org (Self Hosted)

What you need:

1. A domain name
2. A website host
3. Patience

Think of your domain name as your home address. Think of your host as your landlord.

Recommended set up:

1) Buy a domain name

Most sites will be similarly prices ($10 on average per month for a .com - recommended)

1and1.com (Worldwide)
123-reg.co.uk (UK)
Not recommended: GoDaddy.com

The reason I strongly advise against the very popular GoDaddy.com is because (1) they're needlessly more expensive than most other registrars and hosts, and (2) they make you pay extra for SSL. This is the thing that makes your site super safe, should you want to take visitors payment information or any personal details for that matter. Let's just say, it's ruddy important and it should be free. The other companies I recommend will let you add this free of charge, at the time of writing this.

2) Buy your website hosting

Even though your domain registrar will likely offer you hosting too, I advise you going through a separate company for this. The reason for having a separate domain provider and host is just incase one company ever goes under, or their services change. You don't lose both your domain and your hosting all at once.

You'll likely only ever need a starter package with any service provider. Most will do deals – starting as low as a few bucks a month, then ramping up to $6–10 a month.

I recommend crocweb.com – a tirelessly patient Canadian company

Regardless of who you choose, don't bother with any added extras! Walk away with JUST the hosting.

3) Make sure your domain name is pointing at your new hosting site

I don't want to get into the weeds here, but your host will walk you through this. It's basically a matter of grabbing your name servers (another kind of address) from your host and entering them over on your domain provider's DNS settings. Again, all service providers will have support if you get lost here. Use it, you're paying them!

Just send emails like 'Help! Name servers! DNS! What do I do!'

It will take a day or two to get the two talking to each other, but then you're all set!

4) Install Wordpress

Now the fun begins.

Again, most hosts these days make it super easy with '1-click installs' that do all this for you.

1. You log in to your cPanel (at your hosting provider)
2. Then find the Services/Software section and click on the Wordpress option.

You can also find a guide to walk you through the process here: https://www.betterhostreview.com/easiest-way-install-wordpress-hostgator.html

Just remember you can't do this step until your domain name is pointing at your host server.

Wordpress Set Up

Pick a Theme

The beauty of WP is for me, in the themes. There are so many options... You can spend weeks – or months – deliberating.

You can go for a free or premium (paid) option, and the best way to decide is simply budget. If you CAN push for 60-80 (one off) on a theme, then do it. The support will be better and you can guarantee customisability.

I'd go straight to envato marketplace. There are others (I've used Restored 316 in the past, but I honestly feel it was a rip off for the quality and support delivered!)

TheCreativeintrovert.com uses the Story theme, which is around $60. If you're on the fence and just testing the waters, go for free. There are loads out there - and they can be brilliant. Have a google for "best free wordpress themes 2020" (or whatever year it is) and seeing what comes up. Usually you'll get some listicles that will give you a good idea of what's on the market.

What to look for in a theme

- Responsive layout
- WooCommerce ready
- Portfolio section

Some I've found:

Astrid: https://athemes.com/theme/astrid/
Flash: https://themegrill.com/themes/flash/
Rife: https://apollo13themes.com/rife/

Have a play with the demos (they'll all have these) and decide from there.

Top tip: Give yourself 24 hours to make a decision! People sit on this for way too long (myself being the worst for this!) and you won't know until you install it and try it on yourself.

Part 2: The Content

The Bare Necessities

These are the pages I recommend you have:

1. About
2. Portfolio
3. Hire me/Shop
4. Blog
5. Contact

1) Your About Page

This is likely the most emotionally painful page you'll have to add to your site, but it really is a necessity. People prefer to buy from or want to work with people they already know, like and trust. It's a hackneyed expression because it's true!

What to include:

You might want to treat your About page much like a resumé – a list of your education background, work experience, clients... and whilst I'm sure that works for some, I'd urge you to bring a bit more YOU into it.

Try to add at least a few sentences explaining your True North (see: Part 1, chapter 5.) You can use these prompts:

- Why do you make the work you do?
- What are your influences?
- What lights you up?
- What change do you want to see in the world?
- Who is your work for?
- What would you like to achieve?

If this feels long, break it up. You could have a brief bio at the top of your page, and below you could have a heading saying something like: The Backstory or Want to Learn More? After which you add your longer bio.

You can find more about writing a killer About page in chapter 4.

2) Your Portfolio

I'm mostly referring to visual artists, but this is still true for musicians, writers, performers. You'll want a section to show off your work – that's kind of the point of this website thing.

If you're using Wordpress and picked a theme with a 'portfolio' set up – it might be called a gallery – then you'll be set. If you don't have that option, then I still believe Behance is a good online portfolio option out there, even if it's changed a bit since back in the day. It looks great and is easy enough to use. If this is your choice, then you can simply add a navigation menu item (in Wordpress: Appearance > Menus) and link to your Behance portfolio there.

This would also work for musicians who want to link to their Soundcloud or Bandcamp page.

Q: How many pieces of work should be in your portfolio?

Er... it depends! Hah, no. I won't leave you with that.

Honestly, I've seen a mixture, from 6–7 pieces on the entire site, to seemingly hundreds of pieces. I would err on the side of 'less is more' and focus on trying to create a body of work that looks like it all comes from the same person!

This was a big problem for myself as I never had a 'style' in my opinion. I couldn't decide who I wanted to work for or what type of work I wanted to make. Finally one day I settled on cute/grotesque creatures and I went with it. Did that mean I stopped making work in other styles ? No: I just kept that stuff somewhere else.

Maybe you use your website for your core style, or the one you feel is most popular or commercially viable, and you keep your 'experimental' work on Behance or DeviantArt, or under a separate Soundcloud account.

This can be another real emotional battle and a reason I believe in paying for portfolio reviews. Yes – paying. I did this a few times when I was starting up, and each time I felt like I'd had a spiritual revelation. Associations for illustrators like the AOI (UK) offer this, and it's worth searching for 'portfolio review + YOUR CITY' on Google.

3) Hire me/Shop

Unless you are making art purely to make art, and you want people to see it because... it would make you feel good? Then ignore this step.

But I'm willing to bet the majority of folk wouldn't say no to making a few bucks from making work they love. So: what action do you want your website audience to take? Do you want them to commission you? Do you want to work for an agency? Do you want to sell some t-shirts or prints or get a record deal? All these things need to be super clear on your site.

Hire me pages:

- Explain HOW you can help them: 'I can do X, Y, Z for you'
- Give examples of previous work experience or clients (ideally giving visual examples of the work unless you signed an NDA)
- Give testimonials from happy clients (if you don't have these, it's rarely too late to ask)
- A contact form (I recommend the plugin WPForms for this)
- And contact info (some folk hate forms!)

Great example: https://www.maijintheartist.com/hire/

Shop pages:

Option 1: WooCommerce

Make sure WooCommerce is installed (and your WP theme is shop/woocommerce ready.) This tutorial will explain everything better than I can: https://kinsta.com/blog/woocommerce-tutorial/

Advantages: avoids distributor fees AND means you can connect to your mailing list (very important for future sales!)

Disadvantage: bit of a pain to set up.

Great example: https://www.minilearners.com/

Option 2: Link to distributor

Use the link in the menu to go to a distributor (like Etsy.) I also recommend sites like RedBubble for selling art prints on products without paying upfront for the print + production

Example of links out to multiple shops: http://cuddlesandrage.com/shop/

4) Blog

Blogging isn't dead! Ok, it's getting pretty long in the tooth – but that doesn't let you off the hook. I still believe if someone is coming to your site for the first time, it's a great way for them to know (1) you're still alive and (2) who you are. You can give visitors an idea of what you're about and that you actually care about the work you're making.
Plus, it's still good for SEO (search engine optimisation – what Google is giving you points for so you can be found in search results.) If you paid attention in the previous chapter, you'll already have an idea of what kind of content you can create for your blog.

Q: How often?

Once a month. If you wanted to be a blogger and actually use it to monetise the site, then 2–3x a week, but that's not necessary if you're just trying to make a living from your art.

5) Contact page

If you don't create any of the other pages, at least remember to add this one!
This should read like a business card: It just needs your email address, possibly your phone (if you're happy with phone calls!) and (optional but recommended) a contact form (again, WPForms is a great plugin for this)

And... your done!

Part 3: Plugins and Optional Add-Ons

Plugins

Plugins are the extra tools that make Wordpress so great. Never download an untrusted plugin - stick to ones you find in the WP repository (Plugins > Add New)

1. Yoast SEO - https://wordpress.org/plugins/wordpress-seo/
2. Easy Forms for MailChimp - https://wordpress.org/plugins/yikes-inc-easy-mailchimp-extender/
3. Really Simple SSL - https://wordpress.org/plugins/really-simple-ssl/

1) Yoast SEO

If you've heard people talk about SEO and got confused and/or bored - I don't blame you. Luckily, Yoast have made it super easy to optimise your site so Google is happy to help you out and make you easier to find online.

Basically: fill in the details Yoast gives you in each blog post or portfolio item. It's worth knowing what keywords (the words we type into Google's search) you want your site to rank for (or show up in the search results for.)

Be specific: 'Children's digital illustrator Nebraska' is better than 'illustrator'

Lots of free info here: https://yoast.com/cat/seo-basics/

2) Easy Forms for MailChimp

These days if someone finds your site and aren't ready to take action straight away, there's a good chance they'll leave and forget you completely. It's sad but true.

But! When you give someone a chance to leave their email address: the ball's in your court. You can still provide them with useful information, updates and start a conversation with them. Even if you aren't keen to write your own weekly Museletter, I still think a quarterly update to your email list is worthwhile: in the same way an illustrator might send direct mail campaigns out each quarter.

Great example of mailing list capture: http://www.janeheinrichs.net/

Note: you will need a way to store and send these emails, and because Mailchimp.com is my... email management chimp of choice, Easy Forms is a great way to make it even easier to grab email addresses. You can find a tutorial for easy set up here: https://en-gb.wordpress.org/plugins/yikes-inc-easy-mailchimp-extender/

If you don't use Mailchimp, Ninja Forms is another great option: https://ninjaforms.com/

3) Really Simple SSL

Remember I mentioned this SSL thing in the part about choosing a domain registrar and host? This plugin allows you to generate a free SSL certificate.

Nice to Have Website Features

These are optional, but nice to have if you decide to grow your online presence.

1. Press/Media page
2. Patreon - https://www.patreon.com/
3. Page Duplicator - https://wordpress.org/plugins/duplicate-page/
4. Thrive Architect - https://thrivethemes.com/architect/

1) Press/Media Page

This is optional but recommended if your work has been published or if you've had any luck guest blogging for someone or been interviewed - may be in a magazine or a podcast. Any hype about you and your work - put it here!

Great example: http://www.ianingram.com/press/

2) Patreon

This is something many creators are using as a neat way to let people fund their creative work, like an actual patron, and unlike straight-up paypal donations, Patreon users can reward their supporters with cool bonuses.

This is my set up for the Creative Introvert podcast: https://www.patreon.com/creativeintro

A great place to add a link to this is at the end of blog posts or in the 'widget' area on your Wordpress site.

3) Page Duplicator

This is a massive time saver if you have a particular set up format for a blog post or portfolio item – it lets you very easily duplicate any page/post on your site for future use.

4) Thrive Architect

Some pages on my site look a little... fancier than others. And they didn't get that way because I'm a pro coder. There are several high quality WYSIWYG page editors out there, but the one that I've been in a long-term, loving relationship since 2016 with is... Thrive Architect.

This is great for those of you who want to create a fancy landing page or customise any page beyond the limits of your Wordpress theme allows. Thrive Architect makes it super easy to add different sections, layouts and all kinds of things I have no idea how to code myself.

It isn't free, but it's more reasonable and extensive than other page builders I've seen on the market.

Phew! I know that was a lot, and you might have scanned this and thought.... NOPE. But! I'm hoping this has given you at least a bird's eye view of what you *could* achieve on your own, or with minimal help (read: no fancy, expensive web design agencies.)

ACTION STEP:

If you don't already have an online home, and feel ready for one, decide on your single next step. Don't plan too far ahead, just consider what your next step is.

For example, you might decide to pick your website builder of choice. I'm clearly a Wordpress proponent, but you might be prepared to pay extra, save yourself some time with tech, and go for Squarespace. Whatever you decide, make a call, and sign up. That's your first step.

I'm also happy to answer questions on all of this website stuff, as this has been my day job for nearly a decade now. Email me: hello@thecreativeintrovert.com and ask away.

Troubleshoot: Procrastination

We've all been there. We put something off to the last minute, looking for anything that might provide a worthy distraction. Sometimes we don't even know we're doing it. We can so quickly justify our change of focus, raising our distraction's importance far above our primary goal in an instant.

The problem is that procrastination, much like binging on too many cookies, just leaves us feeling like crap. At its worst, we raise our stress levels as it dawns on us that that task we're delaying is STILL not getting done.

Some procrastinators claim they do their best work under pressure. I don't buy it. Its just another way to justify their actions. And sure: the thing they procrastinated over still gets done... but at what cost? What would the quality have been, had they dedicated themselves to it from the get go? Not to mention, what's it doing to their stress levels? We know chronic stress isn't good for us, so any ways to reduce it would only benefit us.

What surprised me when I first came across the idea, is that perfectionists make for some of the most extreme procrastinators. It makes sense when you think about it. If a job or project can't be completed perfectly, it's probably best not to start. Our conscious mind might not be aware of this reasoning, but that's what's going on behind the scenes.

By far the most helpful explanation I've ever read about what's happening in the brain when we procrastinate is the occurrence of the 'Instant Gratification Monkey,' a mischievous creature that was dreamed up by Tim Urban of WaitButWhy.com. This monkey only thinks about the present, which may sound all zen, but really it's a problem when you have things you want to accomplish in the future.

The biggest problem is that no matter what substitute activity the Instant Gratification Monkey distracts us with, we're still not satisfied. Are you really having a great time scrolling through Instagram? Are you really enjoying yourself by the fourth trip to the fridge in the past hour? No matter what, we are left in a kind of limbo between having completed our goal and doing nothing at all. And then we panic.

This level of sheer terror is just about the only thing that kicks us into action, but it comes at a cost. It can result in exhaustion as we stay up all night trying to get this holy grail task complete, as well as an arguably less quality resulting piece.

In addition, the more reliant we become on this panic-monster showing up in time to pull us into action, the less motivation we are left with to take care of the less urgent, but more important, projects in life. Like learning a new language, getting into better shape or working on that painting. These life-enriching, but less urgent activities fall by the wayside, which doesn't serve us creatively or in life as a whole.

Some tips for tackling procrastination once and for all:

1) Pick one thing

Pick ONE thing to act on next. Just one. And forget the rest of the items until that one thing is complete. When you make your to-do list, think about ordering each of your items, rather than using bullet points or any other cute symbols. Numbers are our friend here!

Of course you'll need to prioritise urgent tasks, but make sure they rank highly on importance too. Urgency is often a figment of our (or someone else's) imagination.

Double check your order by asking yourself:

- What happens if this never gets done?
- Could someone else do this?
- What's the least I can do to classify this as done, and move on?
- Does completing this task make getting anything else done easier or more expedient?

2) If it feels too big, break it down

Some tasks may have been hovering on your to-do list for quite some time. These are things you know you'll be satisfied with when they're done, but you might feel strong resistance to them.

A common problem is that these tasks are too vague or too big to feel like you can get a good grip on them and make progress. Learning Japanese had been on my to-do list since I went to the country in 2013, and it wasn't until I found the app Duolingo in 2017 that I felt that tackling it might be manageable, all thanks to Duo's short, bitesize lessons.

Ask yourself:

- What's the smallest, easiest first step I can take on this big task?
- Do I need more information to begin?
- If so, what exactly do I need to know and who do I need to ask? Can I act on that now?

If in doubt, go smaller! the more micro the task, the better. When we take the first step, momentum starts to build and our Instant Gratification Monkey starts to quieten down.

3) Create your own panic monster

I've always known I work best to deadlines, and actually require them if I'm going to even make a start on a project. A client who says "I need this ASAP" will be *less* effective at getting me to work for them than one who says "I need this by 5pm next Tuesday." You must be as specific with yourself.

It can also help to tell someone who will keep you accountable. In the League of Creative Introverts, I offer everyone an opportunity to share their #1 goal for the week on Monday. On Friday, I'm all ears to hear from you whether you have or haven't accomplished your goal.

4) Minimise distractions

It's worth making a list of your go-to procrastination devices. Your phone, Netflix, certain apps or websites. It could be things around the house, like cleaning your desk or going to the kitchen to make a snack.

Then, do what you can to put them on lock-down while you work. It sounds obvious, but it really does make a difference when you remove the obstacle. Out of sight, out of mind. Apps like Self Control and Rescue Time are wonderful for blocking certain distracting sites or from checking email for set times during our day.

5) Start a success tracker

Particularly for long projects, where you chip away a day at a time, it's a great idea to keep a visual reminder of how far you have come. I use a writing tracker to track how many words I've written each day while working on my book, and I love apps that keep track of certain daily habits or tasks, like Todoist or Strides.

ACTION STEP:

Take action on one of the tips above and apply it to something you've been procrastinating on.

Resources mentioned:

Self Control - https://selfcontrolapp.com
Rescue Time - https://www.rescuetime.com
Todoist - https://todoist.com
Strides - https://www.stridesapp.com

Chapter 5:
What the Heck Do You Say?

If the thought of posting a snap of your breakfast on Instagram induces nausea in you, take a deep breath. I don't want to confuse content marketing with self-indulgent exhibitionism. However, I'm also not going to let you off the hook just yet in terms of sharing a bit of your world on social media or whatever platform you choose for your content marketing.

In my books, creative content marketing falls under the following categories (and if you read chapter 2, of this Part, this might ring a bell):

1) Educational

This is the content that helps people solve their problems. It can be a blog post or Facebook post about something you've found helpful, an advice article, a podcast or video explaining how to do something. 80% of my content falls under this category, but if I was primarily plugging other services or products like my mandala paintings, this percentage would be much lower, something like 30-40%.

However it wouldn't be zero. So even if you're a jewellery designer, there is an element of education that's worth including in your content. For example, telling people how and where they can find your products is educational. Showing people your work station or what materials and tools you use is also educational, and can be incredibly effective when it comes to attracting a sale.

The following two categories are the ones that most classic creative work (visual art, literature, music etc.) is most likely to fall under:

2) Entertaining

I follow many comic book artists and illustrators on Instagram for the very purpose of this: I want to be entertained. Great art entertains, in my opinion, and there is nothing trivial about that. Figure out what way your work entertains: does it make people laugh? Does it fill them with awe? Does it invoke a sense of beauty and wonder? Does it give them the creeps? (You know, in a good way!)

Whatever flavour of entertainment your work takes, it's likely deeply connected to the third category I'm sharing, Emotive, because entertaining things trigger emotions in us. But there's a reason I'm giving Emotive a separate category altogether

3) Emotive

The origins of the word 'emote' comes from the Latin *emot-* or 'moved' and to be moved is what this final category attempts to do. Arguably, it's the most difficult to achieve. Motivational speakers (see that 'mot' come up again?) move people into action, or try to. When I listen to a great TED talk that reminds me it's OK to be an introvert or hear a podcast from someone who has been through hell and back, I'm motivated to act in a certain way. I'm triggered emotionally, and this can have a real lasting impact.

In many ways, this category will have overlaps with the previous two, but it cover much more than a simple how-to article or a snap of a sunset. To really achieve the art of Emoting, a piece of content usually has to include a healthy dose of humanity. This means... getting vulnerable. Telling our story, or someone else's. Revealing what we really think. This is not the time for Instagram filters or stock photos. To really emote, we need to get real.

The truth is, unless you're planning on selling a commodity item through a big conglomerate who doesn't even acknowledge you as the creator behind the work, you'll do much better in injecting some of YOU your art, or at least your promotion efforts. We buy people, not products.

"In order for connection to happen, we have to allow ourselves to be seen – really seen."
- Brené Brown

7 ideas for content that sells creative work

There are many different ways to create content that checks off at least one of those categories, and there's no one best solution for any creative. You will need to play with this, and reflect on what worked, what didn't, what felt good, what didn't and so on. But hopefully these ideas will provide you with a jumping-off point, so that you can make a steady start.

1) Introduce yourself

You don't have to save your introductions to your About page on your website alone. Particularly when you're looking to attract new eyes (or ears) to your work, it usually takes time for someone to find your About page anyway; the first contact may be on social media. Many creatives I follow use a certain day of the week to say hello to new followers, and give a little background to their work.

It's also an opportunity to let your audience introduce themselves to you. My approach is using my podcast to occasionally publish episodes that talk more about my background, and what led me to do the work I do. Whatever you decide, don't underestimate the value of a friendly introduction: people will be more interested than you might expect.

2) Share what inspires you

As much as you might love the illusion of complete originality, the truth is no art is created in a vacuum. Something has to go into us, in order for something to come out. Have a think about your current inputs: what books are you reading? What would you recommend to friends? What music or podcasts do you listen to? Are there any films you've watched multiple times? What sites do you regularly visit? What social media accounts make your day?

There might be TV shows or books or films you loved as a child, that are still influencing you today. Start to collect all of these, no matter how obscure or untrendy you think your collection is. Can these be shared with your audience in creative ways? It's amazing the kind of response from my audience I've had when I share a love from my childhood, or a book I'm currently obsessed with.

I occasionally mention my 'Japanophilia' and my progress in learning the Japanese language. From that alone I've forged closer bonds with like-minds in my audience who share this fascination with the Japanese culture and who have given me invaluable help with learning the language.

Not only does this help connect you to your audience, it also gives you a chance to divert the spotlight from your own work briefly. I won't pretend it's easy to continuously create content that centres around yourself, but this is a way to point the spotlight towards someone or something else for a moment, whilst still telling your audience something about yourself.

3) Share the process

Regardless of whether you're a parent, you'll probably understand the urge of many new parents to snap as many pictures and take all the home movies they can of their newborn as it grows. What if you treated your work that way; with love and patience (even when it makes bad smells)?

Try to capture your work at different stages, from different angles, in different spaces. You can take screenshots if you work digitally. If you don't have a physical project, you can still find ways to share samples, whether it's music or writing or even ideas. If you work with clients, you don't need to reveal any personal details in order to reflect on something you learned from working with them.

Another advantage to sharing the process is that you can look back at the end of a project, and see how far you've come. Like family albums, there's something charming (if sometimes a bit embarrassing) about seeing your work grow.

4) Share your tools and tricks

I'm not recommending you give away all your secrets, but a hint of the kind of care and consideration – even the challenges – that go into making your masterpiece, is going to be compelling to your viewer.

People are fascinated to see how the dish gets made. I know I watch cooking shows with no intention of making the food, and this is no different. It's worth remembering this when you get the willies about sharing a part of your process that you think someone might rip off or copy. Remember imitation is the highest form of flattery, and anyone deliberately trying to pass your work off as their own, won't get very far.

If you're not keen on sharing your process, focus on your tools. Simply showing your preference for a certain type of pen, what music you listen to while you work or what tools or apps you just can't live without, tells your audience the care that goes into making your art.

5) Share a story about your work

This is a really lovely way to introduce a finished piece to your audience. I've found that every work of art has some kind of story attached; work generally doesn't fall from the sky onto our laps (and if it did, even that would make a great story.)

Have a think about the motivation you had to make it. Did you hear a tune as you were reemerging from sleep? Were you out for a walk in nature when you saw a bird that sparked your latest illustration? Who was this character in your story based on? If you're stuck, see if you can get a loved one to interview you about your work. You might be surprised by what people are curious to know.

6) Share something you've learned

This could be something you've learned from the past, or something that your current project has revealed to you. I love this idea in particular because it means every mistake I make in my creative work gives me an opportunity to learn something and then share what I learned.

It could also be the answer to a question you get asked often about your process or how you do what you do. Answering questions is a great way to connect with your audience, regardless of the kind of creative work you make. It's also worth prompting people from time to time, letting your audience know they can ask questions, and that you'll do your best to answer.

7) Share an experience that has informed your work

This is a great opportunity to get personal (and emote!) and really connect with your audience on a deeper level. Instead of talking about your work on a surface level (which you may have experimented with in idea #5) this prompt asks you to go deeper. You may recount an experience you had in your childhood, that informs the work you make today. Or perhaps there's a burning issue in the world that you are called to address through your work. Whilst it's great to let our work do the talking, sometimes people on the outside need a caption (think about work in great art galleries) to provide a context that enriches our understanding of the piece.

Remember: be consistent!

The last thing I'll harass you about in terms of content marketing, is the importance of being consistent. I often have the experience of finding a podcast, and thrilled with what I've heard, I decide it's worth subscribing for future shows. Then I check the last recorded date, and if it's over a few months ago, I won't subscribe. I assume the host behind the show is probably not in it for the long game, and won't be updating us any time soon with new material. However, if the most recent show I hear states that the podcast will be back again by a certain date, I'm happy to subscribe because I know I will get my fix if I stick around.

This is the danger of not not being consistent with your content, and worse, not updating your audience if you do have any breaks. It doesn't need to be a massive declaration, but a habit of putting out an update at least every month is a good rule.

Derek Sivers is famous for many things, being the author of the brilliant *Anything You Want* as well as the founder of CDBaby, and the originator of the trend to have a 'Now Page' on your website. The idea is to use a page on your site to keep people up to date with what you're currently up to. Not what you've done, but what you're working on now. This doesn't have to be super personal, nor does it have to exist to impress people – it could just be a few lines about the projects or interests that you're currently giving your attention to.

ACTION STEP:

Make a list of things you can share with your audience.

Here are some ideas to get you going:

- The idea that inspired this work is…
- When I'm working, I love to listen to…
- A tool I can't live without is…
- Last weekend, I went to…
- When I make art, I feel like…
- Someone who really inspires me is…
- Here's how you can purchase this or commission me…

Chapter 6:
How Do You Plan Your Promo?

Planning ahead is something I take great pleasure in – in fact, sometimes I find the planning is a lot more fun than the actual doing. I wind up indulging in elaborate planning, only to find out that the reality of taking action brings up a whole new set of challenges. That said, when I have a plan I can rest much more easily knowing that I don't have to make any more critical decisions before taking action, and I am much more likely to overcome those waves of self-doubt that hit just before hitting 'publish' on a blog or social media update.

Other creatives I know despise the planning part: they would much rather take action spontaneously, go with the flow, see what the spirit sparks in them. This too can backfire, because there will be times – great expanses of time – when the spirit simply doesn't strike. This seems all too common in my own experience when it comes to personal marketing.

I believe in finding your own sweet spot: planning enough in advance that you feel prepared whilst still retaining enough flexibility for spontaneous creative input. This is exactly what a solid content plan will give you.

What is a content plan exactly?

In case you haven't come across content plans before, here's a brief overview. They can be presented in different ways, and there are multiple options for fancy software and apps that will make a pretty picture of your content plan, but it could just be a simple spreadsheet or a paper calendar.

The idea is just to work out what you want to say and when you want to say it, then mapping it out in a way that makes sense to you. Then you can act on the plan when you please: it gives you the option to batch your promotion efforts into a day a month or an hour or two a week, and schedule blog posts, podcasts, social media posts and emails in advance.

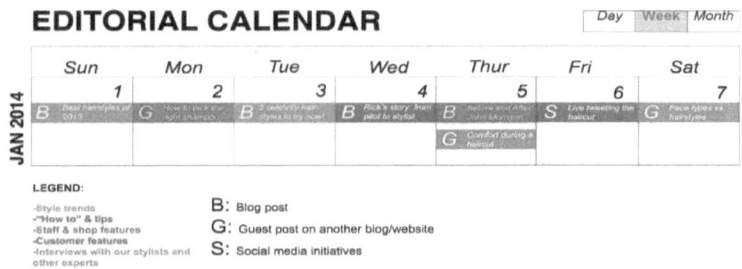

Now we're on the same page, let's dig into the how-to.

How to begin content planning

There are multiple approaches to content planning. My aim is to give you a walk-through to the simplest and most effective route, with plenty of options to customise it to suit your needs.

1) Get clear on your why

You might start to see a pattern in my process: I tend to start with 'why.' This not only serves to direct your content plan so you don't go off course from your aims – I certainly don't recommend this just for the fun of it – but it also takes the pressure off any concerns you might face about any past efforts. The truth is, even if you haven't had any luck with social media or blogging or whatever your outlet has been in the past, chances are you didn't have a plan. At least not one that was truly directed and stick-to-able.

That may not be a word, but hopefully you see the value in starting with the goal in mind. If your aim for the next 90 days is to get 10 sales from your artwork, that's your overall goal for this content plan. But within that goal are your micro-goals. Remember them? Your micro-goal might be selling at a local crafts market. Or it could be getting featured in a magazine your Superfans are likely to read. Each of these could generate multiple pieces of content that help make those possible.

I urge my clients to stay away from creating any expectations about numbers in terms of followers or subscribers for now. After all, these numbers don't generate sales if your content isn't right. Focus now on Push Goal, and the reasons WHY it is important to you. From there, you can take a look at your micro-goals, and the content you could create to fulfil those.

It might help to make a mind map, with arms spreading out from your Push Goal:

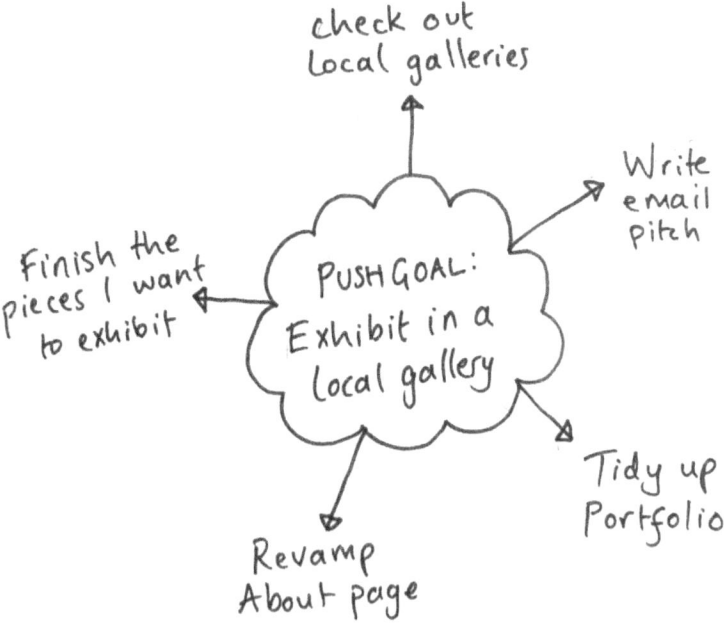

2) Create your content categories

This is mostly a way to minimise decision making on your part, but it also has the advantage of giving your audience what they'll come to expect from you. If someone follows someone after seeing a recipe post from them, they'll likely expect more recipes – and understandably will be a bit disappointed otherwise.

Some of the categories to think about are:
- Work in progress
- Behind the scenes
- Coming soon
- Lessons learnt
- Offers/sales

- What inspires you
- Opinions

Have a look at what other creatives in your industry do for inspiration. Notice that the most successful are likely to have a consistent look and feel, without being boring or overly repetitive. In some cases there will be very clear offers being made, and in other cases it's clear that they are focussing on raising brand awareness first and foremost. Ideally, you want a mixture of content categories, so over the next 90 days you can determine what works best for your audience.

You can also decide how often you want to include each type of category in your content calendar. Ideally, you don't want too many offers or sales posts in any social media feed, but as long as they're distributed amongst other interesting, informative or entertaining posts, you'll be fine.

To make life even easier, you can create styles or templates for your categories, if there is a certain style of image that could work well. Pretty much every medium you choose (see the previous chapter) for creating content will benefit from visuals of some kind.

I use Canva.com to create images for my blog and Instagram posts in particular, and it's been a huge time saver – and regardless of whether you have any experience in design, it's something I promise you can do!

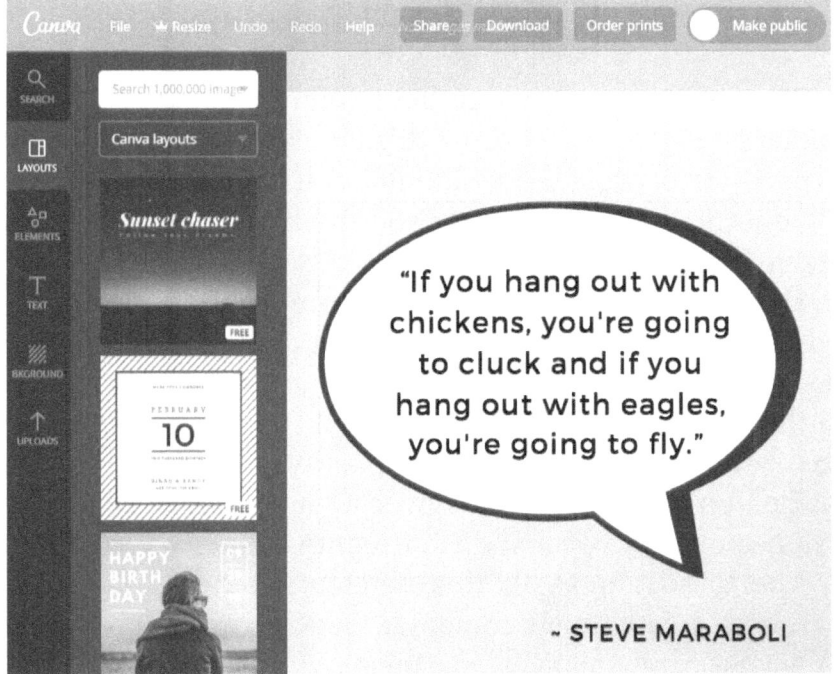

3) Jot down any important dates

Now you have some ideas of what you can be adding to your calendar, it's worth thinking ahead about what's going on in your world and the wider world over the next 90 days or so.

You might have certain project deadlines, and can plan ahead for how you want to share that with your audience. You can make a note of any significant dates, whether they're seasonal or those novelty days – I like to make sure International Donut Day (June 7th, for your information) is firmly in my content plan, for advance donut pun-planning!

It's remarkable how quickly you'll be able to fill up your calendar once you have some of these events marked in, and how content will flow once the structure is in place.

4) Decide how often you'll be posting content

How often you decide to have content going out to your audience is, like with all of this, totally up to you. In my experience, more is better... only up to a certain point. The big question is how much do you think you realistically can create?

Keep in mind that **you don't need to be creating content daily** in order to drip it out daily. I've settled into the routine of creating all my social media posts on one day of the week, and I schedule each post to go out every day or so. I've also batched my podcast: planning, writing, recording and editing an entire series over a few days, which is then dripped out each week for a few months.

The disadvantage to this batching content is that it's harder to create timely content, around an event in the news or in your personal life. It also means you can't take your eyes off your feed entirely, in case you're posting something kind of inappropriate on the day of a national tragedy, for example.

But on the whole, having at least a week's worth of content planned, created and scheduled in advance is going to make consistency a real breeze - and take a load off your mind if things get busy.

Your schedule might look something like:

- 1 x Instagram posts a day
- 1 x Instagram story a week
- 1 x blog post a week
- 1 x email newsletter a month.

You can also be 'visible' on other platforms without needing to create additional content. For example:

- Connecting your Instagram to Twitter and/or Facebook
- Republishing blog posts for Medium or guest blog posts
- Creating an eBook or eZine of a collection of blog posts
- Recording an audio version of your blog posts for a podcast.

And remember, all of this can be batched on one day a week or month to save time and make sure it gets done.

Some of my favourite scheduling tools:

- Hootsuite - best for managing multiple accounts on social media
- Buffer - best browser extension for sharing content from other websites
- Later - best for Instagram scheduling

What's the best time to post?

This is a bit of a "how long is a piece of string" question, because it really does depend on your audience's habits. Factoring in timezones is something you may need to consider. You might be based in the USA, for example, and have four time zones to take into account even if you're only targeting your USA-based audience. Little factoids like: 80% of the USA's population is in Eastern and Central Time is worth noting, when scheduling your content.

Another aspect to consider is people's viewing behaviours. A video is more likely to be watched in the evening, around 8–9pm in your timezone – which makes sense, given that it's hard to watch a full video at an office for most people. It's also worth considering late night insomnias checking, at 2–3am. One of the most popular times for people to check social media is just before work really begins, 8–9am and the end of the work day final check, 5–6pm.

There are plenty of ways to find out what time you're most likely to catch your audience online, depending on what platform you're using. If you have a business account (worthwhile on Facebook and Instagram) then you can view your analytics to show you what your audience are up to . Same with Twitter, Pinterest and many blog hosting platforms, like Wordpress.

As for external analytics, Iconosquare is an Instagram analytics tool that has a feature to help you understand when to post to Instagram to reach more of your own followers. Followerwonk from Moz is a great option for Twitter.

Do a bit of research, but unless you've been posting frequently for a long time, you likely don't have super reliable stats. Consider adding the goal for your first 90-day plan to experiment with multiple posting times and determining at the end of 90 days, your personal optimum time to post content.

ACTION STEP:

Download your Content Planner template from the Resources and make a start on your first 90-day content plan. It might be worth booking out a day or an afternoon in the next fortnight to really buckle down and get this started –

you'll thank yourself when you have your first week scheduled.

Resources mentioned:

Canva - https://www.canva.com/
Iconosquare - https://pro.iconosquare.com/
Followerwonk - https://followerwonk.com/
Hootsuite - https://hootsuite.com/
Buffer - https://bufferapp.com/
Later - https://app.later.com
Medium - https://medium.com/

Chapter 7:
How Do You Grow Your Audience?

Let's say you're on board with the content marketing business. You're sharing your work, sharing your process, and maybe even... enjoying it. And yet... the only person who seems to see your stuff is still Aunt Pauline. What's the use in all this content creation if no one is there to connect with? Fear not!

The rest of this part will be dedicated to helping you grow your audience by getting on other people's platforms, spreading the word to their audiences, and attracting a bunch of new eyes and ears to your work. This is the more extroverted end of the promotion spectrum, but I promise there are ways to make this relatively stress-free and introvert-friendly.

I remember being intensely frustrated that my content marketing efforts were simply not paying off, at least not as quickly as I had hoped (and needed.) So I had to sit down and have a long, hard think about where my ideal audience, my Superfans might be.

Eventually, I figured out it might be – just might be – in similar places to where I discovered my favourite artists, authors and general creative gurus. I made a list:

- Podcasts – I loved listening to interview shows and found myself becoming a fast fan of someone within half an hour of listening to them
- Video – the YouTube algorithm seems to know me better than I do, and with the more recent IGTV, there are more ways than ever to discover people through video
- Guest blogs – Occasionally a blog I already read will have a guest article from another creative. At the end of the article, I can see who that new name is, and find ways to connect with them for more great content.
- Magazines – I love fancy, hipster art and design magazines, and I know that the barrier to entry can be pretty high to get published in them. Instantly, I'm filled with respect and admiration for the products or creative work I see featured in these.

Of course, there are more places, but it's well worth having a brainstorm yourself. Where do you find people? Where do you find products? What makes you decide to invest in someone? Are these places your Superfan might investigate?

In any case, one of the best ways I've found is to contact the creatives that already have an audience of people who are very similar to my Superfan. Now, if you're worried that being an introvert might make this 'contacting big wigs and strangers' part tricksy... have no fear. Did you know we're actually at an advantage? It's true!

For one, we're more likely to spend time writing a considered email than an extrovert might. I've received countless badly worded emails from top CEOs and people much wealthier and more powerful than myself, which have been enough to turn my stomach and actually lose respect for that person.

On the flip side, I've received thoughtful, sweet and humble emails from people I don't know at all, often asking me for much more time and energy in return for nothing, which I've responded to immediately because of the clear attention they put into writing the email.

In addition, more and more people are preferring the written word for it's convenience, than answering their phone. Janet Murray, podcast host and PR extraordinaire, insists that even journalists are preferring emails now, due to the flexibility it allows them. Don't feel like you need to pick up the phone, especially in the first instance of reaching out to someone. Finally, the classic introvert trait of expressing ourselves best through the written word is working for us.

Now that you've had your pep talk, let's get to business. There's a system to getting featured or published somewhere, and I've been crafting it for several years now. Here goes:

1) Research

This can be what makes or breaks your pitch, so don't skimp on the research! Here are some questions to answer while you're in Sherlock mode:

- Where is your Superfan finding people like you? For example, if you create graphic tees and prints, where do you find similar products? Could it be that your Superfan might look there too? Sometimes you'll have to find places that you might not look yourself, but that do attract a wide audience.
- Who is the best person to contact? If this is a smaller operation like a podcast, it's usually pretty

obvious (you contact the host!) but if it's a store or a publication, you might need to do some digging and send some emails first, asking who is the best person to contact. In printed magazines, the front or back covers is the place to find the editor. It's also worth trying to contact relevant contributors and find out if they have any advice about who to speak to. On the web, usually you'll find a contact page or a page for submissions, but in some cases the email addresses will be hidden and you'll be stuck with a contact form. Personally, I much prefer email addresses to contact forms because you have options to attach files, add your email signature and keep track of opens with other extensions. My secret weapon in these situations is hunter.io - it's a fantastic extension for your web browser that reveals any email addresses it can find on a website.

- What are the requirements? The larger the platform, the higher the standards. Printed publications have to be economical with space, so naturally the bar is high for getting featured. Some online publications need you to prove your track record in order to guest blog. It's worth researching this, so you don't waste your time with pitches that don't meet the mark.
- Where do you fit? Take note of the categories that your chosen platform splits its content into. For example, if this is a magazine or website, you might find content under different categories such as News, Opinion, Features, Interviews... Are there any that you would fit into? There's no point in submitting a press release designed for a local magazine to someone who just wants to sample one of your products. This might

mean you have very different pitches, depending on the publication and what they currently offer.

When you have your contact information and research, start to keep a little black book or a spreadsheet. You could also try to find them on Twitter and/or Instagram, and follow them to get an even better idea of who they are and what they want.

Top tip: Create lists on Twitter to easily filter and keep track of those you follow.

2) Resonate

In some cases, you might find a platform that has a huge audience, and could really reach a lot of potential Superfans. But... something about it rubs you up the wrong way. This feeling you get – even if it's kind of irrational – is worth listening to. If you're not a fan or at least an appreciator of the platform you want to be featured on DO NOT CONTACT THEM!

Our minds can be pretty dense, but our intuitions are crystal clear. If I receive an email from someone who hasn't taken the time to listen to the podcast and just wants to flog their wares, I can pick up on it quicker than I can figure out whether they would be a good guest or not. It's difficult to fake enthusiasm, so keep on researching until you can find platforms that you genuinely resonate with.

It helps to note down the ways you resonate with them too. You might be a genuine fan of that magazine or clothing store. You might have something in common with that blogger or podcaster. These little points of connection will be invaluable when it comes to writing your email pitch.

3) Reason

No matter how sweetly you word a pitch, if there isn't something of value there to give your platform of choice, what reason do they have to feature you? If you sell a physical item, can you give this person or business a percentage of profit? If it's an online content creator, what value can you give to their audience?

Something I've found useful when I'm pitching online platforms is to look back through that creators archives. What videos or blogs get lots of views or comments? What questions do their audience ask? If I know this, I can shape the content I'd like to speak about and prove to the host that I can provide content that their audience is clearly interested in. Some examples of what you can offer as a creative are:

- **Product Reviews.** These aren't as effective as they were in the early days of blogging, with influencers getting bombarded now by brands who often have very little relevance or story that the influencer can run with. That said, if you form a relationship with a blogger or Youtube or Instagram influencer, you can have a heck of a lot of impact. The trick here is to be considerate to them and their audience, provide something of value and make it easy for them to share.

- **Personal Stories.** A personal story can be effective because it gives you the opportunity to craft your story and talk about your product or service with enthusiasm and a passion that no one else can match. After all, no one cares as much as you do about what you do! If you've ever read an article or listened to a podcast and thought, "Yes! Me too! I'm so glad he/she said that" then you know the feeling you want to elicit in your audience. Before you dismiss the idea of baring your soul to an audience of strangers, keep in mind this doesn't mean you have to share your deepest, darkest secrets. It just means putting your work in context. I ask guests to do this all the time on The Creative Introvert Podcast, and no one has ever declined to share. In fact, in many cases they probably surprise themselves with what they bring up – and those real stories about their journey, their challenges and why they do what they do – that's what draws the audience in.

- **Teach something.** This is an opportunity to give real value to this publication's audience as well as educate your potential buyers, getting them to a place where they are ready to hire you or buy your thing. I take this approach all the time for guest blogging or being a guest on a podcast.
- **Share research.** This is a great way to create informative content that people are likely to share. In fact, this is some of the content that people are most likely to retweet or share to their friends, because people like to appear smart and helpful. We're that simple. The important part is presenting the information in a fun or visually pleasing way. A great example Ben the Illustrator's Illustration survey.
-

In short, always give your platform host a reason to say yes.

Now you've got phase one out of the way, you should be ready to write your first email. Gulp!

Step 0: Warm up

Before you do, something worth considering is writing a warm-up email. In fact, this doesn't need to be an email – you might have better luck contacting your big shot via Facebook or LinkedIn or Instagram. Have a think about where this person is most likely to hang out. Regardless, sending a warm-up message is a great way to start building a relationship before you go in for the ask.

Most of the time, going straight in for the ask is not the best approach for most people. But in the case of bigger journalists, suppliers or influencers: you'll want to make contact before asking for their time. This doesn't have to feel awkward or forced either. A simple thank you goes a long way in showing your respect for someone, as well as getting on their radar.

For example, when I sent my email to Janet Murray pitching myself as a podcast guest, I had already sent an email to ask about a missing link to a resource on her site as I genuinely wanted to share it with my audience. She replied, I got the resource I was looking for, and when I emailed a few months later in regards to being a guest on her podcast, she remembered me and that really gave me an advantage.

Now, I will admit that this is NOT a vital step for every single email you send. For example, if you're pitching a creative director, who doesn't have much of a presence on social media and whose agency has little content to reference: you might cut straight to the chase.

However, if it's a fairly well-known influencer who has a strong online presence and puts out informative emails each week, who probably gets solicited by PR companies and others looking to guest post, then take five minutes to warm them up.

Step 1: Write a clear and creative subject line

The email subject line is incredibly important as it can be the make or break decider between your recipient opening your email or not. In any case, it sets the tone for what's to come.

Particularly in the case of guest posts, press pitches and podcast interview requests, I make it VERY clear what I'm asking for in the subject line. For example: "GUEST POST SUBMISSION: How Introverts Can Thrive in Open Plan Office Spaces." The recipient can decide immediately whether they're interested or not, and I'm not wasting anyone's time. I've actually been told by a big name podcast host that this kind of formatting was very much appreciated – so I'm sticking with it!

In the case of emails with a softer ask, or your thank you/warm-up email, you have the opportunity to be cuter.

Step 2: Write your personalised introduction

Personal means you HAVE to write this in a way that could not be used for any other platform. No templates! At least not for this first paragraph. Include how you came across them, and yes, get a little gushy. You're a fan, after all. The thing I see a lot of people doing is leading with a paragraph all about themselves. To the person reading this, what's going through their head is likely: "that's nice that you're so talented... but why on earth should I help you?" It helps to lead with something that at least lets the person reading know they're speaking to a human, and that they've done their research.

Step 3: Lay down your offer

This is less of a: "PLEEEASE HELP ME" and more a "Here's what I can do for you..." kind of vibe. In your second paragraph, let your recipient know that you have something of value to offer them or their audience.

I usually break this down into bullet points. For example, if I want to be a guest on their podcast, I lay out 3–4 talking points that I think will be useful or interesting to their audience. This is a section that can be a little more generic across different pitches, but it's still worth customising as every platform will have their own quirks.

It's also worth considering the type of language used on this platform - is it casual or more formal? Is it poetic or more scientific? Are they speaking to all genders, or women only for example?

Step 4: Make a clear call to action

Don't leave them hanging now, you've come so far! Let your recipient know what the next steps are. Do you want them to arrange a call with you? If so, have a booking calendar like Calendly or Acuity ready to link to in the email. This will really help save email ping pong.

Step 5: Sign off with no pressure

This is personal, but something like "I look forward to hearing from you" always feels a little presumptive to me. How do you know you'll hear from me, hmmm? Instead, I default to a no pressure sign off. Literally. "No worries if this isn't a good fit for your publication. Thanks for all you do!" Or something. Basically, be nice.

OK so now you know my secret sauce! Of course, every pitch is a little different, and over time you end up refining your own approach. This is just the format that works for me.

ACTION STEP:

1) Download your cheeky email contacts sheet from the Resources.

2) Set aside some time to start researching publications; magazines, blogs, podcasts, social media accounts that you would love to have your work featured in. Try to add 20 names to the Contacts spreadsheet and ideally start following the key influencers and journalists on social media. Creating a Twitter list is a massive timesaver, even if you aren't a big Tweeter.

3) Aim to email one contact a day each week day for the next month.

Resources mentioned:

Hunter - https://hunter.io/

Chapter 8:
How Do You Collaborate (and Why Would You?)

Austin Kleon, author of *Show Your Work*, describes the lone genius, as:

"An individual with superhuman talents (who) appears out of nowhere... free of influences... with a direct connection to God or the Muse"

This is, as far as I can tell from Kleon's description, a mythical creature. Simply put: lone geniuses are either rarer than Dragonites or 100% fictional. It seems to be that true 'genius' doesn't just pop into existence from thin air. Even the lone geniuses of history we might think of were actually part of a scene of people doing great work around them; or as Brian Eno sweetly calls 'a scenius.'

Think that 'Eureka!' Moment could have happened alone? After struggling for years trying to develop his special theory of relativity, Einstein got his old classmate Michele Besso a job at the Swiss patent office — and after 'a lot of discussions with him,' Einstein said, "I could suddenly comprehend the matter."

Does this mean we have to sacrifice our own ideas, individuality and introversion in favour of going along with a crowd? Not at all. The internet gives us creative introverts the perfect playground to meet like-minded and complementary geniuses to collaborate with: in our own way, at our own pace. Blogs, social media groups, forums and team collaboration apps are all ways you can find, connect and create with your own 'scenius.'

Another objection I commonly hear when encouraging (gently) fellow introverts to team up, is that they live in obscure places: they simply don't dwell in a thriving artistic community.

I understand this problem intimately, because I've been there. Was I living in an obscure hamlet in the English countryside? No, actually. I was living in central London, one of the busiest parts of the planet.

Still, I had no scenius.

Don't get me wrong: I tried to connect with my fellow artists and creators. But somehow... I didn't quite feel like I was part of the gang.

Was it something they did wrong? Looking back, I can see how this was **entirely my doing.** For one, I let my introversion separate me, rather than connect me. In years to follow, I realised how my fellow creatives felt the same way: we were mostly all introverts, shy ones at that, struggling to stay afloat in the harsh London landscape, hating our jobs and just wanting someone to go to a gallery or a gig with on the weekend. Or even better: be at home, making art.

It wasn't until I moved away from London, to the smaller but arguably just as busy city of Brighton. This time, nothing had changed but my attitude. I was aware of how common introverts were, particularly in creative communities, and I knew they were out there.

The problem now was tapping into that quiet community. If they were anything like me, they'd know what's good for 'em and stay home. I found myself doing exactly what I was so good at in London: signing up for events (usually via Meetup.com) and when the day would come, I'd bail. I'd always convince myself I had a good reason, but deep down I was just scared of uncertainty. What if I hated it? What if they hated me? Fear of the unknown got the better of me.

So how did I find my 'scenius'? I didn't – I created my own. After months of moaning about feeling alone on this messy journey, I finally pulled my socks up and decided if I was going to do this collaboration thing: I'd need to remove all my obstacles. One of my obstacles had been time of day. You might recall that I'm an early bird, who thrives at day break and slowly declines throughout the day, so by the time 6pm comes I just want a good meal and to get into my pyjamas. With many events starting at 7pm or later, I had to find a fix for this.

In addition, I needed structure. I needed to know what would happen and when. With my own group, I could set all these little details according to my introverted whims. Alas - my sense of uncertainty was no more.

How to make your own scenius:

1) Set your own rules

It's important that your scenes is actually something you want to be a part of. One of the ways I did this with my Meetup group was having a consistent time and date. This would become Saturday morning, a time for those who haven't been partying too hard the night before, a time when

Brighton city is... relatively peaceful. And a time when I could hold a conversation without fantasising about bed.

I also objected to groups with no clear structure, so I decided that a simple two hour meeting which was short enough to not drain a typical introverts battery, but long enough to get some proper creative work done.

I would also make sure nothing was mandatory: you don't want to talk? Don't talk, just come and do your work, whatever creative pursuit that was. Want to come late, leave early? You're welcome to do that too.

That was my formula for Creative Cafe and it worked like a charm. The start was a bit slow while I worked out my formula, but ultimately nearly every friend I have in Brighton, including some great clients, has stemmed from that little Meetup group.

2) Be clear about your intentions

One more point I'll make about collaboration: you can never guarantee your outcome. There will be ideas that just don't take off, for multiple reasons. Sometimes you'll work out that you and your creative conspirers simply don't click like you first imagined. Other times, a simple chat over coffee will lead to years of fruitful collaborative projects and a friendship you value above all else.

All of this has been true for me: and I can honestly say none of what came from it - the friendships, the collaborations - was planned. But that doesn't mean I had no plan whatsoever. I had set my intention quite clearly at the beginning: I wanted to:

1) Have accountability to show up somewhere outside my house or favourite cafe

2) Start making art again, which again I needed accountability for

3) Bonus: meet some like minds to talk about the creative industry with

Other than that, nothing else was in my control.

3) Be patient

My Meetup group wasn't a hit from the start. The group was cautious, as you rightly would be if you go to a Meetup group for the first time, and one that has just launched. Plus, I had no idea what I was doing... which probably didn't fill them with a sense of ease either.

But as I proved to those early attendees, bit by bit, what they could come to expect from the group, and rely on (a low pressure, super friendly and accepting space to create freely in, every week, come rain or shine) I saw the numbers grow.

The time I put into this group, and practise I got with meeting new people each week, has also made me a much better judge of potential long-term collaborators. The more you meet up with fellow creatives, the better you'll get at determining who you should work with and what skills you bring to a partnership – which is crucial when you're used to being a mythical lone genius.

What to do with your scenius

Of course, you're not done yet. You might have a growing group of fellow merry creatives to have a chat with, but you might still be working solo. The next step is to team up and actually collaborate with one or more of those people in your scenius.

While you don't have to go into an intense collaborative project just yet, I do recommend having a real think about how you could expand your experience in this area, even as a test run.

I took a bit of a leap when I met Théa Anderson through a friend from Creative Cafe. After one chat over wine, I could see why our mutual friend suggested we meet. We had a lot in common, despite her being an extrovert. We shared a love for comedy, thought creatively and had big, absurdly big, dreams.

It wasn't long before we were making plans to host a two-day live event in Brighton, featuring 21 speakers, seven workshops and two live performances. Oh and a band of flamenco dancers! I'm still not sure what we were thinking, and I can see how this was a total fluke, but it has made me see what's possible when more than one mind can work on a goal.

Here are some things to think about when hunting for potential collaborators:

1. Do you share the same values?
2. Do you share a similar vision?
3. Do you share a similar level of self knowledge (if not, lend them this book for part 1 and get them up to scratch!)

Ideally, I want two or more of these answered with e a wholehearted 'YES', if you're trying to find a collaborator who's serious about working with you.

Of course you don't need to both be introverts. In fact, I'll recommend finding someone who has plenty of opposite skills and traits to you. I'm not sure I could have created a live event with another introvert, I relied so much on Théa's tolerance of meeting new people.

In addition, your collaborative project could be something super small. I've collaborated with several fellow creatives from diverse fields to co-present webinars or sell our online courses as a discounted bundle to our audiences. Little experiments will help give you an idea about how you work together.

ACTION STEPS:

1) Have a look at your existing contacts. Is there anyone who you know might be up for collaborating? If not, go to step to. If so, skip to step 3.

2) Have a look on Meetup.com for groups that could be a source of your scenius. If one doesn't exist, create your own!

3) Start to make a shortlist of potential collaborators, based on the three test questions I gave you earlier. You don't need to know exactly what you want to create together yet; you just need to talk to them about your goals in general, and see where your interests overlap.

4) Consider reaching out by email first, then a coffee or Skype meeting to discuss your vision and values further.

Troubleshoot: Asking

Asking for help is difficult for most people. It forces us to admit our shortcomings; our weaknesses; our vulnerability. It reveals us as the bruised peaches we are – not the shiny, unspoiled apples we wish to be seen as.

"Vulnerability sounds like truth and feels like courage. Truth and courage aren't always comfortable, but they're never weakness."
~ Brené Brown

For me, asking certainly fits into that 'uncomfortable but good-for-you' category. A common, though somewhat sexist assumption I grew up hearing was, 'men will never ask for directions.' Ridiculous as it sounds, I did notice my own father would never, EVER ask for directions (he was even resistant to getting a GPS.) In fact, he voiced proudly, that he never asked for anything.

One day I pointed out that he had asked me to tidy my room. His response was: "That wasn't a request, it was an order." Fair point. In recent times however, I wonder if it's not his gender that leads this resistance to asking: but the fact that he is **also an introvert.**

For the longest time, I too found it nigh impossible to ask for anything without feeling like I was taking up space, time, or resources. Asking made me feel I was a crab without a shell.

It's understandable, given the many traits associated with introversion that could make the psychological aversion to asking more extreme:

1) Self-sufficiency

One trait common to introverts is our self-sufficiency. We draw energy from within, not from our external environment.

We think. A lot. Often to a fault. For me, that means I'm used to coming up with (often unnecessarily elaborate) solutions on my own. It's not that I believe my solution will be better: I'm just more familiar with looking inwards for help.

2) Heightened self-awareness

This is up for debate of course, as many would say this inward focus could make introverts *less* concerned about the outside world, but it hasn't been the case in my experience!

I believe that it's this strong inward attention that can make an introvert highly self-aware, a wonderful trait, but it can cross the line to self-consciousness, which is less helpful. It's almost like the light we shine into the cave of ourselves reveals so much that we get terrified of others seeing what's inside. Because of this, we can become overly concerned about looking weak or foolish when asking for help.

3) We like being alone

Finally, there is a practical reason: we work best alone. Physically, we don't do our best problem-solving around people. Particularly now that we are able to consult the online compendium of knowledge, we can do most of our asking alone.

Working on problems in groups, or asking others for help in person however, requires us to be around people! If I can take my answers from Quora, I will.

So what does all this mean: do we, introverts, just accept that we aren't great askers? Well, no. Fortunately, I learnt a lot from Amanda Palmer, and her excellent book, *The Art of Asking*. In the book, she accounts tales from her experience as a living statue: 'The Six Foot Bride,' a character she adopted after finding an affordable second-hand wedding dress for sale.

Having to ask strangers ever day for support, their spare change as well as their attention, was something she simply had to get used to. She didn't have a choice if she wanted to make rent. It's that practise that taught her how to be vulnerable enough to ask her audience for support as an artist in the Dresden Dolls, raising over $1million in support of her crowdfunding campaign to record an album, free from the restraints of her old record label.

Amanda flies the flag today for all artists who are bold enough to attempt to make a living from their art - supported by their fans, their patrons. She may be an extrovert, but I don't believe that you need to become an extrovert to be a pro asker: we introverts have our own inner resources that make us great at asking, if we decide to give it a go:

1) Inner resilience

Because we're less affected by the external world than extroverts, we can depend on being okay inside, regardless of the reply to our ask. It may seem like a farfetched idea, but you won't know until you've tried. What I've learned from asking and receiving countless no's, is that it never feels quite as bad as I expect. I look at myself and realise: oh hey, I got another 'no' and I didn't die!

2) Empathy

The ability we have to put ourselves in another's shoes makes us great at asking, because we are considerate about what someone else might get in return. Asking isn't a one-way street. In every ask, you have the opportunity to give. Even if you can't repay the favour immediately, it's quite likely that simply your appreciation is enough for someone - they get to feel like they've done a good deed, supported an artist or lent a hand to the future generation. That's a gift in itself.

3) Creativity

This is less to do with your introversion, and more to do with your ability to come up with novel ideas, creating value for others in ways that feel new. There are countless ways now to ask online, and I'll lis just a handful below. But it was Amanda's creativity that led to ideas from the Bride character to fund her musical career, to her crowdfunding campaigns to fund her new records when her record label let her down.

With your inborn creative introvertedness, you are equipped with natural asking skills.

Now all skills must be practised, so I want you to start practising the art of asking. You can do this at any and every stage of a creative project; there are millions of people who have gone before you and plenty of platforms and tools to help make this simple:

1) Ask before you create

From what I hear, the music industry has been undergoing some rocky times in the past decade or so, and even a major recording artist can have their livelihood swept away in one fell swoop from a record label. Amanda Palmer was in a sticky situation herself with her punk cabaret act Dresden Dolls, leaving her major label in favour of fan-supported artistry. It's then that she stumbled upon Kickstarter, the crowdfunding platform that ultimately allowed her to raise over $1.2 million to produce an album independently. Now on Patreon, she is close to having 15,000 fans backing her - financially contributing to her 'making stuff' from as little as a dollar.

Of course it isn't easy for someone to reach this height of generous support - just having a crowdfunding campaign up doesn't guarantee you an audience. But the fact that this is an option means you have the option to at lest try it. You can put an idea out into the online ether, and rather than go into serious debt trying to make something people ultimately don't buy, you can actually test your idea first. If people are willing to fund it, you know you have something. If people don't put their money where their mouth is, you still haven't lost anything: you've just figured out what won't work.

It's worth having a look at what you're already doing, and see what people will give you for that. The next step is thinking about what you'd like to create IF you had the cash and the knowledge that people will pay for it. That's when you can think about creating rewards on Patreon or creating your own Kickstarter campaign.

2) Ask while you're creating

Even if you don't have any big expensive project or idea you'd like to fund, there is no harm in giving your Superfans the option to show you their support. Patreon is great for this - I personally support a handful of podcasts who I love and appreciate, because I know personally the effort and cost and time that goes into creating a podcast. I know my monthly donation won't exactly buy the podcast hosts a fancy recording studio, but I do know that every little helps and I'm going to behave in a way that I wish others to: if you can spare it, support your favourite artists.

Patreon is one option, but so is a simple 'donate' button, via Paypal. You can quite simply add this to just about any website. If you can put an image up on your site, and get it to link out, you can add a Paypal button.

Note: you can't expect people to dig deep and donate if you don't ask. This all comes back to making it clear, not begging. Rather than get resentful that people aren't supporting you, think about the ways you might be missing an opportunity to ask. How clear is it that someone CAN support you, and that their support will be greatly appreciated?

3) Ask once it's out there

I have a suitcase of shame in my house. It contains almost £1000 worth of merchandise: t-shirts, posters, tote bags and zines... that I once thought would sell like hotcakes. After all, my friends and fam told me they liked my designs.

Agh. Turns out, the general public were not so keen. I just missed the mark. And I don't believe this is because my designs were horrible. But I do know that I had my marketing all wrong, and honestly didn't give people enough reason to buy.

Hopefully you don't have quite as much wasted efforts sitting in your garage or attic, but you might also be sitting on some great ideas for products that you're too fearful of putting out into the world, in case you do end up in that pricey mess.

I want to encourage you to create, to market to sell. I want your creative work to see the light of day... whilst also playing it safe. Fortunately there are now loads of print-on-demand options for creatives to explore.

When I realised my printing in bulk error, it wasn't long before I found out about sites like Redbubble, Society6, Teespring and so many more - whilst the markup is high, there's little to be lost in putting an idea for a t-shirt or print online on one of these sites. Then, when you realise people are keen enough because they're buying, you can move forward and print a small run yourself, with a better markup.

But you won't know what people want, until you ask. Sites that let you print on demand and strip out the middleman are fantastic, partly because they do some of the asking for you. That said, your designs aren't going to fly unless you also make it clear that people can buy them. Linking to your designs on these sites from your own website, social media and in emails will also be key to getting any momentum on online sales.

4) Ask people to share

Another way to ask isn't directly related to selling your products or services, but to getting the word out about what you do. Again, I don't expect anyone to share an episode of The Creative Introvert Podcast or a blog post if I don't ask. It's not that people don't want to help you or spread the word about what you do: it's that they don't think to do it.

If you catch someone on a good day, in a giving mood, and ask them for a retweet or to forward something to a friend, if they can spare a second: they absolutely will. Telling yourself the story that no one wants to support you or that everyone's too busy to help, isn't going to get you anywhere. Thinking this way is seriously damaging: it means you're less likely to ask, therefore less people will help and there you go: you get more evidence to support that belief.

I had to really shake myself from this story, and some days it's easy for me to slip back into it. I send what I think is a thoughtful email to a friend, thinking they'll most definitely share this one... and I get nothing. I email a bigwig journalist a great story that I definitely think will be perfect for their publication... and nothing comes back.

This is the nature of asking: and unfortunately there is no guarantee that each ask will get the response we desire. However, each ask increases your chances of that positive response. It's a simple numbers game. What's more, the more you ask the better you get at asking! And guess what happens when you get better at asking? Yup - the more of those 'of course I'll share!' responses you'll get.

ACTION STEP:

Where are you in your 90-day push goal? Which of the above four methods would be most helpful right now? Do you need funding to get something off the ground? Do you have services or products already out there, and just need to make the ask to your Superfans? Have a think about what you need, who you can ask, and what you can offer in return.

Chapter 9:
How Do You Network?

Honestly, I don't know anyone who actually enjoys networking events... but then, most of my friends are fellow introverts who would prefer to be at home, sipping tea (or something stronger) and far away from the din of small talk at an awkward networking event.

Too bad they're pretty unavoidable for those of us who want to take action for our career: we can't do it alone watching Netflix. The good news (yes, I promise there is some) is that there are strategies you can put in place to make getting through an awkward networking event a breeze – even if you're a hardcore introvert.

Before the event

Here are some things you can do to get prepared for any kind of event with lots of new people.

1) Do your research

We fear the unknown. Do yourself a favour by researching the event in advance. Even researching the event space ahead of time (many will have online galleries) allows you to visualise it. Doing this innately calms us, as we know what to expect.

2) Prepare a side dish

This has nothing to do with food (er – unless you're asked to bring one) this is how you answer a typical question like, 'Have you been on holiday recently?'

You could answer this with a straightforward yes or no, and pretty much kill the conversation there. Instead, always have a 'side dish' prepared. "Yes, Portugal. It was beautiful – the food in particular was worth the trip alone!" **The side dish is your commentary on the food.**

The trickier follow up when your answer must be a negative: for instance, you haven't been on holiday. Rather than an abrupt 'No' you could try elaborating with a positive spin: "Not at the moment, but I'd love to travel more. Have you been anywhere recently?" You can make just about any 'No' a bit more interesting by adding (1) an opinion (ideally positive) and (2) a question, to turn it back on them.

Start preparing yourself for typical small talk questions, and a handful of side dishes (opinions, facts or questions) to tag on to your answers.

3) Prepare your Quick Pitch

We all know it's going to come up at some point. For most of us, it's a question we dread. To be pigeonholed, misunderstood, or simply bore the socks off someone is not what we came here for.

A good way to test out your answer in advance is to try to pre-empt what a typical reply might be. For example, in some audiences, saying "I'm an illustrator" will prompt a reply like "Oh, what type of work do you specialise in?" Harmless enough... but do you have an answer prepped for that?

Rather than seeing these moments of threat (what if he/she asks this...) and getting defensive before you even get asked; try to see these moments as opportunities to test your material. Remember the 'Quick Pitch' in the Troubleshooting guide in Part 2? This is your chance to try it out and see how your pitch is received. From there, you can tweak, try and test again!

4) Decide what you're offering

This is something else you can prepare ahead of time: you know your skillset and what you can offer, the only thing you need to do when you're actually at the event is to play detective, which shouldn't be too hard as you're already in interview-mode.

Some events will have a guest list available (and if not, it's always worth asking the organiser.) If you can also find out who else might be attending in your industry ahead of time, you can do a bit of online 'stalking' to learn about them. Then, you can prepare something to say that is slightly more interesting than 'nice shoes' (though, when in doubt for small talk – compliments go far!)

5) Ask a friend to come

If you can convince a fellow colleague or friend to meet you at the event, you will be much more likely to show up. I find that if no one knows I'm going... I'm more likely to bail on the event.

One word of warning: do not spend the entire event talking only to them. They can be great to help you 'warm up', but don't use a familiar face as a crutch – that's not what you came for!

6) Set your Cinderella curfew

This is one of my favourite techniques, which applies to anything that we don't necessarily enjoy. It's a bit like a reverse Cinderella curfew, in that Cinders had a maximum time she could stay at the ball, whereas you'll have a minimum time to remain at this event.

The effect of this is powerful though. Just telling yourself in advance you only have 45 minutes to stick around makes it a much more manageable feat - you might even decide to stay longer. Even if you do make a dash as soon as your time is up, at least you know you've tried.

It also forces us to make the most of our time, rather than spending it by the snack table, pretending to text someone.

7) Get your excuses ready

When your timer is up and you do feel the urge to bail, have a decent excuse ready. This will reduce your anxiety about leaving, and make sure fellow guests don't feel like they're boring you (even if they are.)

At the event

So, you made it there! Here are some tips to have in your back pocket:

1) Find the wallflower

Many 'networking tips' will tell you to find someone who looks comfortable, confident and extroverted. This can work, but I find it's far too intimidating for many of us – at least at the start of the event.

Instead, find someone who looks equally awkward, and warm up by talking to them. It's comforting to know you aren't the most awkward there, and with this confidence you can move onto bigger groups.

Of course, don't feel obliged to stay talking only to this person all night. Suggest you mingle as a pair. There's also no harm in taking a bathroom break and using this as a break to chat to someone new.

2) Turn on airplane mode

Another crutch we sometimes rely on at networking events is our bestie: our phones. If possible, turn your phone onto airplane mode to make sure you aren't distracted by messages or Facebook when times are getting tough.

3) Pay attention

Rebecca Hendrix, psychologist, makes the great point that: "People don't care about how much you know until they know how much you care."

Being *interested* is far, far more important than being *interesting*. It's an amazing illusion our mind creates: when someone shows interest in us, they automatically become fascinating.

Attention means making eye contact with your conversational partner, giving them your full focus, nodding when you feel it's appropriate and pausing before taking your turn to speak. A good conversational partner will allow for those gaps – and if they don't, move on! Listening is a wonderful quality introverts generally have in spades, but don't let anyone take advantage of your superpower. You also deserve to be listened to!

And on that note about eye-contact, it's worth keeping in mind that when someone else is speaking, looking at them in the eye most of the time is ideal, even if it's the spot between their eyes if that feels easier.

However, when you're speaking, it's perfectly natural to look away most of the time, coming back to their eyes every few seconds for a fleeting moment to check they're still with you. It really calmed me down to realise I could do this and still look like a relatively confident speaker.

"Real listening can't happen unless we have a sincere desire to understand what we're hearing. And that's not an easy thing to manage, because it requires us to suspend judgment—even when we're feeling frustrated or scared or impatient or bored and even when we feel threatened or anxious about what we're about to hear (because we think we know it or because we don't know it)."

~ Amy Cuddy

4) Be an interested interviewer

As a rule of thumb, ask FINE questions: F - Family, I - Interests, N - News, E - Employment. For follow up questions, you can use the classic journalistic prompts: what, how, who and when to dig a little further. There's nothing worse than throwing out a question, them hitting back, and you dropping the ball.

Another part of active listening is to ask questions, following on from where the other person left off. However, too many questions can sound like you're an interrogator. The trick is simply paraphrasing what your conversation partner has said to affirm and clarify: "You must be..." "So what you're saying is..." "That sounds like..."

It shows someone that they've been understood, listened to and basically makes them feel good.

After the event

So it's the next morning – hopefully you're not hungover! This is a great time to put all your hard work to use.

1) Let it go, let it go...

If you did say something at the event you regret or make a little foible, try not to judge yourself. It only makes the situation more miserable for you! Instead, laugh about it (out loud or in your head!) and remember it's just a funny story for the future. It can also help to use your mindfulness practise here. Everything around you is temporary. It too shall pass.

2) Follow, Like, Comment, Share

It's one thing to take someone's business card, it's another to actually do something with it. Until we all agree that these cards are a waste of paper, it's still up to us to translate them into something useful: digital connections.

Usually you can find someone's social media weapon of choice from the business card, or a bit of googling. Then, follow! I recommend using Twitter Lists to keep your contacts in order. For example, if I met a publisher at an event, I'll add them to my list of publishers. Your other option is to use your handy Contacts Spreadsheet (find it in the Resources) and make a note about where you met this person.

Go one more step and actually make contact. It could be very simple, a quick "Nice to meet you last night!" tweet, or a lengthier note on LinkedIn, possibly giving them a link to something you were chatting about, or asking for a coffee.

3) Don't wait for them

If there was one piece of advice you take from this whole chapter, let it be this: don't wait for someone to make the first move. Take matters into your own hands! This is where the introverts can really shine. We might not be the best when put under the spot in a group environment (I know I'm not) but we come into our own when we're back home, with time to craft a considerate email.

Hopefully, that's enough to help you feel more at ease with any networking events you find yourself at. Even though I don't make a deliberate effort to attend formal networking events, I somehow manage to find myself at occasions full of people I don't know, which would once upon a time fill me with anxiety.

I won't pretend my fears of social awkwardness have gone away entirely, but reminding myself of these pointers is a big help. Above all, I remind myself that I'm not there to sell anything or convince anyone of my ability. I'm there to connect. Those moments I've shared with a like-minded creative (often a fellow introvert) at these odd events are priceless, and I'm always willing to recreate that feeling whenever possible.

As much as I love the online world for meeting new people, nothing beats these intimate, face-to-face connections, which, if you ignore everyone else in the room for a moment, are perfectly introvert-friendly.

ACTION STEP:

Find an event local to you and get it in your diary. This doesn't have to be a formal networking event; it could be a coffee morning, a community event, a workshop or a meet up for people interested in a certain hobby. There are plenty out there – Meetup.com is a great place to have a browse no matter where you are in the world.

Chapter 10:
How Do You Speak in Public?

The grandaddy of fears... public speaking. It feels so natural to be fearful about public speaking – a fear that's been put above fears of spiders, plane crashes and depending on who you ask: death!

But it's what mankind has used for millennia to spread new ideas, to command armies and to teach. Even if you don't plan on giving a TED Talk in the near future, it might be something you start considering after you've read this chapter.

After all, public speaking is a very useful tool to have in your toolbox. You can take your creative skills to workshops and events. You can spread your message and talk about your work with ease and persuasion, when needed.

1) Research

The more you know in advance, the more you'll feel prepared. Research where you'll be speaking, who you're delivering to, how long you'll speak for and who else you might be speaking with.

It helps to think about the audience's expectations – what will they want to get from the speech? A group of students about to leave the safe haven of school has very different needs compared to a room of execs.

Don't forget the logistics – will you have access to a projector, the internet, a table? Ask as many questions as you like to the event organiser - they'll be more than happy to clarify (it's their job!)

2) Write your speech

Study TED Talks, Creative Mornings, commencement speeches and anything relevant in your field to get you inspired. But once you've had a decent fill, stop! There's a danger (I've experienced) in watching so many amazing talks from the pros that it puts you off ever speaking because the perceived 'gap' between where you are and where they are is so great. Just remember: they started somewhere. Just use their talks as guides for structure, cadence, poise and so on.

I picked up many tips just from studying some talks from the greats:

- Simple devices like starting with a story work wonders
- Signpost so your audience knows what to expect (I'll be sharing what I learned about X, Y and Z...)
- Throw in a question to the audience (and pause as though you were expecting a reply - don't rush this!)
- The power of 3 (using lists of three are a great device to hold your speech together)
- If all else fails, end strong (for example, simply saying the words 'to conclude...')

3) Practise

It helps to have someone around to practise in front of, but of course this can be just as nerve-inducing (if not more so) when you know the person. Instead, try recording yourself. Just set up your smartphone and hit record. That way you can watch yourself back too, and make adjustments.

No matter how long you have (ideally at least three weeks) before giving the speech, practise every day. I do this after showering, a trigger I use to remind me. Every day during the run up, I get out of the shower and start to get ready for the day, I put the recorded version of my speech on repeat, and talk over it. I have it prompting me in the background, and I rapidly get familiar with the flow of it, the pace, the pauses. For the final few days before the speech, I deliver it solo – no backing track!

4) Prepare for the worst

This is a technique that can be used for all of the following scenarios, and it's one worth practising – the more you do it, the more powerful its effects are.

Before my first Toastmasters speech – 'the Icebreaker' – I made a list of all the things I could possibly think of that could go wrong, as well as how I expected to feel.

Then I came up with – as rationally as I could muster – workarounds and solutions for each, as well as the best case scenarios.

1. Butterflies
Solution: deep breaths, proper nutrition, limit caffeine

2. Dry mouth
Solution: drink plenty of water, practise speech in advance allowing for water breaks

3. Hand gestures are ridiculous and I look like a puppet
Solution: film yourself in advance to check puppet-likeness, watch some favourite TED talks and see what the pros do (many move very subtly)

4. Too quiet and no one hears the speech
Solution: begin by asking "can you hear me at the back?"

5. Forgetting my words
Solution: have back up notes, practise every day – no excuses!

6. Technology fails
Solution: test in advance, bring a back up if possible

7. Total disaster - I pee my pants?
Solution: go to the loo in advance, or just remember that I'll have a great story to tell

5) Day of the speech

This is when it's time for the somewhat cheesy (but actually very effective) advice: visualise. Visualise yourself giving the speech, confidently and with ease. You have back ups for everything that could go wrong, so just think of the best case scenario now – after all, you'll be going on stage soon!

Prior to going on stage, it helps to have someone to talk to – there's nothing like trying to talk when you've barely said two peeps to anyone all day. Professionals recommend vocal warm ups, which you can find on YouTube. You could also find a space (loos are fine) to pull some 'power poses', which help some people feel more confident. I personally find them helpful to open up so I stand with better posture.

<EXAMPLES OF POWER POSES>

It's tempting for our eyes to connect with the duller looking faces (don't take it personally – some people have naturally moody resting faces!) and be deterred. Find someone in the crowd with a smile on, and use them as a focus point.

Finally, just remember that nerves are not a bad thing! An audience who sees your nerves isn't going to turn on you: in fact, the opposite is much more likely. People want you to succeed, and they'll appreciate the fact you care enough about them to be nervous!

6) Post-speech

Plan a way to celebrate your accomplishment, even if it's in a small way. You've done something that sends the most confidence extrovert into cold sweats: so give yourself a good pat on the back, and bask in the post-adrenaline glow.

ACTION STEP:

If public speaking is something you might be considering, have a brainstorm for places that you could cut your teeth on. I do recommend Toastmasters, as a free to low cost option for a safe place to get in front of people and be OK with potentially making a fool out of yourself. It's not for everyone, but I have found it's a great resource in virtually any city that can provide the motivation and structure to at least get you on a mic.

Resources mentioned:

Toastmasters - https://www.toastmasters.org/

Part 4:
Progress

Chapter 1:
How to Keep on Keeping on

Let's say you've been at this game for a while now. You've been taking action, journalling, finding a supportive community, showing your work. But... Things aren't moving as quickly as you hoped. In fact, they've stalled. They might even look like they're moving backwards, like when planets go into what astrologers call 'retrograde'. Planets never *actually* go backwards by the way, it just looks like it does from our perspective.

It's exactly the same with our work: I promise you, no matter what it looks like, you're *not* going backwards. Everything that happens is simply more data. More information for you to use to move forward again real soon.

I'll admit it might look bad. You might have set a goal months ago, a SMART goal, even. It was: Specific, Measurable, Actionable, Realistic and Time bound.

Or so you thought. That deadline has come and gone and you haven't achieved that goal. I know how that feels. I can't tell you the number of times I've missed the mark. And it sucks. It does. I won't try to sugarcoat that one.

The only upside – and actually, it's quite a big upside – is that in every case, in every missed goal or disappointment, I learned something or I grew in some way. More confidence, more skills, or something totally crazy came out of left field.

This part will cover some of the best ways I've found to stay on track, through the good times and the bad. We'll also tackle some of the ways in which we often get set back: criticism, self-doubt and stagnation, and how to learn from those little (or large) bumps along the road.

1) How Do You Review Your Progress?

I'll share my process for reviewing your wins and losses, and most importantly: how to use these reviews to move forward, bigger and stronger than before.

2) How Do You Deal with Discouragement?

It can feel uncomfortable at first to start celebrating personal wins, but I encourage you to make this a habit. I'll share various ways of making sure your successes don't go unnoticed by you.

3) How Do You Handle the Haters?

On the other end of the stick, we have criticism. Eek. Not to worry: this chapter will outline some simple and timeless strategies for handling whatever the peanut gallery throws at you.

4) How Do You Work With Difficult Clients and Customers?

These are the clients and customers that make you want to pack it all in and change your name. But before you do that, read this chapter! You might find a way to remedy even the most difficult situation.

5) How Do You Change Direction?

I don't recommend flogging dead horses, for multiple reasons, but nor do I want you to bail out too soon on a project that isn't meeting your expectations. The trick to developing this awareness is the art of the pivot.

6) How Do You Keep To Your Word?

I used to think all my motivation came from within... until I discovered the power of making myself accountable to others in my life. Suddenly, I stopped bailing on events I said I'd attend, I stopped skipping the more challenging tasks on my to-do list, and – best of all – I started feeling like my effort was being acknowledged and supported. Find out how you can form your own accountability partnerships and start reaping the benefits straight away.

7) Who Do You Go To For Help?

It doesn't matter if you aren't connected to some high-flying business mentor, or if you can't afford to pay for the support. There are people out there who are at least a step ahead of you and you'll be surprised to find out just how willing they are to offer a hand up. We'll talk about how to get help from a mentor, without being a bothersome brat.

8) Who Do You Surround Yourself With?

I know, the idea of having a group of people you meet with – virtually or in person – might not sound terribly introvert-friendly, but I've found a real pleasure and massive business benefit in a well-crafted Mastermind. The trick is making sure it's well-crafted. I'll share my tips on making sure your Mastermind works for you, and you look forward to each meeting.

There are Action Steps at the end of each chapter so be sure to have a pen and paper next to you! You can also download your accompanying Creative Introvert workbook and all the resources mentioned throughout the book at: www.thecreativeintrovert.com/book

You will also find Troubleshooting chapters peppered throughout the book, to help you overcome any challenges that may arise in working through the exercises. And if you have any questions for me at any point, don't hesitate to email: hello@thecreativeintrovert.com

Chapter 2:
How Do You Review Your Progress?

When I first started down the online business route, I didn't even consider making time to look back and review my progress. After all, I was all about moving forward: when I got to where I wanted, that's when I'd take a break and look at how far I'd come.

This was a huge mistake, because even in those early days I had a lot to learn, simply from my own actions and results (or lack of.) In addition, by not pausing to reflect on my past successes (even if they were minuscule) I was unknowingly undermining my own inner motivation. D'oh!

Not only could I learn from my successes and failures; I could look at the sheer amount of moxie I was demonstrating by even *attempting* to make a business from doodling animals, and that would have done a lot of good for my self-esteem.

Now, no matter how much or how little I think I've achieved over the course of a week or a month, I make time to review my process. I urge you to do the same, no matter how far along in your creative pursuits you are.

Here are some ways to structure progress reviews:

1) Focus on valuable metrics (not vanity metrics)

Looking at the numbers – whether its sales or followers or email subscribers – is valuable, yes. But it's not the only thing you should be paying attention to. In fact, I usually put it at the bottom of my priority list on progress reports.

Why? Well, for a long time I found looking at the numbers more depressing than motivating or informative. It would make me see how short I fell of my bold expectations, and put me off doing another progress review any time soon.

This is why I recommend getting very clear on your micro-goals (see Part 2, chapter 4) and reviewing your progress in terms of those. For example, if my Push Goal (overall goal, 90 day goal) is to finish my book, one of my micro-goals is to write 500 words a day. I can track word count every day, and review that, sure. But I can also recognise the fact I managed an average of five days per week where I made an effort to write some words (even if I fell short of 500.)

This tells me a lot for my progress goal. I can celebrate that fact, and I know I'm not having a problem in sitting down to write. But because I'm not hitting the full word count, maybe I add a second writing session in, three days a week for the next period of time before the next review.

2) Focus on quality, not quantity

Another way to look at my word count writing goal, is in terms of the quality of my writing experience. I might consider how I felt when I was writing. No matter what your creative work is, I believe in using your sense of enjoyment as a real metric, not just focusing on numbers as a measure of progress.

Ask yourself some questions like you might ask a loved one. Was this an enjoyable part of your day? If not, what could you do to make it more enjoyable next time? Did you have more fun when you wrote in a certain cafe, or were you more effective and happy when writing at home? Again, these could show you variables to play with next time.

3) Get a date

This is super, super important. If you finish reading this chapter and even went and downloaded your progress tracker, and you DON'T set an actual date in your calendar to go through this progress... well then I apologise, because I've most definitely wasted a good half hour of your life.

Please, for the love of chocolate, do set a date to do this. Of course, you still have to take the next step and do it, but if you're anything like me, if it isn't written down somewhere, it won't happen.

Rant aside, when you do decide to schedule your review you're going to have to decide when and how often you take these reviews. Of course, this is all up to you. Personally I have experimented with multiple review periods. Daily, weekly, monthly, quarterly, yearly... you name it. At different times, these have all worked, so I encourage you to experiment too.

Currently, I lean towards the daily, monthly and yearly reviews, and naturally the daily ones are more brief and the yearly reviews are more in-depth and provide me with a big picture view.

4) Create a review journal

I've found it helpful to keep my reviews in one place. Now if you're a traditionalist, you might want a physical paper planner or a fancy notebook, and I highly encourage going stationary shopping especially if you know you're motivated when you have something nice to write in and write with – a good pen makes a lot of difference. They're not a sponsor but I've been obsessed with Pilot V5s. Best pen ever, until further notice.

Alternatively, you might want to save the paper and do this all digitally. I use Evernote for this, I create a Notebook which is for all review or life based stuff, and I create notes within it, usually just titled with the date. It's been amazing to look over these when I feel like reminiscing on past business successes (and fails) and the major advantage is: it doesn't take up any physical space! Very helpful when you're homeless, like me.

And of course, the free Progress Tracker I've made for you will be a helpful tool to look at each time you come to review your progress, so be sure to download that and print it or keep it safe on your desktop so you have it at hand.

What to ask yourself in your review

One thing to consider is how extensive you make your review, which will greatly depend on (1) your tolerance for this and (2) how often you decide to review.

For example, a daily review might simply consist of:

1. Did I get my #1 task done today?
2. Did I learn anything?

3. What's my #1 task for tomorrow?

Alternatively, a monthly review might take into account multiple areas of your creative goals, and even your life as a whole.

My monthly reviews usually mean taking a look at each of my life areas (e.g. Work, Play, Relationships, Health) I go back through my journal, any relevant spreadsheets, as well as my Asana calendar (or Google cal) to see what I managed to get done.

This takes a little while, but I book it in my calendar for a Sunday afternoon near the end of the month and make sure not to miss it. I actually find it a great way to wrap up the month and go into the new month with renewed focus and a clear slate.

5 Questions To Ask Yourself Every Month

- What/when did I do my best?
- What challenged me?
- What can I learn from the challenges?
- Did I treat myself with care?
- What decisions can I make for next month?

In terms of yearly reviews, it's probably worth me recording a separate episode about how to do these, but in some ways you can adjust the monthly questions and apply them to the year. I also like to review each of my monthly reviews to give a better overarching view when it comes to the end of the year.

This is also when I set my goals for the month or year ahead, and one thing I've found is that I've become a way better, more realistic goal setter since I've started taking my reviews more seriously.

ACTION STEPS:

1) Decide what kind of review schedule you would like to start with. I recommend weekly for now, but you know you. Get it in your calendar!

2) Download your Progress Tracker from the Resources, and start using it to keep an eye on the prize.

Chapter 3:
How Do You Deal with Discouragement?

Now even if you're a pro at goal-setting, at checking off your to-do list items and reviewing your progress, many of us forget this crucial step: acknowledging your wins.

After all, we've been taught to spot our weaknesses, working on those rather than highlighting our strengths and making the most of what is working for us. Plus, it's in our genes! We have built-in cognitive biases or shortcuts our brains take to make sense of the world, and keep us alive. One of these is known as Negativity Bias.

It's the tendency to forget the things that go well for us, and remember the bad. Sound familiar? The reason we do this is really quite... reasonable.

For example, let's say you've gone on a beautiful bike ride on a nature trail. You spot rare birds, butterflies, plants and are having a lovely time. Then, you spot a rattlesnake! You evade the rattler, but when you get home – what do you remember best? Likely, the snake. We remember the **threats** in our environment, because that's what keeps us safe.

It may have been helpful to our ancestors, but chances are it's not helping us when we've had a review from our boss at work – we forget all the positive and focus on that one negative point. Not great for our self-esteem. This is why we need to make a deliberate effort (it will become a habit with time – promise!) of recognising our successes.

The more we **celebrate our wins**, record our **achievements** - no matter how small - the more we start noticing them. Fortunately, there's a cognitive bias for that too! The Positive Bias isn't just for people called Pollyanna... it's something we can actually train our brains to do. Simply by paying more attention to these positive outcomes, the more we spot and the easier it gets.

I'm not telling you to lie to yourself either. This is just a way of rebalancing our tendency to focus on the negative, in a way that helps you move forward. When you start focussing on your wins, you naturally increase your confidence and are more likely to go for what you want, and actually achieve it.

There are a few simple ways to speed up this process of retraining your brain's biases:

1) Share your wins (and own them)

Being public about what we've achieved builds confidence and encourages us to continue to make an effort to progress further.

Yes, this is scary. Many of us have been brought up believing we need to be humble. Whilst humility is a strength, we can take this too far. That's when we get into the murky waters of guilt and shame.

Remember not to discount your successes by putting everything on Lady Luck. Professor Martin Seligman has shown that if you don't train yourself to recognise the connection between your actions and efforts and the positive results you get, you may end up thinking your achievements were just down to good luck.

While luck may feel like it plays a role: it's important that we see our behaviours as impactful, and that we can make a difference. Those self-deprecating comments like "My boss must have been in a good mood and taken pity on me" may get a laugh, but they can be harmful to your confidence in the long run. Instead, remind yourself "I put a lot of time and energy into that proposal, that's why my boss was so happy with it." That way, you'll increase your chances of future efforts, that get similar rewards.

2) Take pride without the guilt

One of life's many paradoxes is around how to handle pride. We're told in an abbreviated and oft quoted Bible verse, 'Pride goes before the fall' but simultaneously told to 'make our parents proud' or 'be proud of your nationality, your profession, your work, your lineage, your race' etc.

So which is it?! The truth is, pride is a tricky subject, and depending on your culture or upbringing or simply life experiences, we all respond differently to the problem of pride.

Tara Swiger points out there are multiple different definitions of pride, including:

1. "a feeling of deep pleasure or satisfaction derived from one's own achievements, the achievements of one's close associates, or from qualities or possessions that are widely admired."

2. "unreasonable and inordinate self-esteem (personified as one of the deadly sins)"

I'll take the first one, thank you! As with many traits, we can take pride too far. To be proud of what we have accomplished, what we've worked for and what we deserve, does NOT automatically make us arrogant.

We know how bragging feels: we've seen it done by others, and seen the effects it has. Bragging actually comes from a place of *insecurity*. If you're worried about bragging or seeming arrogant: chances are: you aren't in any danger of doing any of that! Sharing your work and your successes with others doesn't make you arrogant or cocky: it builds your self esteem – and may be the inspiration that helps an other see what's possible for them.

3) Create a Pastport

No, that was not a typo. Your 'Pastport' is a record of your past successes, achievements and triumphs. The only way to build trust in your skills, abilities and potential is to acknowledge and remember what you've already done. No one else is going to award you for these little wins: it might have been this way at school or as a child – but now it's up to you to give yourself a gold star for your hard work.

ACTION STEP:

Make that Pastport! Get a nice little (or big!) notebook and maybe start by jotting down answer to some of the following:

1. What have you been proud to have achieved recently?
2. When did you keep to your word, even though it wasn't easy?
3. When did you do something driven by your Values?

Even if your Pastport is looking a bit empty right now, start making it a habit to add to it. You can do this on a daily basis or you do it during your weekly or monthly review.

You could include certificates from your past, rewards, souvenirs – anything that reminds you of a time when your confidence was ramped up.

Chapter 4:
How Do You Handle the Haters?

"Criticism locks us into the very pattern we are trying to change. Understanding and being gentle with ourselves helps us to move out of it."
~ Louise Hay

We aren't always going to be showered with compliments and support from others: sometimes, we'll face judgement and criticism from others. It's something everyone experiences throughout their lives. If you get any kind of true success or are in the spotlight... you'll likely get criticism. You might get criticism from strangers and internet trolls, but you may also get it from those closer to home: the 'who do you think you are doing X?' comments.

How we respond to what we hear or read or pick up from others, is however 100% up to us. We have the choice to see it as a threat or not.

Questions to ask yourself before taking on board criticism:

1) Who was it from?

Brené Brown talks about the time she read all the online comments on her famous TED Talk. It hit her hard to read the criticism from envious trolls, and that's when she found the 'man in the arena' speech from Theodore Roosevelt.

She acknowledges that you can't keep critics out of the arena, and we can't stop caring what people think, but we can still show up in spite of them.

"If you're going to show up and be seen, there is only one guarantee. And that is: you are going to get your ass kicked."
~ Brené Brown

Rather than focus on trying to win over the critics, surround yourself with those who will lift you up and bolster your confidence. Be clear about who the critics are and who your fans are. Who was the criticism from? What were their intentions? Make sure you aren't sacrificing your work to the critics at the expense of your fans.

2) How many times have your received that criticism? Was it from one person? Or multiple times from multiple people?

One of the few ways to identify a word of criticism that might be worth taking on board and doing something about is to start to recognise how often you get this piece of criticism. For example, I had to face facts early in my work career that attention to detail was not a strong point of mine.

As a designer, this was a hard pill to swallow. But I couldn't deny it: for one, the people who delivered this criticism had my best interests at heart. It came from multiple people over the years, and over time I've improved slightly, building in extra checks to make sure I don't miss dotting an 'i' or crossing a 't' (and thank the good lord for spell check.)

But attention to detail will never be my strong point. What I lack in the details department, I make up for in eye for balance, cohesion, originality, colour and speed. In that sense, I learned to double down on my strengths, and not ignore my weaknesses, but not to be deterred because of them.

3) How personal does it feel?

Remember: **it's never about you.** Nearly any piece of criticism (even constructive feedback) is in some way a projection of the critic's beliefs, fears, desires. It's up to you how you want to feel or respond to it: whether or not you can see it in yourself and want to change it, or whether you leave it with the critic and go on with your day.

"If it feels personal then it's probably nothing to do with you."
~ James Wedmore

This is a really helpful way I've found to sort out whether or not I should pay attention to the criticism. Using the example of being pulled up on my attention to detail: if this is in relation to a website I've designed, I'll happily take it on board. However, if it's in relation to what shoes I've chosen to match with my bag, I'll likely take the criticism with a pinch of salt. It's personal, and not shouldn't matter to anyone, so I can leave that one at the door.

4) Does it come from within?

Oh no! The biggest, hairiest, scariest critic of all: our Inner Critic. This critic is old; older than us, in fact. It's comprised of society's fears, neuroses and biases, as well as what junk we've picked up in our own lives. It might come from a magazine article, a thoughtless word from a parent or bitter teacher. Over time, we internalise these words of venom, and begin to think they are us.

Ultimately, the inner critic wants us to 'fit in', and thereby keep us safe from harm. After all, our ancestors survived by showing the rest of the tribe "I'm like you too!" But for people today, trying to express their creativity, the critic is more of a pain than a handy helper.

One of my favourite articles ever on WaitButWhy.com, describes the Mammoth (basically your Inner Critic) and how finding our Authentic Voice is the best way to 'tame' the mammoth.

To get clear on your Authentic Voice, I recommend going back to part one, in which you created your Alter Ego. This part of you signifies what you truly care about, what you truly want and what you're truly capable of. Your inner critic must learn to stay out of these areas of your life, and while you're going to have to take it along for the ride, it doesn't get to sit up front. Imagine a car with your Alter Ego sat next to you, and your inner critic firmly buckled down in the back (or better, the trunk.)

What to do about the trolls

So let's say the criticism isn't helpful or constructive or from someone you love and trust... it's from the TROLLS. You're out there in the online world, sharing your stuff and making new connections with a growing audience. Your inner critic may have even piped down, now it's learning you can't be stopped.

But then you have a run in with an *outer* critic, also known as a troll. A real person (even if they aren't acting like it) who has words that hurt, that you can hear or read. What then?

Unfortunately this is one of the very real, very challenging aspects of the digital age. We may have freedom of speech online, but this also leaves us vulnerable to attack. One way people deal with these attacks are through digital detox, or terminating their accounts with a social media site or forum altogether. Whilst I do recommend breaks from the digital world from time to time, I'm not convinced this ostrich-in-sand approach is the best. For one, it means the bullies win.

"Without others sharing good work and encouraging words, the scene itself dies."
~ Austin Kleon

I know it isn't easy. I know there will be times where one thoughtless comment throws you for a loop. But I urge you to stick with it! Fight the good fight, and know that no matter what, you shared what's true for you.

Even if you remove all the social media apps from your phone, block the comments on your site and stop reading the news: there will still be people in your life who won't understand you. They'll form their image of you (and you of them) and nothing you can do can change that. Instead of fighting, there are ways to mitigate the damage they try to do. Here are some more tips to protecting yourself, whilst still participating in the game:

1) Take out the trash

Something I do on a regular basis is sift through social media accounts I no longer want to follow. I go through my feed and check in with myself as I scroll. How does this post make me feel? Does it provoke stress, anger, jealousy? If these unhelpful emotions arise, I know what I have to do. Unfollow. It really can be that simple.

Twitter has a great feature of Lists. Having my interests in list format mean I can add accounts to these lists and only view updates from the lists I choose. This is not only convenient for managing contacts, it's great for managing stress and overwhelm!

Set aside some time to have a really good clear up, and make a date with yourself regularly to comb through and filter out the unhelpful sources.

"Whatever excites you, go do it. Whatever drains you, stop doing it."
~ Derek Sivers

2) Batch, schedule and recharge

One thing I do to keep my sanity in check as well as saving time, is designating one morning each week to batch create my content. This means writing, creating images and scheduling my posts for the week ahead. Batching and scheduling posts can be done for most platforms: I personally focus on Instagram but Facebook and Twitter can be prepared for in the same session without much extra work.

Scheduling tools such as:
Bufferapp.com
Hootsuite.com
Later.com (my current choice)

This will allow you to quickly and simply say all you want to say in advance, and without actually opening an app or visiting a website other than the tool you choose.

It also means you can take extended breaks to recharge between batching sessions where you don't have to think about social media if you don't want to.

You can have another session each week in which you check in on comments and do your own work to support you creative community (more on that in chapter 8) but at least you can do this at a timer you're feeling at your most courageous, and not at 3am when you can't sleep.

3) Reply with caution

You owe no one a response. Sometimes the most effective way to deal with online bullies is the age old technique of... ignoring them.

This does not mean tolerating them. It might be a matter of hitting 'delete' on the comment, or blocking the offender, even reporting them, and moving on with your day.

At other times, you might feel the need to respond. For example, if someone simply has their facts wrong, there's no harm in correcting them. I've written one article that's received some critical but thoughtful comments, and I've approved and responded to each one because I believe in freedom of speech, as long as it's not simply bullying. I've also seen negative reviews for local shops and cafes where the owner has responded thoughtfully, apologising for the customer's experience, and going as far to invite them back to make it up to them. I see this as a smart choice: it not only means the owner has taken the higher ground by not losing their cool, but it also looks great to future customers who appreciate the owners kindness in the face of (often ridiculous) criticism.

However, there is the danger of adding fuel to the fire when you start to reply: if you let your temper get the better of you, it only serves to bring you down to the level of the trolls.

There are also many options to turn off comments, whether it's for an Instagram post or your personal blog. It's no surprise that one of the most popular blogs online, Seth.blog from Seth Godin doesn't allow comments to be posted.

That said, you can't delay the inevitable: you simply can't be out in the world without at some point running into folk who just don't get you.

4) Practise loving kindness

Loving kindness? To the trolls on the internet? Sounds like a walk in the park... if the park was on fire.

When I first came across the concept of loving kindness meditation (also known as 'mettā' in Pali, I was all kinds of dubious. For one, I tend not to get on well with guided meditations (which isn't vital for practising this technique, but it's a good place to start.) Plus, I couldn't see how forcing myself to send loving 'vibes' to someone I was mad at would be possible, let alone calm me down.

But I trusted Tara Brach (a wonderful meditation teacher) enough to give it a whirl... and I was shocked by its effect on me.

The commonest form of the practice is in five stages, each of which should last about five minutes for a beginner.

1. In the first stage, you feel mettā for yourself. You start by becoming aware of yourself, and focusing on feelings of peace, calm, and tranquillity. Then you let these grow in to feelings of strength and confidence, and then develop into love within your heart. You can use an image, like golden light flooding your body, or a phrase such as 'may I be well and happy', which you can repeat to yourself. These are ways of creating the feeling of mettā for yourself.

2. In the second stage think of a good friend. Bring them to mind as vividly as you can, and think of their good qualities. Feel your connection with your friend, and your liking for them, and encourage these to grow by repeating 'may they be well; may they be happy' quietly to yourself. You can also use an image, such as shining light from your heart into theirs. You can use these techniques - a phrase or an image - in the next two stages as well.

3. Then think of someone you do not particularly like or dislike. Your feelings are 'neutral'. This may be someone you don't know well but see around. A local coffee shop barista, for example. You reflect on their humanity, and include them in your feelings of mettā.

4. Then think of someone you actually dislike - maybe that internet troll - someone you're having difficulty with. Try not to get caught up in any feelings of hatred; think of them positively and send your mettā to them as well.

5. In the final stage, think of all four people together - yourself, the friend, the neutral person, and the enemy. Then extend your feelings further, to everyone around you, to everyone in your neighbourhood; in your town, your country, and so on throughout the world. Imagine waves of loving-kindness spreading from your heart to everyone, to all beings everywhere. Then gradually relax out of meditation, and bring the practice to an end.

After practising this to a guided meditation a few times, you'll likely be able to practise it on your own, and even throw it in throughout your day. The whole thing can take less than 10 minutes, if you give one to two minutes per step.

The effect this had on me was an ability to detach from my hurt little ego mind, and see the big picture. Hating on others won't do me any good, nor will stewing in my own self loathing that might be triggered by a thoughtless, jealous comment. Instead, taking the higher ground and remembering we're all imperfect creatures who deserve a bit of love, helped me regain my power and sense of peace.

Give it a try. Even if you don't get through stage three on your first few goes, stick with it. Try it at a time you aren't feeling too bad, and see how far you get. Over time, I promise it gets easier.

ACTION STEPS:

1) Make your list of five people that you listen to. If the criticism comes from someone else, remind yourself: only the list counts.

2) Have a think about what you can take from this chapter in terms of protecting yourself from the haters. Are there any accounts you can have a clear out of? Is it time to start that batching and scheduling approach? Maybe spend 10 minutes on mettā practise?

Resources mentioned:

Loving Kindness meditation - https://www.tarabrach.com/guided-meditation-metta-lovingkindness/

How to create Twitter lists - https://help.twitter.com/en/using-twitter/twitter-lists

Chapter 5:
How Do You Work With Difficult Clients and Customers?

Freelancing or running your own business can be tough. Really tough. There are some months when you aren't guaranteed a paycheck – at least that's how it was for me. So turning down a client is often out of the question, and we'll bend over backwards to avoid refunding a customer. The result of this scarcity mindset is that we end up burnt out and resentful, all because we didn't set clear boundaries with the client or customer.

In this chapter I'll focus primarily on dealing with difficult clients, as a service-based business tends to have greater (and more nuanced) challenges in terms of boundaries, than a purely product-based business does. However, the suggestions I give will be applicable to both service-based gigs and to those of you who sell products to customers.

Back to boundaries. For me, boundaries have become clear only through experience. From getting burned, basically. The client who didn't pay in time means I have boundaries in my contract that state 50% of payment is upfront, and only then will work begin. Or there might be project deadlines, and an invoice is sent when each milestone is met. Invoices also come with a deadline, and you could think about penalties for late payments.

In order to start laying down your own boundaries (as these will be unique to you) have a think about what could go wrong before you jump into working with a client. And trust your instincts! I've had hunches about people before and I wish I'd paid attention to them. This doesn't mean rejecting the job, it just means stating at the start how you work and what you expect... with respect for the client, of course.

The key to a lot of this is empathy; which introverts tend to have plenty of, so it's simply a matter of tapping into those resources. To start, have a think about what the client's issues are. Are they scared you'll run off with their money without doing the job? Maybe they've been burned before and that's making them want to micromanage you and be snappy in their emails.

For each issue your client might have, think about how you can put them at ease. That way, when an issue comes up, you've already addressed their fears and they're way more likely to act appropriately.

For example, you might tell a client that you'll have an update for them each day or each week at a certain time. This alone will alleviate those clients who are scared you aren't doing the work you promise, and make them more likely to leave you be, and not keep calling you every 15 minutes.

The same goes for selling products. Do you have a refund policy on your website? Do you have a process for handling refunds and exchanges? Do you have a frequently asked questions page? All of this work will save you heaps of time in the long run, and your customers will appreciate it.

Now, that's all good and well before you start working together. But what if the deal is sealed and you're already working for a difficult client, or have a mess of customers breathing down your neck? Here are some things to try, during these moments of madness.

1) Communicate (even if you don't feel like it)

One of the biggest issues with client relationships, particularly with us introverts, is that we can tend to avoid communication where possible. I like to use the fewest possible emails to make something happen, and phone calls – well, I avoid them at all cost.

That said, I know how many clients DO feel better when they can speak on the phone, so I will get over my phone phobia for them. Personally, I prefer video calls, even though that doesn't sound super introvert-friendly. I just find you can read your client's emotions better and they naturally see you as more of a human when they see your face, and are more likely to treat you like one because of it.

I also recommend scheduling updates, especially if you're on a longer-term project. Just letting someone know you are working on their thing, seems to help to put them at ease.

2) Get it in writing (or record conversations)

A lot of issues also come from miscommunication. Someone thinks the deliverable is this, someone else thinks it's this... Email is great because you have it in writing.

But even phone calls are worth recording. I record my Skype calls using a piece of software called eCamm, you can also use Zoom, and there are other ways to do this. Of course, legally you ought to tell your client you're recording the call, and most will be fine if you explain it's so you don't have to worry about taking notes or forgetting what's been said.

If any trouble comes about because of a misunderstanding, at least you have evidence to show what you heard or said.

3) Assume the best (but prepare for the worst)

Assuming the best is a lovely outlook, but it can land you in hot water. Equally, just assuming the worst can end up backfiring because putting out those negative vibes can be detected. And I don't mean in a woo-woo way. I think we've all had conversations with someone who's annoyed at us or just generally in a bad mood, and everything we say ticks them off. Don't let that happen to you and your client!

The trick I've found is to assume the best, that they're a human like me and they're trying their best in spite of their own problems. But I also prepare for the worst, because I know humans like me are fallible! I know the client may forget the 10 am meeting we have booked, so I remind them at 9 am. I know they might have forgotten that invoice I sent, so I send a friendly reminder – I don't ignore the situation and hope it goes away, nor do I snap at them because the due date has passed three weeks ago.

You know what buttons your difficult clients have pushed in the past. You know they're likely to push them again, so how do you mitigate that? Is their feedback unhelpful? Maybe you start sending a Typeform (an online survey application) which helps guide their feedback in a more structured way.

Realise they're unlikely to change, but they probably don't mean to be dicks. So do your best to help them not be dicks.

4) Let them go

I started this with saying how hard it can be to turn away or fire clients, but sometimes it really is the best policy. I've told you before about the client I tried to fire, and the email I wrote. I basically explained my issue (the fact he hadn't paid me) and why this was a problem for me (I was counting on it to pay bills.)

I didn't make him wrong, I just laid out my problem and why that meant I could no longer work with him. He ended up turning round and was very apologetic, paid immediately and we worked together until the project ended. So sometimes it takes trying to fire a client to make them fix up and behave themselves, and other times a letter like that will bring out their shadow side – and you'll have saved yourself a lot of future hassle.

So don't hesitate in sending a 'break up' email, if you're at the end of your tether. It can go two ways, but either way it's better than staying in a shitty client relationship.

ACTION STEPS:

1) Decide what your boundaries are. What limits do you need to put in place around client or customer service? Is it limiting your hours of availability? Limiting your refund window? Limiting the number or revisions on your designs? Think of everything that has been an issue in the past, and create a boundary to mitigate each.

2) Have a look at your existing client on boarding process, or your policies (or lack thereof) on your website. Can you incorporate your new boundaries somehow?

Resources mentioned:

eCamm for Skype (Mac) - https://www.ecamm.com/mac/callrecorder/
Pamela for Skype (PC) - https://www.pamela.biz/
Zoom - https://zoom.us/
Typeform - https://www.typeform.com/

Chapter 6:
How Do You Change Direction?

How do you know when to carry on and when to quit altogether? This has been one of, if not THE most difficult questions I've had to face in me business and freelance history.

My first instance of the when-to-quit-when-to-stick scenario was in my agency job. I had a lot going for me. I was technically head designer – and I loved my colleagues – but oh jeez... The reality of the office life, the commute through London and the less-than-inspiring clients... I knew my time was limited. But when to go? The 'perfect time' never seems to come. It actually took me over two years of on/off should I stay/should I go to finally throw in the towel.

I've also struggled since in freelance side projects, like my pet portrait company and my old healthy living blog. All of these start off with a honeymoon period, and basically fall to pieces as my enthusiasm drops.

The toughest part is not wanting to be seen as a 'quitter' – which, for whatever reason, has been deemed in our society as failing or the opposite of success.

Since then, I've totally shifted how I approach quitting, and no longer live in fear that quitting = failure. Sometimes, it's simply the next necessary step. For me success is the art of the pivot. Sometimes that pivot looks pretty huge: quitting a job to go freelance. Other times it's smaller: changing a direction on a blog. In any case, it's knowing that you've done your best, and learning from any and all experiences, before moving forward.

Now, I want to share the five tools I use to decide on whether something is worth sticking with, or letting go.

1) Intuition

Without getting too hung up on what intuition is... let's just say for now it's the little voice – or feeling – you get about someone or something. It might come from your belly or your heart. It doesn't sound like reason or logic.

It might be a feeling in your gut that says "Euuurgh - I don't know about this person." Or the goosebumps you get when you have an idea, or hear a certain truth spoken. It's the voice that might come through when you journal or have been journaling for a while.

My suspicion is that whatever it is, it's far removed from the 'I' or the ego self which often gets very confused and can make it all the more difficult to hear our true inner voice.

I have two tips for using your intuition when it comes to decision making.

1. Meditation. I know I'm probably the 57th person who has told you to meditate, but honestly – it really is a powerful way of helping your noisy thinking mind to quieten down. Even if it's for a split second today, it might be a whole second tomorrow.

I say this, because I need that reminder. I really struggle to quiet my overly loud mind, but I'm fully aware of the difference when I go even a day or two without meditating - or at least attempting to. I am host to a crazy overthinking monster, my 'thinking brain' and I can see the difference over the years that meditation has made to giving me a break from that.

2. Writing. My second tip when it comes to using your intuition is... writing. Yay! The introvert's friend. I learned to do this from Jess Lively, who like myself has come from a very left-brained, analytic, scientific approach, and who has let more esoteric ideas and more right-brain thinking in.

She recommends writing to your intuition as you would a friend. Ask a question by writing it down, and when you hear an answer, start writing! It does feel really forced at first, at least I found. But as soon as I start moving my pen, like automatic writing (google that if you're not sure what it looks like.) I start to form words that mostly make sense and actually come up with some pretty great answers, that I don't believe just ruminating about the problem or question would have achieved. Start practising this, ideally first thing in the morning, and see what comes out.

2) Ask yourself: what is it costing you?

Much more of a left brain approach here, incase the last one wasn't your jam. What I want you to focus on is not necessarily the time or the money your pursuit might be costing – thought these are worth considering – but what is the energy cost of you staying in your current situation or working on a particular project?

If this is a shitty client, you may feel like leaving them is going to cost you in cash. But what if staying means it will cost you even more by losing out on a bigger, better client? What will it cost you in energy?

Start journaling this out. Seeing this stuff on paper makes the world of difference.

3) Ask what can you Prune, Cultivate or Exterminate?

By prune, I mean: what about your current situation could you cut back on, rather than give up entirely? I could reduce my old fitness blog, because I could decrease the number of posts I wrote per week.

Or I could cultivate it: I could double down on my efforts, go all at it to see if my energy around it shifted. Or I could exterminate it entirely: write a final goodbye post.

I tried all pruning and cultivating first, before ultimately I exterminated it. The point of this is to know you have options, and that usually, you can run experiments before axing the project or whatever it is altogether.

4) Set a deadline

Too many of us will delay this decision-making process so much that it costs us significant opportunities. This is why setting a decide-by deadline is so helpful for those who are prone to procrastinating. That isn't to say you have to decide everything right now. But ultimately, creating a deadline will help.

Return to your question, use your intuition, run experiments, until you reach your final deadline. You could also have multiple deadlines. I set weekly and monthly reviews for this purpose. If I have anything that's feeling a bit off or I'm unsure of, I have time booked in to review whether or not I stick with it for another month.

It might be worth telling a friend your deadline so you have some accountability to stick to it.

4) No regrets

This is more of a post-decision tip. Whatever you decide: have **no regrets**. One of my core life rules. Ain't nobody got time for regretting things!

And odds are in your favour you won't regret whatever decision you made, thanks to the cognitive bias of choice-supportive bias. Which basically means, when you choose something you tend to feel positive about it, even if the choice has flaws. So... happy decision making!

"Why do you go away? So that you can come back. So that you can see the place you came from with new eyes and extra colours... Coming back to where you started is not the same as never leaving."
~ Terry Pratchett

ACTION STEP:

At this point in working through the book, you might be ready to take a review of your current ongoing projects or tasks. If there is anything that feels like it's worn out its welcome, or you're undecided as to whether you should stick with it, go through the advice in this chapter and set a deadline for your decision.

Chapter 7:
How Do You Keep To Your Word?

Accountability has never been a word that fills me with eagerness. It sounds an awful lot like accounting (ugh) and responsibility (ewww.) Being held accountable to someone or something outside myself also whiffs of something only an extrovert would need. Aren't we introverts meant to be intrinsically motivated, self-sufficient creatures?

Actually, what I've come to see in years of trying to do everything solo is that... working for yourself is hard. Chasing a dream... defining what and who you want to be... starting something new... switching things up... making it happen... all of these things take work, dedication, patience and there's nothing like accountability to keep you on your path.

If you're a one-creative-introvert band, you may be tempted to do everything all by yourself. It makes sense: you likely do your best creative work solo, in a place free from distraction. If you're anything like me, teamwork has never been your strong suit.

But when it comes to sticking with your creative pursuit when the going gets tough, that's something that even an introvert can struggle with. This is why having someone else you can rely on to keep you accountable is so useful. I call this an 'Accountabilibuddy.'

What is an Accountabilibuddy exactly?

An Accountabilibuddy is a person who witnesses what you are trying to accomplish and holds you accountable to yourself and to your dreams. The kind of relationship you have with your Accountabilibuddy is up to both of you, and can work regardless of whether your buddy is an introvert or an extrovert. The point is to offer support to one another, have weekly meetings, or just share your goals on a weekly or monthly basis.

Having someone who knows what you're up to and what you're trying to accomplish is incredibly helpful.

How to get yourself an Accountabilibuddy

Start by making a list of people you know who are doing something, anything that might require some serious self-motivation to do the work. This could be a friend working on a novel in her part time, or a brother-in-law trying to stick to a new diet where he doesn't eat food that starts with the letter S.

You don't have to limit yourself to your industry. Anyone who is trying to make something happen beyond their basic survival needs, can benefit from some accountability.

Nor do you have to limit yourself to your close friends or family. Heck, they can be internet strangers. In fact, that might be better for you if the idea of saying the word 'Accountabilibuddy' makes your ears turn pink. There are plenty of Facebook groups and online communities out there packed full of people who are also looking for some accountability, but who are too afraid to ask. It's still an important feature of the League of Creative Introverts, because I know how valuable it is.

Before you make more excuses, know that I've created some templates for you (both for email and for social media) that you can play with so NO EXCUSES when it comes to pitching!

How to be an Accountabilibuddy

The first thing to think about is how often you want to keep in touch with each other. It might be every Monday, or every other week. It might be in a longer catch up every month. I'd recommend as frequently as you can. Fortnightly has always suited me well, but I'd still aim for weekly at first to get you into the swing of it.

Then, have a think about format. This could be email, text, Skype, Facebook messenger – anything you both feel comfortable with and will regularly check. Slack is a great application for teams to keep in touch during the work day, but if you use it already, you might consider setting up a channel for yourself and your accountability buddy.

Next you can have a think about the contents of these check ins. This is very much a personal choice, but I do have a structure I recommend to my Leaguers who opt in for the accountability buddying program.

For example, you can simply start with a recap of where you're at. What you got done last week to move toward your goal, what you'd like to improve. Then you could share what your number one focus is for the week ahead. You could share what you think might be a challenge.

On the whole, I like to keep these check-ins brief, light and not too heavy on the moaning. Complaining about why you're struggling with a goal might be too much of a burden for your buddy after a while, though this is totally up to you and I'm all for the occasional vent!

Then you could offer some words of encouragement to your buddy (I don't expect you to force any inauthentic 'Go get 'em tiger!'s but if you feel inclined... go get 'em!) Just let them know you're here for them, and that you know you both can make this happen.

ACTION STEP:

Have a think about who you can ask to be your Accountabilibuddy. Make a shortlist of five people, and take a look at the templates in the Resources if you need a little extra help in making the ask. Don't take it too hard if someone declines: remember this is a reflection on their priorities, and don't let it affect yours. Plenty more potential Accountabilibuddies in the sea!

Chapter 8:
Who Do You Go To For Help?

In my books (specifically this one) the way highly competent people get to where they are is by asking for help. One of the best examples of this is in the field of mentors and mentees.

Marc Andreessen (multi-millionaire founder of Mosaic and Netscape) was mentor to Mark Zuckerberg (billionaire founder of something called Facebook.) Director Ingmar Bergman was mentor to Woody Allen.

I was incredibly fortunate to have access to the Princes Trust Enterprise Program back in 2013, which – if I successfully pitched my idea – would grant me my very own mentor. For free! After a couple of years of banging my head against my desk (ouch) and getting all my information from books and podcasts (fine, but unfortunately they can't listen back) I was eager to find someone who could listen to my struggles, and actually offer me guidance and support. Someone who had many more years of experience than me, and could spot me when I was doing something that pushed my comfort zone a little too far. Fortunately, my pitch was accepted (picture an introvert in an X-Factor audition) and I was granted my mentor.

My mentor, Philip Allison, was not what I expected. For one, he was younger than I expected. My brother's age, with kids at a similar age to my niece and nephew. I realise how agist this sounds, but I was expecting someone who could be my mum or dad, not my big bro. He also admitted to me that he had come from a financial background and is certainly not a 'creative' type (even though we're all creative, really.)

Anyway, despite my expectations being blown, I liked the guy. He was grounded in a way the professors from art school had not been. He had real-world experience with 'business people' and I figured his level of professionalism might rub off on grubby little me. He would always catch me when I was trying to avoid the numbers. Those pesky numbers... The ones us 'creative' types like to ignore; sweep under the rug. He finally made me look at the viability of my t-shirt design business, and whilst he never told me what to do, he would make sure I took off my wishful-thinking-glasses and put my reality-specs on. And above all, he supported me through my madcap pivots, providing the encouragement to plough forwards I so needed.

Whilst you can't guarantee age and background of your mentor, these are some of what you can expect from any mentor worth their salt:

1) Constructive criticism

"Mentors have a way of seeing more of our faults that we would like. It's the only way we grow."
~ George Lucas

Even if your mentor hasn't been in your exact shoes, they're likely to have been in a similar situation or at least had more experience to shine light from. I've never been unwittingly discouraged by the criticism I've had from my mentor, but I'm grateful that I've had someone to hold a mirror up to some of the more... outlandish ideas I've had.

2) Moral support

"A mentor is someone who allows you to see the hope inside yourself."
~ Oprah Winfrey

They are there no matter what and offer moral support sprinkled heavily with cheerleading. There were times that if there wasn't a mentor there for me, I could have easily caved-in emotionally, or thrown in the towel on the business.

3) Perspective

Business is tough enough regardless of what stage you're in – so why reject the offer of perspective from a mentor who has gone forth, had the experiences, made the mistakes and gotten the t-shirts all before you?

In my case, I really appreciated the fact that Phil was not from a traditionally creative background, and could give me the perspective from someone who had worked for some serious 'big fish' companies, and who took the numbers part seriously.

Tips for finding your ideal mentor

1) Look for your opposite

Whilst Phil and I are both introverts, that's pretty much where our commonalities end. And that's a very good thing! If someone is too similar to you, they won't be able to offer you quite the distinct perspective you can benefit so much from.

2) Prioritise connection

Ideally, you want to 'click' on some level with your mentor. They don't have to be your bestie (in fact, it's probably best if they aren't!) so don't rush into a mentorship just because I say so.

Think back to a great one-to-one conversation you once had at a networking event, or someone you've seen deliver a talk, or someone who's writing you love. This is a great foundation for thinking about who you could connect with.

Remember this matters both ways: it's not enough for your mentor to approve of you: you have to approve of the to if you're going to listen to what they have to say!

3) Be specific in your ask

When you go in for the ask, make sure that you are super specific about what you'd like to be mentored on and what is it about them that you're hoping to benefit from. This could be a certain skillset, or experiences they've had.

It's also worth thinking about the practicalities of meeting (e.g. coffee once a month, a call once a week, a meeting every two weeks). They are likely to appreciate your preparation. That said, remain flexible with your logistics and suggest you a no-pressure trial run, just to see how you both get on.

Once your mentorship has begun, continue to set check-ins with yourself and with each other to make sure you're both happy with how things are going and if anything can be tweaked.

4) It's a reciprocal relationship

What can you offer them? Whilst many mentorships are often free, it might be that you pay them a small fee to start with. Why? Well, be honest. Do you really value what you don't pay for? Compare a free event you signed up to as a whim, to the investment of a £250 workshop you've had booked for months. How reluctant are you to cancel on the latter? If you're anything like me, even if you attend both, you'll likely feel like you got more from the priced event, because we tend to value things we pay for more.

In addition, have you ever worked for free out of the goodness of your heart, then come to resent the relationship as you don't feel you're being fairly appreciated? Regardless of whether you pay your mentor, think about how you can show them your appreciation. Respect their time, their commitment and their generosity.

Even if you have a very limited ability to invest in a mentor, there are many consultants and coaches who offer a reduced rate for students and those on low income. There are also various programs that have systems in place to set this up. If you're in the UK and aged between 18 and 30, you could look into the Enterprise programme from the Princes Trust, that offers support and mentorship for no cost, as long as you've got an idea you're willing to put in the work on.

5) Don't expect answers

"The type of mentors who tend to be the most helpful are those who don't necessarily give you an answer."
~ Tim Ferriss

What I've learned from my own mentors, coaches and random brilliant minds that cross my path is that the best answers come from within. The best you can hope to get from outside sources, no matter how wise or experienced they are, is a provocation: a poke that will help your answer rise to the surface.

Simply expecting the answer from your mentor is not going to lead to the decisions that are truly best for you. After all, they are NOT you. No one has your particular preferences, personality and – if we want to go that deep – soul. Only *you* really know what's best for you; your mentor is simply there to give you more information, tools and support that will help fuel any decision you do ultimately make.

ACTION STEP:

1) Have a look into some formal mentoring programs in your area or country. If you qualify for one, go for it! There's nothing easier than having a system to get yourself set up with a mentor.

2) Failing that, have a think about people who you know who might be able to offer mentorship – even if they don't already. It could just be one coffee chat or call. You don't need it to be a regular meeting for the mentorship to work.

3) Write your first email to a potential mentor. As always, buckle yourself up for a no or a no reply, but use it as an experiment. No matter what, you'll learn from writing this first pitch.

Resources mentioned:

Enterprise programme from the Princes Trust - https://www.princes-trust.org.uk/help-for-young-people/support-starting-business

Chapter 9:
Who Do You Surround Yourself With?

Not long ago, the word 'Mastermind' to me meant a black leathery chair, a stressful spotlight and... John Humphrys. Then, as the word started popping up in books I was reading (Napoleon Hill's classic 'Think and Grow Rich,' being one) and podcasts I listened to.

It turns out, a Mastermind is actually just a group of people who all have goals or aspirations they're trying to achieve. The group meet to discuss ideas, work through problems, support each other, share resources, and basically help each other achieve their goals.

It was actually the day after hearing an episode of the Online Marketing Made Easy podcast that I started to really consider creating my own Mastermind group. Until that time, I thought it would be impossible for me to be in a Mastermind group. I didn't know anyone in a Mastermind, and any groups I found online were either for the super-elite or simply full up.

My other concern was: I'm an introvert! Why on earth would I want to surround myself with *more* people?

I've never liked team sports...

I always do my best work alone...

Plus, don't too many cooks spoil the broth?

Well that is definitely what the introvert in me thought to begin with. But as I discovered more and more successful people who absolutely swore by their Mastermind, I had to admit: there must be something in it. I also knew from being part of a few private Facebook groups, that there was something special about an intimate group of people who genuinely wanted to scratch each others backs. (Well, not literally.)

The other problem I was facing in my business at the time was lack of support in 'real life'. As much as I love my friends and family: none of them even owned a business – let alone an online one.

Trying to bounce ideas off them around email lists and algorithm changes would have been like someone trying to tell me about the rules of Cricket. It doesn't interest me and leaves me confused. Ultimately, my Mastermind itch became increasingly intolerable and I am SO glad I finally scratched it.

I finally realised I didn't have to be the one waiting for the invite, or selling organs to pay for it. I could set up my own Mastermind group – a group of peers who were at a similar place in their business.

Thanks to the Princes Trust Enterprise Program, I knew plenty of amazing business owners who I fit the bill. Note that this wasn't my creative scenes, but a sea of fellow newbie business owners who could also likely benefit from some group support. I started emailing and making calls, and within a week, I had five other savvy business owners to bounce ideas off, support and learn from.

These are the reasons I think any creative (even introverts) can benefit from being in a Mastermind group:

1) Motivation

Particularly when you work for yourself, in a grand old business of one, there are days when you need reassurance. I do anyway.

It might be just having someone else to moan to about taxes, or someone to tell you 'I know it's hard, but I believe you can do it.' Just having that encouragement come from someone in a similar boat makes a huge difference for me.

I know friends and family support me, but having someone who can fully relate is invaluable for keeping me motivated.

2) Accountability

Some of us are superb at getting things done just because they're on our to-do list. Some of us just need to know why they have to do the thing. Others just need someone to be relying on them – to hold them accountable. To text them "Where the f*** are you?!" when they don't show up. You might have discovered your Tendency if you took the test from Gretchen Rubin I mentioned in Part 1, chapter 2.

Regardless, having a Mastermind meeting in your calendar – whether it's in person or on a call – can be a game-changer, from helping you hit goals in business to just doing that thing you've been putting off for weeks.

3) Unbiased feedback

A problem I've always found (even as a child, holding drawings of mangled cats up to my parents) is where to get honest feedback. I can't say I've always found criticism easy to take – but I still value it. I might not follow all the advice I'm given – but I'll certainly consider it.

Trying to get an outside perspective from someone who 1) isn't close to your business and 2) doesn't love you SO much they couldn't hurt you is key to improving anything you're working on.

4) New perspectives

Just like getting feedback from unbiased peers, getting ideas from those who aren't even in the same industry as you can be a huge help.

It brings fresh, unique perspectives into your business that you wouldn't find alone, no matter how many hours you spent mulling over a problem.

Note: I wouldn't recommend joining a group that is SO far removed from what you do. For example, physical product sellers might be best suited to a group of other product sellers, rather than those selling services. The products can all be very different, but the challenges and experiences aren't too far removed. I also recommend starting with a group who are at a similar place in their business, in terms of profit, for example.

5) Shared resources

One of my favourite parts of any Mastermind meeting is the excitement that surrounds a shared resource. I recall my Mastermind meetings when I was banging on about my love for Periscope, which I think convinced some of my fellow Masterminds to get on board with the live video content.

I've also discovered loads of books, apps, plugins and tricks that my group has shared, and I love that we do this without fear that someone else is going to know 'our little secret'.

I think that's the key to any successful Mastermind group: never come with a scarcity mindset. There is enough of the pie to go around for us all to have a slice – and then some.

6) It teaches you to talk about yourself

Amazingly, even though I set up the Mastermind, on our first meeting I didn't even introduce myself. I asked the group to explain what they did, what they were currently struggling with and what they could bring to the table. Somehow we called the meeting to an end by the time it got round to me – typical introvert fail! I think I secretly wanted that to happen though.

Since then I've become much more vocal about my business, and it really wasn't so bad. In fact, it was hugely encouraging and every meeting it gets easier to have everyone's attention.

Your Mastermind will likely reflect back to you things about yourself you've been overlooking, and that you couldn't spot on your own.

7) It's flexible

Even when I'm not feeling up to talking too much about my own struggles, I can kick back and listen. The perfect introvert indulgence.

This allows me to do what I do best: listen to what others are struggling with, and then offer my advice. For some reason, this doesn't feel awkward at all – it never does. Even if you are having a more 'quiet' day, know that it's more than OK to take a back seat and show up as more of a giver than a taker.

8) You can do it from the couch

Not all Masterminds can meet up in person, but thanks to Google Hangouts, Skype or services like Zoom – you can totally do this from your office or a coffee shop… or at home on the couch.

Yes, I do think that meeting up in person is beneficial, for accountability as well as how much more people open up, but I don't think location should restrict you. I love the idea of connecting with Mastermind members all over the world, and we should totally take advantage of our ability to do so.

ACTION STEPS:

1) Make a list of at least 10 folk you could ask to be in a Mastermind. Your ideal number will be closer to five or six, but assume that there will be some declines.

2) Decide how often you would like to hold meetings, how long they are and what format they take (e.g. In person, on Skype etc)

3) Use the template in the Resources to help you in structuring the meetings. You can also adapt the Accountability buddy email template to help reach out to potential Mastermindees.

Not interested in setting up your own Mastermind? The League of Introverts offers you the opportunity to take part in a fully formed Mastermind, led by me, Cat! To find out more, head to https://www.thecreativeintrovert.com/lci

So You've Made it to the End... Now What?

Oh crikey – you made it here. The end. I wasn't entirely prepared for this, so I hope this doesn't strike you as an anticlimax.

Basically, you've got everything you need. You had it already, but hopefully this book has helped you identify exactly what that inner gold is, and how to extract it from yourself. I also hope it helped you get clear on the junk you no longer need, and helped you let it go so you can continue your creative introvert journey.

The journey to living the life you want on your terms isn't always a walk in the park – you probably know that by now. But even if you are an introvert, remember that you don't have to go it alone. I hope you find support in this book, but there are some other places I'd love to share with you too:

The League of Creative Introverts, my online community of likeminds: https://www.thecreativeintrovert.com/lci

Book readers can save 20% forever, if you enter the code: IREADIT at the checkout!

www.ingramcontent.com/pod-product-compliance
Lightning Source LLC
Chambersburg PA
CBHW031607210526
45464CB00004B/1464